D0313537

BLACKSTONE'S
BOOK OF MOOTS

BLACKSTONE'S
BOOK OF MOOTS

Tim Kaye, LLB, PhD,

and

Lynne Townley, LLB, LLM

BLACKSTONE PRESS LIMITED

First published in Great Britain 1996 by Blackstone Press Limited, 9–15 Aldine Street, London W12 8AW. Telephone: 0181-740 1173

© T. Kaye and L. Townley, 1996

ISBN: 1 85431 516 1

British Library Cataloguing in Publication Data
A CIP catalogue record for this book is available from the British Library.

Typeset by Montage Studios Limited, Tonbridge, Kent
Printed by Bell & Bain Limited, Glasgow

All rights reserved. No part of this book may be reproduced or transmitted in any form or by any means, electronic or mechanical, including photocopying, recording, or any information storage or retrieval system without prior permission from the publisher.

The publishers are prepared to allow mooting competitors to photocopy moot problems in Part III of this book, provided that they are for competition use and provided that prior permission is sought from the publisher.

CONTENTS

PREFACE

Mooting seems to have gained markedly in popularity in the last few years. It has also come to be seen as increasingly important in the development of oral presentation and practical skills throughout each of the academic, vocational and practical stages of legal education. Yet there seems at the same time to be a marked scarcity of suitable material available for prospective mooters to learn how both to prepare and to present a moot. Moreover, since the well-known *Observer Book of Moots* is now out of print, there is an even more acute shortage of widely available problems which can be used to form the basis of a moot.

This book attempts to help fill these gaps. Part I comprises what we hope will be seen as a very down-to-earth and thoroughly practical guide to the development of general mooting skills, placing particular emphasis on the essential legal research methods and the skills and tactics of oral presentation. It also takes prospective moot organisers through all the steps to be taken in organising a mooting competition from the initial organisation right through to the smooth running and judging of the competition itself. Part II attempts to put some flesh on these bones by not only presenting a problem actually mooted within the Law Faculty at Birmingham University, but also by following that with reproductions of the speeches of the first-year students who took part in that competition. A commentary on the various aspects of that moot is also included.

Finally, Part III provides a large number of sample moot problems which may be photocopied for use in competitions. Some of these have been provided for us by various contributors; those that are unattributed have been prepared by Tim Kaye. These can either be used exactly as written, or varied in certain aspects as the person in charge of mooting at each institution desires. Originally we had thought of including moots on as many different areas of law as possible, but our own experience of moots and mooting told us that this would probably be a fruitless exercise since so many of the more esoteric moots would then remain unused. Instead, we have concentrated on those areas of law which we know to be most popular among mooters and which will therefore prove most useful. We should, however, point out that our general categorisation of moots into subject areas is not intended to be taken too rigidly. Some of the moots on tort, for example, contain elements of contract too (and vice versa). Similarly, agency issues are raised in a number of different moots. We also urge users of this book not to be afraid of tinkering with the moots in this book to suit their own requirements.

We are both greatly indebted to all the contributors, without whom this book would not have been possible; to Nadene Scott and Mary Ballard for typing so many of the moots; and to Alistair MacQueen at Blackstone Press for his patience and consistent good humour. Lynne Townley would also like to thank Miss Anthea Tatton-Brown, the Students' Officer at the Middle Temple, and Miss Sue Phillips, the Students' Officer of Lincoln's Inn for their enthusiasm and helpfulness; and Nitzan for encouragement given with regard to this project. Tim Kaye would like to thank his wife Jan and children Nia, Zoë and Tristan for their suggestions, comments and general loving support.

Part One

HOW TO MOOT

One

WHAT IS MOOTING AND WHY IS IT IMPORTANT?

WHAT IS MOOTING?

Mooting in its earliest form dates from about 1485 when moots were organised by the Inns of Court, then the centres of legal education. These early moots differed from the format familiar today, where moots are generally concerned only with points of law. The early moots set by the Inns of Court were perhaps best viewed as a kind of pleading exercise.

The core of this exercise was to decide which action to bring in the particular case and thereafter to draft pleadings which would bring out the essential points of the moot. Also, unlike today's moots, these moots could last for up to one whole term — as did the case of 'The Greyhound', a discussion which took place at the Inner Temple in 1480, according to The Seldon Society Records. Students at the Inns of Court took part in moots in order to enhance their standing at the Bar.

Today moots are set to test the ability of the mooter to present a legal argument. The standard of the mooter is judged by paying particular attention to the mooter's ability to make use of the available legal authorities, answer questions, observe the etiquette of the courtroom and generally appear competent as an advocate.

A typical moot problem is solely concerned with a point (or points) of law. Normally it will take the form of a case heard on appeal with the grounds of appeal clearly stated. Unlike the ancient moots, a modern moot speech will have a strict time limit of 15–20 minutes.

A 'moot' usually consists of four speakers. The speakers are divided into two teams of two who argue each side of the case. One team becomes the leading and junior counsel for the appellants and the other the leading and junior counsel for the respondents, although the mooters may be judged as individuals or as a team.

The speakers are each in turn given a certain time limit in which to present their arguments. The moot is presided over by at least one judge who delivers a judgment at the end of the moot both on the law and on the result of the moot itself.

·The organisation of a moot requires a good deal of advance preparation on the part of both mooters and the moot organiser. It is necessary for the mooters to prepare their arguments in advance of the moot and to select the most appropriate legal authorities for the purposes of this argument. The rules of mooting require that these authorities be exchanged with the opposing team (the mooters arguing on the other side) in advance of the moot. The moot organiser has to make arrangements for the staging of the moot itself and any communications between the mooters.

The moot 'court' should reflect, as far as possible, the courtroom scenario in reality. The presiding judge is supported by the clerk of the moot who is responsible for providing the judge, when required, with a copy of each authority cited by the mooters. The clerk also times the moot speeches. The two teams of mooters sit at separate tables, taking turns to stand to present their arguments to the court.

For the duration of their arguments, mooters are required to maintain an appropriate courtroom manner (remembering, amongst other things, to address the court and fellow counsel in the accepted form). Further, to add a touch of authenticity of the moot, the participants are often required to wear gowns.

WHY IS MOOTING IMPORTANT?

Many students ask why they should take the time out of their academic schedule to make what can often be the time consuming and demanding preparations necessary before taking part in a moot. The mercenary answer to this question is to invite those students to glance at application forms for jobs in the legal profession and beyond, where they will see for themselves the frequent demands made by employers that applicants have some public speaking or mooting experience.

But whether students wish to pursue a career in the legal field or otherwise, they should take the opportunity whilst in higher education to gain some experience either in public speaking or in a more specialised type of advocacy such as mooting. The ability to present an oral argument coherently and within a strict time limit will be an asset to students regardless of the career they eventually choose. At some point in their working life most people are required to give a presentation, a lecture or even a short talk, therefore those few hours devoted to preparing for the odd moot or two will be time well spent.

With regard to students intending to become practising barristers or solicitors, it is not an exaggeration to say that some mooting experience has almost become a prerequisite for entry into some sections of the legal profession (particularly for those students wishing to attend Bar school and thereafter secure a pupillage). So if a career in the law is what you aspire to, you should take any opportunity available to moot whilst at university. It will pay dividends later on. Having 'broken the ice', as it were, with regard to public advocacy, that first appearance in court will perhaps be a little less daunting.

THE ADVANTAGES OF MOOTING

Mooting also provides students with what is perhaps a unique and unparalleled experience during their time in legal education. There is little scope in most traditional degree courses to nurture the skills of oral argument in the way participation in mooting can.

Preparation for a moot also helps develop good basic research and presentation skills, in that compiling a moot speech requires the mooter to acquire the ability to identify rapidly the legal issue or issues posed by the moot question, before sifting through all the available cases and other material and presenting a structured and coherent argument, often under the pressure of time. In conducting their research for a moot, many students will also become familiar with certain legal materials and information retrieval systems, which might otherwise have escaped them throughout their time in higher education.

With some experience, skilful mooters become well able to 'argue both sides of the case', which involves identifying with ease not only the arguments in their favour, but also those less favourable to their side of the case. A mooter must be prepared to attack any opposing authorities head on by, for example, finding a way to distinguish them from the particular case being argued. Often mooters with a seemingly hopeless case have ended up winning the moot comfortably — simply because they have not been afraid to advance novel arguments.

This ability to recognise and seize upon the weaknesses of any counter-argument is one that will, in time, prove a valuable skill on many occasions. As 'real life' advocates improvise as a matter of course, the mooter likewise learns to make the most of his or her situation. As one author, explaining the skills of an advocate, explains:

> ... no matter how hopeless the cause, however unmeritorious the client, notwithstanding the antipathy of the judge, irrespective of the risks to his own reputation, and despite the pressing concerns which may be preying on the mind of the lawyer, what counsel must do is to follow and defend the great tradition of advocacy: to make mountains out of molehills, to find a point of law where none had previously been known to exist, to ensure that his client does not lose the case without everything possible (and, on occasion, some things impossible) being said on his behalf. (Pannick, D., *Advocates*, Oxford: Oxford University Press, 1993, p. 5.)

In order to argue effectively in a moot, it is necessary to read the relevant cases in much greater detail than perhaps the average student would normally be inclined to do (or indeed would have the time to) in the ordinary course of his or her studies. Thus the ability not only to read a case, but also to understand its structure, is enhanced. For the purposes of mooting the finer points of the case must be noted and, in searching for favourable arguments, the student becomes familiar with perhaps previously uncharted territory such as dissenting judgments. This can only be of benefit to the student in the course of his or her academic studies.

Few exercises can provide the practical experience and encourage a growth in the confidence of the law student in the way that participation in mooting can. In short, mooting goes far to bridge the gap in a system of legal education which, for the most part, places greater emphasis on the written argument. In the words of Glanville Williams:

much stress has been laid by educationalists on literacy and numeracy, but we hear little about the importance of being articulate. Footballers practise passing and shooting, singers and clowns practise assiduously. Why is it supposed that speaking comes naturally and needs no effort or concentration? Fluency and clear enunciation are particularly important for the lawyer, when our forensic practice is largely oral. (Williams, G., *Learning the Law*, 11th ed., London: Sweet & Maxwell, 1982, p. 160.)

FURTHER GENERAL READING

Hyam, M., *Advocacy Skills*, 3rd ed., London: Blackstone Press, 1995.
Sherr, A., *Advocacy*, London: Blackstone Press, 1993.
Evans, K., *The Golden Rules of Advocacy*, London: Blackstone Press, 1993.

Two

HOW TO ORGANISE A MOOTING COMPETITION

WHO IS RESPONSIBLE?

Most law faculties and other institutions of legal education will have a student committee, one member of which will be responsible for mooting. This central figure (commonly called the 'Master' or 'Mistress' of the Moots) may also be supported by a member of the academic staff who will assist with the 'red tape' aspects of organising a moot competition (such as obtaining permission for the use of rooms for mooting, use of the fax machine and so on). In larger faculties it may be helpful to appoint an assistant to the Master or Mistress of the Moots in order to share the administrative burden. An assistant is a particular asset if one or more internal mooting competitions are planned.

The Master/Mistress of the Moots plays a pivotal role in the organisation and success of any planned mooting venture. Although it is not always the case, it is nevertheless worth adding as a word of warning to anyone wishing to take on the job, that the bulk of the administration as well as the clerking and general preparation for a mooting competition tends to fell upon the Master or Mistress. Therefore any prospective candidate for the job should consider whether this is a burden worth having in addition to existing academic obligations. However, one of the present writers, speaking from experience, can certainly assure anyone wishing to become an official with general responsibility for mooting or organising a mooting competition, that it is a most rewarding, stimulating and even highly enjoyable experience!

In addition to this central figure who is responsible for the overall organisation of the competition, it is also useful to have a 'support staff' of individuals willing to help out either by clerking moots or by searching out in the library in advance of the moot the particular materials required for the moot.

A successful moot will require a clerk who is responsible for timing the moot speeches and providing the judge with the particular authorities at the precise moment when the mooters refer to them in their respective speeches.

In addition to these duties it is necessary for someone to search for and provide all the law reports and additional materials required and place them (with markers at the required citations) on the clerk's desk in the moot room ready for the moot. Somebody will also have to arrange the furniture in this room in order to facilitate the moot; and the materials will have to be returned to the library afterwards.

GETTING THE COMPETITION OFF THE GROUND

The key to organising a successful mooting competition (as with actual participation in mooting) is preparation. This section will concentrate on a few general points to be considered in advance of scheduling any competition. The remaining sections of this chapter will go on to provide a more detailed chronological overview of matters to be considered as the proposed date of the competition draws closer, and the final section contains a quick check-list of the most important obligations and is designed particularly for the benefit of the organiser.

First of all it is worth engaging in some 'market research' with the aim of gauging the degree of interest in mooting within the student body concerned. There is no point wasting time and effort in organising a competition if there are no participants. This task need not be a complicated one. It is often sufficient to ask interested students to 'sign up' for mooting on a sheet of paper passed around a lecture hall or placed on a central notice board. The organiser should thereafter be able to communicate with the interested students via the trusty student pigeonholes or any alternative method in existence for the receipt of student mail.

Once the level of interest has been noted and considered sufficient, it is then possible to make the preliminary arrangements for the competition. It is a good idea to publicise the competition within the department (or departments) concerned. This may also encourage more students to participate.

The next point to be considered is the timescale of the competition. What date will be set for the final, for example? How many preliminary moots will be necessary and how many moots can be held each week, bearing in mind all the relevant logistical problems? It is also best to schedule moots for the 'quiet times' in the academic year because few students will be prepared to moot when the academic workload is particularly heavy, or during preparation for exams.

It is also highly advisable that you should consider whether it will be possible to provide judges for all the moots which you are about to schedule. This largely depends on the goodwill of the academic staff, although it is the experience of the present writers that there are usually enough friendly academics around to save the day. For certain moots it may be fitting to consider inviting a qualified barrister or solicitor to judge the moot. On special occasions it may also be appropriate to enlist the experience of a 'real' judge to bring a touch of authenticity. There is also no reason why postgraduate students and even seasoned mooters from amongst the student body (save where this would be potentially embarrassing to the judge/ mooter or both) cannot be called upon to adjudicate moots. The organiser is best advised to send a courteous note to all those available for judging, asking those in agreement to suggest dates which would be most suitable for them to attend to judge a moot. A note of the responses should then be kept by the organiser for future reference.

Finally, you should consider running a 'mooting workshop' or at least producing a fact sheet or similar type of introduction to mooting, because in most educational establishments there will be students who are new to the law and many who have never mooted or experienced anything akin to a moot before. It is therefore necessary to provide such students with the most basic tools of mooting, such as the formal methods of opening, closing or structuring a moot speech, the accepted method of citing cases, and the precise manner in which to address the particular court in question. Best of all, of course, would be to advise all potential mooters to obtain a copy of this book!

If the mooting competition has become an established event in the institution concerned it is a particularly good exercise to stage a demonstration moot. This may be achieved by asking former competitors to moot using speeches originally prepared for a previous competition, or by persuading experienced mooters to tackle a relatively simple moot purely for demonstration purposes. Where there is sufficient enthusiasm to run a short series of workshops, it is perhaps a good idea to commence with a demonstration moot and thereafter to organise students into small groups within which they can discuss moot problems, practice and comment on the oral presentation of each other's arguments. Above all it should be remembered that mooting is a practical exercise, so the best preparation is this type of 'hands-on' experience. There is little to be gained, beyond the very basic principles, by providing a programme of lectures for interested students. Indeed, this method may have an adverse effect on the level of interest.

Once you are satisfied that the preliminary tasks have been successfully completed, the time has come to commence the competition itself. The most efficient way to organise a competition is to formulate a timetable which is tailored to the circumstances of the particular competition or academic institution involved. The following chronological check-list contains all the basic guidelines and tasks which should be accomplished at particular times. It may be helpful for the organiser to follow these guidelines or alternatively to adapt them to suit his or her own particular requirements.

ORGANISING THE COMPETITION

The following matters should be considered and decided upon at least two to four weeks in advance of the competition.

Which rules should be adopted?

It is vital that you decide which rules will be used for the particular competition. At the end of this book we have included the rules for the Blackstone Herbert Smith Mooting Competition, but there is no reason why you cannot formulate your own set of rules for a particular competition. By way of guidance, it is usual that a moot consists of four speakers who will be divided into two teams, each consisting of a leader (leading counsel) and a junior (junior counsel). The two leading counsel are then each permitted a time limit of fifteen or twenty minutes in which to deliver their speeches; and the two junior counsel are usually allowed fifteen minutes each.

The order of speakers which has been previously adopted in national mooting competitions has been as follows:

(i)   leading counsel for the Appellant (or Plaintiff, if the moot case is being tried nominally at first instance);
(ii)   junior counsel for the Appellant (or Plaintiff);
(iii)   leading counsel for the Respondent (or Defendant);
(iv)   junior counsel for the Respondent (or Defendant).

This order may of course be varied so that the speech of the leading counsel for the appellant could be followed first by the speech of the leading counsel for the respondent and then the speeches of the respective junior counsel. This order of speaking has the advantage of facilitating the clarity of the moot because moot problems are generally divided into two exclusive grounds of appeal which are argued by the two leaders and the two juniors respectively. Alternatively, the order of speaking could be determined from one moot to the next by the Master or Mistress to ensure that each moot is argued in the most appropriate manner. This flexibility is incorporated, for example, in Rule 6(b) of the rules for the Blackstone Herbert Smith Mooting Competition.

It is also often the case that leading counsel for the appellant (who had the opening speech) is permitted a five minute right of reply after all the speakers have completed their original submissions, during which not only matters raised by the leading counsel for the respondent may be dealt with, but also any issues raised by junior counsel for the respondent.

This is the traditional moot court scenario although, in the opinion of the present writers, it can be unfair to impose such rules where the competition is individual (in that the mooters are to be judged as individuals rather than as a team). Where the mooters are competing as individuals in this way it is suggested, in the consideration of fairness, that they be given equal time for their respective speeches and that the advantage (or otherwise) of a right of reply be denied to the opening leading counsel.

Provision should also be made for the asking and answering of questions during the moot speech. It is the usual practice to 'stop the clock' when the judge asks a question. The clock remains stopped while the mooter is answering the question posed by the judge. This is sensible because it is inevitable that some arguments and points of law will attract more questions than others and 'stopping the clock' ensures that all the mooters have equal time in which to deliver their submissions, irrespective of the number of questions they have been asked during their speech. Time then begins to run when the mooter has finished answering the question and returns to the body of his or her moot speech.

Once a set of rules has been decided upon for a particular competition, it is good practice for the organiser to have them typed up in as brief, clear and precise a manner as possible. This document can then be furnished to all the judges and prospective mooters in advance of the competition. As a minimum, the matters already referred to in this section should be dealt with in the rules. They should therefore clearly state the time allowed for each moot speech, whatever provision is to be made for any time taken up in the answering of questions, and the order in which the mooters are to address the court. Such written documentation eliminates any confusion on the day of the moot.

It should also be possible at this stage to estimate the number of 'knock-out' rounds necessary (which will depend on the number of prospective mooters who have signed up for the competition) before the four finalists are selected. Excluding the final itself, three rounds are usual in a competition providing there is an appropriate number of participants. The organiser will then be able to schedule the moots in relation to the time-scale within which the competition has to be completed.

Who moots when?

The list of prospective mooters should first be divided into sets of four. Each set of four participants will argue together in a moot. It is worth bearing in mind the status of each mooter, that is their particular year of study and whether or not they have studied or omitted particular subjects. Where possible it is best to choose opponents who are in the same year of study and who have studied similar options. More often than not, particularly in internal competitions, students will refuse to moot on an unfamiliar topic against an opponent who has had the benefit of having studied that topic as part of their academic course. Where there is sufficient interest it is a good idea to run separate competitions for students of varying experience. For example, in a typical university law faculty, a competition for first year students could be run separately from a competition for second and third year students. Students studying for the Common Profession Exam could be accommodated in either competition, although the latter might, perhaps, be more appropriate.

Which moot problem?

It is usual for the moot problem which is set to be concerned solely with points of law. The facts are assumed to have been exactly as set out in the moot problem, so there should be no dispute as to what is supposed to have happened. The moot usually takes the form of a case heard on appeal with the grounds of appeal clearly stated. Generally there are two distinct grounds of appeal which can in turn be divided between the two leading counsel and the two junior counsel respectively (the leading counsel normally arguing the first (or the major) ground of the appeal and the junior the second). The moot court will generally — though not always — be the Court of Appeal or the House of Lords.

The abilities and knowledge of the mooters in the competition should also be taken into account when selecting a moot problem. On the whole students prefer to moot on the traditional 'core subjects' which they have had the benefit of studying. It is for this reason that the bulk of the moot problems in this book are on the core subjects. However, if a consensus can be achieved amongst all those concerned (and where a suitable moot problem is available), other areas of the law can be covered. If the moot is to be against a team from another institution, the normal etiquette is for one team to be responsible for setting the moot problem while the other side chooses whether they wish to represent the appellants or respondents.

What information should be provided for mooters?

Once the organiser has divided the grounds of appeal in the moot between the prospective mooters, the moot problem should be photocopied and a copy prepared for each mooter. The organiser should ensure that the mooters receive copies of the moot problem preferably at least two weeks in advance of the day when they are to moot, although it may be necessary to vary this time depending on the academic commitments of participants.

Along with the moot problems, the organiser should send the following instructions for the guidance of each participant:

(i)   A clear statement of which side of the case the mooter is to argue (that is whether he or she is to argue for the appellants or the respondents).

(ii)   Whether the mooter is to act as a junior or a leading counsel in the moot.

(iii)   The particular ground of the appeal which the participant is to argue (bearing in mind that there are likely to be at least two grounds of appeal stated in the moot problem).

(iv)   The time limit within which the participants must complete the presentation of their speech (normally 15 or 20 minutes): this will also be of assistance to the participants when preparing their submissions.

(v)   The date and venue of the proposed moot.

(vi)   The precise date, time and method to be used for the exchange of authorities with the opposing counsel (stating clearly the name of this individual).

It will also be helpful to supply each mooter with the names of all the other mooters, as mooters often find it helpful to prepare or discuss moot problems together, even in individual competitions.

If there is a preferred method of dress for the moot, the participants should also be informed of this in advance. For certain competitions gowns and fairly formal clothing is required to be worn. If gowns are necessary, the organiser must make arrangements for the supply of the gowns and ensure their availability on the day of the moot.

If the participants do not know the organiser personally they should be provided with the name of the organiser and details of where he or she can be contacted (giving a contact telephone number if possible). Finally, each participant should be informed that they must provide a list of authorities which they intend to rely upon in their submissions to the person responsible for clerking the moot. This list could perhaps be sent to the clerk at the same time as the exchange of authorities with opposing counsel is to take place.

Which judge?

A prospective judge should be approached by the organiser and (presuming he or she is agreeable) notified of the date, time and venue for the moot. It is also a good idea to furnish the judge with a copy of the moot problem well in advance of the moot. It is useful to remember that judges often prefer, like mooters, to be involved in judging moots on areas in which they have a particular expertise, so this should be borne in mind by the organiser when selecting a judge for a particular moot.

Where?

The organiser should also take care when arranging the venue for the moot. For instance, if there is a room booking system in operation in the particular institution concerned, this procedure should be followed. This is a relatively effortless way to avoid the potential embarrassment of being left without a place to moot. If any change in the venue should occur in the interim period, all those concerned (in particular the mooters, the judge and the clerk) must, of course, be informed at once.

Once these steps have been taken the basic groundwork for the moot has been completed and the framework for the competition is in place. Notifying mooters about the moot (and of course the moot problem) at least two weeks in advance of its proposed date will also allow for any necessary substitutions to be made, should certain participants be unavailable at the given time through academic or other commitments.

A FEW DAYS BEFORE THE COMPETITION

The date for exchange of authorities is usually scheduled for between one and three days in advance of the actual date of the moot. Each mooter should provide his or her opposing counsel (and the clerk of the moot) with a full list of the authorities to which they intend to refer in their argument. An 'authority' in this context usually refers to a case. However, references to other sources such as passages from legal textbooks, articles from legal journals, or select committee reports, may also be considered as an 'authority' for the purposes of a mooting competition. It will only become necessary for the organiser to distinguish between the two types of authorities if it is intended to place limits upon the use of one type but not on another in a competition (for example to restrict only the number of cases which each mooter may cite in their argument, as happens in some mooting competitions).

The full citation for each authority should be clearly stated. In some competitions it is the practice to limit the number of authorities per team to a certain number (for example, ten per team). It will be up to the organiser to decide whether there would be any advantage in introducing such a restriction, for mooters would be ill-advised to attempt to use so many authorities in a moot event. For this reason the Blackstone Herbert Smith Mooting Competition limits the number of cases to six per team whilst other authorities are limited to four per team. It also certainly makes the clerk's life much easier when gathering all the authorities from the library. Any single case is usually taken to count as one authority, whether the mooter refers to the decisions of one or more courts in that particular case (for example, when the case has been started in the High Court, thereafter being appealed to the Court of Appeal and possibly also to the House of Lords). However, the mooter should provide all the references for this case, if he or she proposes to refer to them during the moot speech. After exchange the mooters may not refer to an authority which has not been cited on exchange unless the other side agrees.

If the moot in question is an external one or involves mooters from another institution, detailed arrangements should be made for the authorities to be exchanged over the telephone, by first class post or by fax (the receipt of which should be confirmed by telephone). If the competition is internal, student mail will be the usual means of exchange of authorities, unless the organiser wishes to prescribe some other method.

At the same time the mooters should also notify the clerk of the moot of the authorities which they intend to adduce, in order to enable the clerk to make the necessary arrangements with the library regarding the materials required for the moot, in particular where they are on restricted access or where printouts are required from LEXIS. Upon receipt of all the lists of authorities, the clerk should then prepare a 'master' list of authorities cited by each side for the use of the judge on the day of the moot.

It has become the practice of the courts in recent years to require that the opposing parties in a case prepare skeleton arguments which briefly detail (in addition to any authorities which may be relied on) the content of the submissions which they intend to advance to the court. These skeleton arguments are then exchanged with the other side and lodged with the court at a given date prior to the hearing. Bearing in mind this trend in legal practice and in order to ensure that the mooters have full opportunity to identify and address the issues raised by the other side, it may be worthwhile considering the exchange of skeleton arguments at the same time as the list of authorities is exchanged. It is not necessary that the skeleton argument be comprehensively detailed: all it need do is simply identify the particular issues or points which the mooters intend to raise in their submission. For example, the Blackstone Herbert Smith Mooting Competition requires that each side produce a summary of their arguments no longer than one sheet of A4 paper. Further guidance on the preparation and content of skeleton arguments can be found in the *Practice Direction (Civil Litigation: Case Management)* [1995] 1 WLR 262.

ON THE DAY OF THE MOOT

On the morning of the moot your worst nightmare can most easily be avoided by contacting the judge, or sending some sort of reminder, just to make sure that the judge has not been double-booked.

Nerves thus settled, your next task is to ensure that sufficient copies of the moot problem should also be made available, not only for the judge and mooters, but also for any spectators. At the same time the judge will need to be supplied with a copy of the authorities and any rules/guidelines for judging which are to be operated. The furniture in the room where the moot is to be held also needs to be arranged in order to suit the purposes of the moot. This is particularly necessary if no custom-fitted room is available to facilitate mooting or general advocacy, or where refreshments are to be provided within the same room as the moot itself.

The judge should be seated behind a large desk facing the mooters (and any audience in attendance). The clerk also sits behind a large table to facilitate the easy use of all the law reports, textbooks and other materials which will have been placed there. It is also advisable for the clerk to sit immediately in front of, or beside, the judge so as to make it easier for materials to be passed from the clerk to the judge throughout the moot. The two mooters on each side sit together at a table on the opposite side of the room from their opponents. The tables for the mooters may be positioned directly facing the clerk and the judge or at an angle of between forty-five and ninety degrees to the judge's table so that the mooters are equally visible to the judge and the audience, although still able to maintain eye contact with the judge. This latter requirement is particularly important if the mooters are to argue from their table rather than from a centrally positioned lectern, although either is perfectly acceptable.

The organiser may also wish to supply the mooters and the judge with carafes of water, which should be put in place on the respective desks, beside the copies of the moot problem, in advance of the moot. If an audience is expected, arrangements should be made for seating and for copies of the moot problem to be distributed for the use of the audience.

Preferably at least one hour in advance of the moot the necessary materials should be obtained from the library and put in place on the clerk's desk. The law reports and journals should be arranged in chronological order and other materials, such as textbooks, select committee reports and so on should also be arranged in some convenient manner. A paper marker or post-it note should be placed in the law reports (and other books) at all of the particular citations or page numbers supplied by the mooters.

A useful tip at this point is to ensure that all the different reports of a particular case are made available if the mooters have cited different versions of the same case (for example where the case has been reported in both the Weekly Law Reports and the All England Law Reports). This is necessary because one or more of the mooters may wish to quote a portion of the case, which may be difficult for the judge to find if supplied with a different report of that case from the one being used by the mooter.

The clerk should also be supplied with a stopwatch or other means by which to time the moot. A stopwatch is the most accurate means of timing, particularly if the rules adopted state that time is to cease to run when the mooter is required to answer a question posed by the judge. Time cards are also useful in a competition and should also be provided for the clerk. The idea is that the clerk can produce the time cards at different intervals in order to warn the mooter of how long he has before he must finish his speech. Three cards printed in large, bold letters with '5 MINUTES', '1 MINUTE' and 'TIME' will usually be sufficient.

Finally, before the moot begins, the judge should be informed of the particular method of judging which is to be employed. This essentially means informing the judge whether the mooters are to be given individual marks/positions or to be judged as a team. It may be sufficient for the judge simply to select one or two mooters to go through to the next round if it is a 'knock-out' competition. The judge should also be informed if a judgment on the law is required (it normally is) in addition to the judgment given on the ability of the mooters. It is usual for a moot judge to pronounce first on the law and then on the result of the moot, as those mooters who win on the law may lose the moot itself (and vice versa). Be sure to give clear and precise instructions to the judge in order to avoid having to give embarrassing explanations to the mooters later on.

The role of the moot judge is, in short, to select a winner (see Chapter six) after taking into account a number of factors such as the presentation and structure of the legal argument, the use made of any authorities, and the ability to answer questions. There is much to be said for supplying guidelines to each moot judge as to how precisely you wish them to arrive at their decision. At the very least, it will encourage a degree of uniformity in the judging of moot competitions, which is particularly desirable in a 'knock-out' type competition where the mooters involved will necessarily present their arguments in front of different judges. Any such guidelines should be placed on the judge's table, along with the moot problem and list of authorities, prior to the moot. In addition the judge should be given the names of each participant and their respective status as counsel in the moot.

DURING THE MOOT

It is useful for the organiser to be on hand should any assistance be required such as the fetching of a stray authority from the library or to explain some ambiguity in the competition rules. However, in the experience of one of the writers, the moot organiser will always be available during the moot — firmly in place in the clerk's chair!

AFTER THE MOOT

First, particularly if it is a 'knock-out' competition, you should make a note of the name(s) of the winner(s) and obtain the score-sheet from the judge if he or she has kept one (it may also include comments which may be useful for the future reference of the mooters).

Where required, the organiser should ensure that the mooters (and guests, where applicable) are provided with hospitality, whether it be of a gastronomic or alcoholic kind (sherry or wine are particularly acceptable after a moot, although best avoided before). This also encourages both judge and mooters to 'hang around' after the moot which can often become a pleasant social occasion for all those involved. However, even where no material hospitality is provided, it is good policy to encourage the mooters to talk individually to the judge in order to be provided with some constructive criticism, comments or general feedback regarding their performance. This is an effective way for the mooters to be made aware of any weak points or mistakes in their argument or its presentation so as to enable them to learn from their experience and avoid such blunders in the future.

You should also ensure that arrangements are made for the return to the library or some other safe storage of all the mooting materials. This should never be overlooked because the goodwill of the librarian may forever be lost if the privilege of removing law reports and other 'valuables' from the library is abused.

Above all, you must remember to thank the judge. A verbal 'thank you' goes without saying but a short written note of thanks is also generally very much appreciated and is an excellent way of maintaining good long-term relations with those who have acted as moot judges, should you (or your successor) need to call upon their services again in the future!

A QUICK CHECK-LIST FOR THE MOOT ORGANISER

Before each moot

Select the mooters (randomly or with reference to any previous round of the competition).   [   ]

Set date, time and venue for moot (book venue, if necessary).   [   ]
Select a moot problem.   [   ]

Send the following to all the mooters

The moot problem, together with a copy of the moot competition
rules, if necessary.   [   ]
Details of the time, date, venue of moot.   [   ]
The time, date and method of exchanging authorities.   [   ]
The name of the opposing counsel with whom exchange of authorities
is to be effected.   [   ]
The side of case and the grounds of the appeal which each mooter is to
argue.   [   ]
State whether the mooter is to be a junior or a leading counsel.   [   ]

Other arrangements

Make arrangements for a moot judge. Send the judge a copy of the
moot problem and all the arrangements for the moot (plus any
guidelines for judging, if necessary).   [   ]
Arrange for any hospitality to be provided.   [   ]
Arrange the furniture in the moot room.   [   ]
Place a copy of the moot problem, copy of the rules, a list of authorities
(and any guidelines or score-sheet, if appropriate) and the names of
each moot counsel on the judge's table.   [   ]
Collect all necessary material from the library and place it in order on
the clerk's table.   [   ]
Provide a stopwatch and time cards for the clerk. Ensure that the
stopwatch is functioning correctly.   [   ]

After the moot

Take a note of the name(s) of the winner(s) for the competition
records. Obtain any score-sheets kept by the judge.   [   ]
Ensure that any law reports and other materials are returned to the
library or secured in a safe place after the moot.   [   ]
Send a note of thanks to the judge.   [   ]

Three

HOW TO PREPARE FOR A MOOT

WHERE TO START?

It may seem obvious, but it is true nonetheless: the only way to start when preparing for a moot is by reading the moot problem carefully. Since moots are always argued as appeals, it is particularly important that the participants understand what are the precise grounds of appeal. Sometimes the grounds will be stated explicitly in the moot problem itself. On other occasions the problem will give the reasons for the decision of the lower court and then say simply that the losing party now appeals against these findings or rulings. Whatever the style of the moot problem you are given, the only way you can really be sure you understand the basis of the argument you will be expected to present is by rewriting the grounds of appeal in your own words.

It is surprising how often mooters go astray not because they present a poor argument but simply because they have failed from the outset to grasp the essence of the case. In our experience such failures have rarely been due to a general lack of understanding of the area of law in question, but have usually resulted from mooters' unfamiliarity with the language used to describe the grounds of the moot. If you get into the habit of rewriting the grounds of appeal in your own words, you should avoid this problem at one stroke. You can now base the rest of your mooting preparations on these rewritten grounds of appeal and need return to those stated in the problem only if you find it necessary to check a precise point of detail.

Remember too that mooting is normally conducted as a contest between two teams of two. Although you may well find it easiest to divide the moot between yourself and your leader/junior so that each of you has exclusive responsibility for researching the particular argument which he or she has been allocated or has chosen, this clearly presupposes that you both know what it is that you are expected to be arguing. The one essential element of cooperation between you, therefore, is to ensure that you both understand the grounds of appeal. If you then wish to disperse into opposite corners of the law library, you can at least do so in the knowledge that your teammate cannot spoil your chances by getting hold of quite the wrong end of the stick.

But just before you get carried away with your library research, stop and think. Do you represent the appellant or the respondent? It is no good putting some thought into rewriting the grounds of appeal in easy-to-understand English and then setting about trying to put together an excellent case for such an appeal, only to realise the day before the moot (or, even worse, just hours or minutes before the moot is to start) that you are supposed to be arguing for the respondent. If you are, indeed, to represent the appellant, all well and good. You need do nothing to your own version of the grounds of appeal. If you represent the respondent, on the other hand, you will now need to write out a second version which directly contradicts the grounds of appeal. Sometimes this can be accomplished simply by putting an occasional 'not' in the appropriate place, but sometimes this will not work because the language becomes too convoluted to be easily comprehensible, so a complete new draft will be necessary. Once this is written you will know exactly what it is you are trying to persuade the moot judge to accept.

Knowing your objective is not, however, enough. Having decided clearly what view you are expected to persuade the moot judge to accept, you must now work out how your argument is to progress to that conclusion. This involves reasoning backwards, as it were, because you start with the conclusion and then work out how to get there. Many of you probably feel that judges do this all the time, so it should hardly be unfamiliar to you. And if you need any inspiration, you can always read a judgment by Lord Denning.

The easiest way to note down the required stages of the argument is by the time-honoured formula of arranging each discrete point in a sensible order and then numbering them accordingly. The one problem with this method is working out where you should start, i.e., what should point number one be? One of the authors of this book once attended a moot in a national competition in which one of the mooters began his speech by trying to explain to the moot court (which for the purposes of the moot was supposed to be the House of Lords) what was meant by the doctrine of precedent. Needless to say, it was an argument that met rather short shrift!

It must be said that this was an extreme and unusual example, but it is still often true that mooters, particularly the less experienced, commence their argument at too basic a level. The usual advice that we have heard given to mooters is that they should assume that the moot judge is familiar with the area of law in question, but in our view it is difficult for anyone who has not mooted before to put this advice to practical use.

A more pragmatic way of working out what the first point in your argument will be is, having started with your desired conclusion, to keep on working backwards step by step until you get to a point which is legally uncontroversial. Since the other side in the moot will not, by definition, wish to dispute this point of law, it can be stated very simply in an opening sentence or two and then 'You're off', as they say in racing circles, without fear either of being contradicted or of boring everyone silly (particularly the judge) by reciting law which they consider to be obvious.

Of course, rewriting the grounds of appeal and using them in the way suggested here makes it imperative that your rewritten versions are accurate. If you are unsure about this, there is nothing to stop you consulting others, including your tutors, for confirmation. It will not take up much of their time and will demonstrate to them that you have put some thought into what you are doing. Indeed, such consultation is often a particularly good idea if you are preparing for your first moot, since the inevitable apprehension that you probably feel when confronted with the moot problem can at least be tempered with a feeling of confidence that you are now sure that you are starting on the right footing.

WHICH BOOKS SHOULD BE CONSULTED FIRST?

The key here again is to start with those books with which you are most familiar. This usually means reading the appropriate sections of the textbook(s) you have been using during your course. This has two advantages, especially for the less experienced mooter. The first is, of course, that since you should already be familiar with the style and layout of the textbook you are using, at least the early stages of research for the moot should not appear too formidable.

The second advantage, however, is rather less psychological and correspondingly more practical. You have probably noticed that textbooks are always stuffed full of notes (whether placed at the end of each chapter, or at the foot of each page) and may even have felt that they are rather in the way. For the mooter, however, they are a godsend for, once you have read the appropriate section in the textbook (and bearing in mind the version of the case to be argued which you have already prepared in accordance with the previous section in this chapter) it will become obvious to you which of the footnotes are relevant to the moot in hand. You should now make a note of the particular principles or points of law to which each of the footnotes are apparently relevant and write against each point the name and citation of each statute, case, article or book to which you are being referred.

At this stage, you may feel that there are one or two 'gaps' in your case in the sense that the textbook either does not cover some of the issues adequately for your purposes (or even at all) or else the author has made some interesting points but given no adequate reference to justify his argument. If you do find yourself in this position, you should make a note of these 'gaps' on a fresh sheet of paper. In the case of points canvassed by the textbook author but inadequately justified you should also make a note of the page on which those points were made. This is because if your subsequent research turns up no authorities on which you can rely to make the same point, it may well be that in the moot you will have to fall back on a quotation from the textbook itself.

Some mooters like to repeat this process of 'grazing' through all the competing textbooks until they feel that they have entirely exhausted this source. Such an approach is particularly valuable if your reading of the first book generated rather a long list of 'gaps'. It is also true that the major textbook writers often disagree and so you will sometimes gain greater insight into an area of law by reading several different authors who all approach the topic from a rather different perspective.

An approach that is often overlooked, however, is to consult old editions of textbooks. This may seem odd in light of the fact that the moot itself will be concerned about the present state of the law in this area. Nevertheless, it is surprising how much more you will come to understand the particular points of law to be mooted once you have traced their historical development. If you have already realised, for example, that the Misrepresentation Act 1967 is important for your moot then you will probably find it useful to go back to an edition of a textbook published soon after the Act became law to discover what the author considered to be the Act's main purpose and what, if any, problems could be foreseen in its implementation. You can then trace the operation of the Act in court through subsequent editions up to the present day, gathering both understanding and new references to footnotes as you go. Even if this method does not render up information which can be imported directly into the argument you wish to present in the moot court, you may well find that you are better able to respond to questions from the moot judge because you will know both how problems foreseen at the outset have been overcome (or, perhaps, have not been overcome) and how and why others have developed in the way that they have.

Whether you have chosen to consult one textbook or several, you will now have quite a long list of references for further research. There is no rule about working out which you should look at first, so just try those that look most interesting or useful or convenient. As you consult each reference in turn, it will itself yield further references. Note them down in the same way as was described above for your textbooks, keeping a separate sheet for recording 'gaps' in your research. Of course, you will hope to fill in most, if not all, such gaps during the course of such research but if they stubbornly remain, pause and think again.

Consider once again your easy-to-understand outline of your case which you prepared at the very beginning. Do these gaps really matter, or are they just interesting points of law which are at best marginal — and at worst quite irrelevant — to the real issues to be mooted? If they are irrelevant you can simply forget them and stop worrying. If, however, you are sure that a proper understanding of these apparently uncharted waters is essential, you should now focus your research effort on them.

HOW TO RESEARCH A TOPIC WITHOUT INITIAL REFERENCES

The basic problem with carrying out research in the way advocated in the section immediately above is that the initial sources of information (i.e., the textbooks) are not primarily designed as aids to mooting, nor even to the presentation of cases in court. They may therefore deal with the moot topic in a way which is only superficially useful as far as mooting is concerned. Following up the footnotes and endnotes in textbooks often overcomes such problems, however, particularly as each new reference yields further references of its own. But it does not always work out like that, particularly if you still have a considerable number of gaps to fill in.

The way round this problem is to behave like a real advocate. Practitioners have little time to carry out research on anything like as systematic a basis as students and therefore rely heavily on texts which are regularly updated with everything that the editors think could possibly be relevant. Such works are nothing like as discursive as the average textbook and tend to prune information almost to the bone but, provided that both the publishers and your librarians are efficient and conscientious, these primarily practitioner-oriented texts will be comprehensive and (almost) up to date.

The best known such work is, of course, *Halsbury's Laws*. (Make sure that it is *Halsbury's Laws* that you are looking at and not *Halsbury's Statutes* or *Statutory Instruments*.) This multi-volume work claims to record all the law of England and Wales. The right volume of the latest edition is easily chosen by considering the headings on the spine of each one. *Halsbury* is crammed full of even more footnotes than the average textbook, so any flagging research is likely to be given new impetus immediately. But there are two other general works often overlooked by mooters (and, indeed, by academics in general) which may also yield useful information. These are *Atkin's Court Forms* (which has 41 volumes plus an index and a supplement) and *The Encyclopaedia of Forms and Precedents* (*EFP*, which has 42 volumes plus an index). Both *Atkin's* and *EFP* are designed primarily to enable practitioners to draft documents in the most effective and legally acceptable manner, but they also provide explanations as to why the documents proposed — known as 'precedents' — are drafted in this way, and such explanations usually involve demonstrating that some element of the substantive law is more likely to be satisfied. Thus *Atkin's* and *EFP* may well suggest not only what needs to be proven in a particular case but also potentially the best means of doing so.

Some readers might feel, on learning of the virtues of *Atkin's* and *EFP*, that it would be a useful short cut if they began their research with one or other work rather than coming to them after considerable work has already been done. This may well be a sensible approach on some occasions for the more experienced mooter (provided it does not justify sheer laziness) but for the beginner and intermediate mooter there are likely to be great dangers in adopting such an approach. In particular, there will be a great temptation to shoehorn the particular facts of the moot problem into the form or pattern set out in *Atkin's* or *EFP*, so that you end up trying to argue a case rather different from the actual problem with which you are supposed to be dealing. Indeed, both works carry warnings to practitioners not to fall into this trap and suggest that it is best avoided by first drafting a case independently of these texts and only subsequently using them to check both that important stages of the argument (and of procedure, though that will seldom be important to mooters) have not been omitted and that the appropriate phraseology has been used.

Three other works of a general nature may also prove useful in preparing an argument for a moot. The first is *Current Law* with its Yearbooks and citators. The Yearbooks use a system of straightforward headings which enable the reader to find the relevant area of law without difficulty, so that it is possible to trace legal developments from year to year with a minimum of work. The one drawback with the synopses in the Yearbooks is that they are usually rather brief and certainly unsuitable for citation in the moot court. This problem is overcome by the citators, however, which provide citations for the standard sets of law reports for each case mentioned in the Yearbooks, so that you will be able to consult the primary source itself.

The next source of material worthy of discussion is *The Digest* (formerly *The English and Empire Digest*). The arrangement of the volumes in this work is similar to that used in *Halsbury*, *Atkin's* and *EFP* but the particular function useful for the mooter and performed by *The Digest* is that of tracing the history of a particular case. So you may be able to discover with relatively little effort whether and when the ratio of a case has been applied, followed, disapproved, doubted or distinguished.

Finally, you should not overlook *Current Law Statutes Annotated* for any moot in which a relatively recent piece of legislation is involved. This contains not only the text of the statute in question but also full annotations explaining why each particular provision was enacted, what its impact on the previous law is (or is likely to be) and how individuals' behaviour may be expected to change as a consequence of the provision. On occasion, the annotation may also refer to differences between the Act which gained the Royal Assent and clauses initially proposed in the Bill before parliament, together with an explanation as to why the changes were made and the practical effect of doing so. One of the authors of this book has personal experience of a real-life case of an application for judicial review which a local authority had every intention of resisting until its counsel was made aware by the applicant of such a change having been made to the Bill in question, whereupon counsel for the authority recommended to his client that they accede to the relief sought by the applicant. Although a full hearing was therefore unnecessary, the time and cost of attending the Royal Courts of Justice could also easily have been avoided if the local authority's legal team had just taken the trouble to consult *Current Law Statutes Annotated*.

WHAT ABOUT LEXIS?

Those addicted to information technology will probably be wondering why no mention has so far been made of LEXIS. For the uninitiated, LEXIS is a computerised data retrieval system, on which is stored an enormous number of statutes, statutory instruments, law reports and even some (mainly North American) law journals. Searches can be made by, for example, case name or keyword, thus allowing you to generate long lists of cases on the most vaguely defined subject area on the one hand — which will, frankly, be too broad to be of any use to you — or the most technical point of legal detail on the other.

Computer fanatics will think this a godsend and the obvious place to start, but our own experience suggests that this would be quite the wrong move. For one thing, it is nothing like as easy to read words on a computer screen as it is to read those on the printed page. Even if you wish to get LEXIS to print all the material it has to offer you, you will probably find that (unless you command the printing to take place at Butterworths' offices to be sent on to you) the print quality will be little better — it may even be worse — than the typeface showing on the screen. And if you request the printing of anything other than the briefest selection of materials, it is likely to take an unbelievably long time. Moreover, the cost of so doing (especially if the printing is to be done at Butterworths) will be so great that your librarian will probably refuse in any case.

Finally, there is always the very real danger that if you turn to LEXIS at the beginning of your research, it will either simply generate so much material that you will be swamped and will not know where to start, or you will be forced to so restrict your enquiry that you will miss important points while lulled into a false sense of security that because you have consulted a computer you must have discovered all there is to know. Remember: as with all computer retrieval systems, LEXIS will only tell you what you have asked it to tell you. It is therefore much the best ploy to save a LEXIS search for somewhere near the end of your research endeavours, so that you can then be fairly sure that you are asking LEXIS the right questions. Used in this way, LEXIS becomes an important 'longstop' enabling you to check that you have missed nothing of importance and, in particular, that no recent developments have been overlooked.

HOW TO PUT THE INFORMATION TOGETHER

If you are anything like most mooters we know, you will now have far more information than you can possibly cram into the fifteen or twenty minutes' speech that you will be expected to make at the moot itself. Experience will make you more selective after a while, but it's almost inevitable in your first few moots that you'll be so concerned not to miss anything that you'll go over the top and decide to make a note of far more than is really necessary.

But do not despair. None of that work has really been wasted. The more you understand the general framework of the law and the context in which the particular dispute to be mooted is set, the better you are likely to be both at presenting your argument to the moot court in the first place and also at answering questions from the judge later on. You just need to follow some simple principles in deciding what precise pieces of information (probably case law in the main) you will rely on for your speech. These principles are dealt with in Chapter 4.

Four

HOW TO WRITE A MOOT COURT SPEECH

WHERE TO START?

When you are confronted by so much material, it is exceedingly tempting to start construction of your moot speech by picking out the cases you consider most important and trying to build your speech around them. It may be tempting, but it is invariably the wrong approach, because the result tends to be a disjointed 'shopping list' of cases which appear to have little or no underlying theme and which is therefore incredibly boring to listen to. Moreover, if you take this approach, there is always a tendency to feel that an inordinately large number of cases are important, and so the 'shopping list' becomes swelled by a number of rather unnecessary or actually irrelevant 'items'. This latter problem becomes particularly acute if no limit is placed upon the number of authorities that can be cited in a particular competition, but even where a limit is set — ten cases per team for example — it is usually unwise actually to cite that number of cases in a moot speech for the simple reason that in the limited time available you will never be able to do them justice. It is always better to make very good use of one or two cases than to give a superficial résumé of four or five.

You must also ensure that you do not fall into the trap of presenting a moot argument in the style of a legal essay. Do not attempt to cover a large area of the law (such as would be found in such an essay or in lecture notes). The rationale of the moot is quite different: it is designed to limit the argument only to (typically) one or two particular points of law. There will thus be no advantage in stating the whole area of law concerned. This only wastes time, irritates the judge and detracts from the quality of the relevant part of the argument. The only real similarity between writing a moot speech and a legal essay is that in neither case is it permissible to quibble about the facts of the problem set. In a moot the facts are to be taken as stipulated in the problem. If there is any doubt or dispute, then the matter should be discussed with the opposing counsel before the moot and a solution agreed upon. You may find a friendly lecturer is prepared to help out here. But if no agreement can be reached, the moot stands as written.

So what approach is suitable for a moot? It is often said that a legal argument, whether presented in a moot court or elsewhere, should proceed from 'principle'. The problem with this rather Delphic statement is that it is both vague and ambiguous, not least because (even if some lawyers would claim that the phrase 'legal principle' describes a fairly precise legal concept) the word 'principle' in practice conveys so many different meanings to so many different people. In our view, some rather more practical advice is required, which can then be tailored to fit your own preferred working habits as you become more experienced.

We suggest that the best method of beginning to write your moot speech involves reading over your notes briefly, so that you are aware of the main issues involved in the case, and then putting them out of sight. For the next step you should now pretend that you are writing a letter to your parents or to a friend who — while perfectly intelligent — knows little about the law, but wishes to know how the moot problem can best be resolved. Unless your private life is a total disaster area, such pretence should make it inevitable that you will avoid being condescending or patronising, which might otherwise strain your relationship with the moot court judge. The second, and most important, effect of imagining yourself in this position, however, is that you cannot really cite many cases — if any at all. This is because, as you instinctively know already, case law is the highly esoteric preserve of the lawyer: lay people are interested only in the outcome of the individual case, and any discussion of the nuances of meaning of certain words, or of the distinction between a case's *ratio decidendi* and any *obiter dicta* will simply make their eyes glass over. Finally, you will probably have to write down your own personal views as to why it is right (or wrong) that the law should decide the matter in this way.

In writing this imaginary letter, you will therefore be forced to simplify the issues, to use everyday language, and to produce a comprehensible explanation. You will also be compelled to be brief. When you have finished the 'letter', read it over and see if you need to add or amend anything. In particular, if you are speaking first, you may wish to try to anticipate one or two likely arguments of the other side and attempt to show why they are not really good arguments at all. If you are speaking second, you will have to build some flexibility into your speech so that you can respond directly to any particularly forceful points made by counsel for the appellants. But do not overdo these attempts at destroying the other side's argument: a crisp demolition job with the aid of one quotation from a case is ideal. Otherwise you will end up with no time to put forward your own arguments.

Something else you should bear in mind when reading through this 'letter' is the doctrine of precedent. You cannot ask a moot version of the Court of Appeal, for example, to overrule any decision of the House of Lords. So check that the moot court has both the power to grant the remedy that you are seeking and the status to treat your process of reasoning as valid. Thus, although the Court of Appeal cannot *overrule* a decision of the House of Lords, it may be possible to persuade the Court to *distinguish* a troublesome House of Lords case.

When you are happy with your 'letter', you can begin to incorporate some of the legal material that you had earlier pushed to one side. Ideally, you will be writing both your initial 'letter' and the subsequent drafts of your speech on a word processor, so that you will be able to print out each new draft quite easily without having to start writing a new one right back at page one. However, just because you are now incorporating the distinctively 'legal' material, do not be too keen to complicate your speech, or to use more 'legalistic' language, or to make the speech very long. Remember that, although you are currently compiling a written document, it is not intended for submission as an essay. To put this another way, remember that you will have to read your speech out loud: the judge will not have a written copy in front of him or her from which to read your thoughts. The communication of ideas through the spoken word requires a much simpler vocabulary and syntax than is possible on the written page, so do not over-complicate matters or else you will end up sounding ridiculously pompous — and you will probably get everyone totally confused to boot, including yourself!

RE-INCORPORATING THE LAW

If you re-read your 'letter', you should find that it begins by establishing some basic, uncontroversial truths (much as we advocated in the opening section in Chapter three, entitled 'Where to start?'), and then proceeds with some argument or reasoning about the important legal issues before reaching a conclusion which that argument justifies and which everyone knew you were bound to reach because of which side you were representing. Such a narrative represents an argument 'from principle', unencumbered by the esoteric niceties of case law or statutory interpretation. To adapt the well-known aphorism about the composition of a narrative you should, in other words, have an uncontroversial beginning, a contentious middle and a predictable end.

If you disentangle these three parts of your narrative from each other, it should be pretty obvious that the first and last elements need no particular support from legal authority in order for you to utter them with justification in the moot court. If you have begun from an uncontroversial starting-point then, by definition, there can be nothing that anyone would wish to say to throw doubt on your assertions. And your final submissions should need no extra support since, if your middle section is properly drafted, it should appear pretty obvious. The major additions to your original 'letter' should therefore clearly concentrate on providing extra authority for the contentious middle part.

It is likely that this middle section involves the taking of several intellectual 'steps', each of which progresses the argument a little further in the direction you wish it to go in order to reach the desired conclusion. These steps can now be numbered in the order in which it will be necessary for you to deal with them. However, it is important to realise that simply because it is necessary from the point of view of logic or rational explanation to discuss point one before point two, it does not follow that point one is more important or requires more justification. Since your moot speech will be heavily circumscribed by time, it is vital that you make the best possible use of the time available by concentrating your energy on explaining the most important or most controversial points in your argument. Once you have numbered each successive point, therefore, it is a good idea to mark in some way those points for which you will need, by reason of their importance or controversial nature, to provide the best possible legal authority.

It should now become clear which case(s) you will need to cite in order to give your presentation maximum weight. Ideally, you would like to be able to make use of a section of a statute or a unanimous judgment of the House of Lords to bolster your viewpoint, but they are unlikely to be available since otherwise the point would not be so important or controversial. More likely, you will have to develop the reasoning in some *obiter dictum*, or seek to extend a perfectly sound *ratio* into an area probably not originally envisaged by the author of the original judgment. Whatever is required, your general familiarity with the primary sources as a result of your research should tell you both what is available and where to look to find it.

REWRITING YOUR SPEECH

At this stage you need to take a metaphorical step back and pause to ponder on the following conundrum. Can you possibly deal satisfactorily with all these points and authorities in a moot speech lasting fifteen or twenty minutes? If you are very experienced, the answer may well be 'Yes', because you will have developed the required expertise of being able to sort out what is important and/or relevant and what is not. If you are not so experienced, the likely answer is that you cannot make this speech within the prescribed time limit.

The way to solve this problem is to consider which of the various points that you wish to make is your best or strongest point, which is your next best, and so on. You should now rewrite your speech to ensure that prominence is given to the best points at the expense of the ones you do not really expect to win. It may very well be the case that certain other matters should ideally be established first before your strongest arguments become relevant, but you are not mooting in an ideal court. Instead, you should simply assert these 'steps' without bothering with authority to support them. Clearly, this is very different from what is expected of you in a legal essay. But in the modern real-life courtroom, where skeleton arguments are frequently submitted to the court in advance, the actual advocacy is limited in precisely this way. Once the groundwork has been laid in the form of these necessary assertions, you can plunge full-blooded into your best arguments without the fear of running out of time.

Moreover, if the judge feels that these assertions do need to be explored in more detail, they will intervene and ask you to do just that. This should cause you no problem, since you have already worked out your arguments (with supporting authorities) for each of these points, so you simply need to have your notes handy in order to be able to refer to them. But the big advantage to you of this approach is that if the judge does feel that further elucidation is required, the clock stops as soon as the judge intervenes and does not begin again until you resume the main body of your moot speech. Thus you will be able to get in all the points you originally wanted to make without exceeding the time limit.

GOING BACK TO THE BEGINNING

It should by now have become clear to you that your moot speech is likely to be interrupted on at least one or two occasions. Since the flow of your argument may well be hampered by such interruptions, it is almost inevitable that the logic which you believed dictated the construction of your speech will not be easily conveyed to the judge. It therefore aids the clarity of your argument enormously if you begin your submission by stating in turn each of the basic propositions on which you wish to rely. In other words, you should always begin the main body of your speech (i.e., after the introductions of mooting personnel and the facts of the case before the court) by telling the judge what you are going to be saying over the next fifteen or twenty minutes.

If you have been following our suggested methodology, you will have already enumerated each point in accordance with the earlier section in this chapter entitled 'Re-incorporating the law', so all you need do here is simply to read out each point in turn. The judge will probably wish to make a note of each point for personal use, and your adoption of this strategy will therefore provide a framework by which the judge can make sense of each submission in your presentation, no matter how disjointed it may become through questioning or other unforeseen occurrences. You may be amazed how much clearer this strategy of stating your propositions at the outset of the case makes your argument to the judge. Indeed, this is probably the most important element of your whole speech and, if you have stated these points with sufficient clarity and conciseness you can be almost certain that the judge will mention this aspect of your performance in the judgment at the end of the case. After all, you will have provided a succession of 'pointers' to help the judge to follow what you say. Moreover, you will have gained the added advantage of providing the judge with a ready-made basis from which to challenge the arguments of the other side by causing the judge to refer to each of your stated propositions in turn to see how opposing counsel deals and/or dealt with them.

THE FINAL DRAFT

Something you should not do is to read your address to the court or attempt to learn it by heart. This will detract from the spontaneity of the presentation and can inhibit your flexibility, particularly when the judge interrupts you for some reason or asks a question. Notwithstanding these considerations, you will need some notes to hand throughout the moot as a memory aid, particularly if you encounter problems or your nerve fails. You therefore need to give some thought to the precise form which you wish these notes to take.

Some mooters make very full notes, or even write out the whole speech; others simply make a list of 'bullet points' and rely on adrenalin during their presentation to enable them to flesh out these points with coherent arguments. The former tend to be good at presenting their initial argument but weak at responding to questions from the judge. The latter's presentation of the case from the outset may not be so strong, but their ability to respond to questions is often greater and more flexible. In practice, any method is acceptable provided that it enables you to look at the judge rather than constantly at your notes while also allowing you to find the notes relevant to any point or case virtually instantaneously when the matter is broached by the judge. Thus you cannot read your speech; but it also follows that it is not a good idea to write out your speech in narrative form as though it were an essay in any event, since each page is then likely to deal with several issues, which may not be particularly easy to disentangle if you are put on the spot.

We suggest therefore that you use either cards or loose-leaf sheets of paper, and head each one with the particular proposition which it purports to deal with. Your notes on each sheet can be as brief or as full as you like, but the heading should enable you to find the right page immediately when asked a question. We also suggest that the details of any cases to which you wish to refer should be recorded on a sheet of paper kept separate from the main body of your argument and also from the details of any other case. This is because you may want to use the case to support more than one proposition, and this will avoid you having to write out the salient facts of the case more than once (in case the judge asks you to recite them). Thus you should have two piles of notes: one containing argument, and the other containing the details of all the cases you wish to cite.

If you adopt this method you will also find it easier to deal with any judicial intervention which requires you to refer to a particular case. For if you simply write the details of your case into the main body of your speech, you will have to leaf through your notes to find the case in the first place, and then leaf back again, once the judge is satisfied with your response, in order that you can restart your speech at the point where you left off. It is surely far better to be able just to pause in your speech while leaving those notes untouched and simply turn to the relevant page in your pile of notes on cases. This way you do not run the risk of getting all your notes out of sequence.

MAKING USE OF AUTHORITIES

A word of warning must be uttered here. Do not get into the trap of thinking that the mere citation of the reference for a case or statutory provision will suffice in the moot court. Whenever you refer to an authority, the judge will expect you to make it quite clear what precise proposition of law you think the case or provision is authority for; and will expect you to do this by, at the very least, quoting a passage which you believe sums up the essence of the point you wish to make. If you have no intention of quoting a particular passage from a case, statute or statutory instrument, the safest thing to do is not to mention it at all. Otherwise you will find yourself trying to explain the *ratio* of a case whose details you can barely recollect, if at all; and to no useful purpose since the case says next to nothing which adds import to your submission. As was said at the beginning of this chapter, it is therefore good advice to limit the number of legal authorities (be they cases or references to other materials) to which you will refer the moot judge. Moreover, introducing a large number of authorities into a moot speech often detracts from the argument, and can even reduce it to little more than a patchwork of quotations.

In those instances where you definitely do wish to quote certain passages, make sure that the judge whose views these words apparently represent does not in the immediately preceding or succeeding paragraphs make it clear that their opinion is the very opposite of what you would have the judge believe! It is amazing how many mooters apparently think they can hoodwink the judge by being highly selective with their quotations from a case. Such selectivity hardly ever bears fruit, because most judges are not completely foolish, and they will wish to try to put the words you quote into some sort of context by reading the passages which come immediately before

and after. Getting caught out like this can be highly embarrassing for the
mooter concerned, and can often completely undermine their whole
argument, so make sure that your submissions are built on rather firmer
footings.

USING SECONDARY SOURCES

Once again, our advice here is very different from that which is tendered
when you are working out how best to write a legal essay. In the latter case,
you are expected to indicate the sources of your arguments throughout,
which includes acknowledging the author of any ideas upon which you wish
to draw, even if these views were not uttered in a judicial setting. To pretend
that these views are your own, original thoughts is to commit the academic
sin of plagiarism, which is quite rightly frowned upon since it is essentially
an example of dishonesty.

The problem with complete intellectual honesty in the moot court,
however, is that it can get you into more problems than it resolves. For
academic writings (together with the writings of judges published in learned
journals or the popular press) are simply of no legal authority. The response
of the judge to whom you cite a learned article is therefore likely to be
something like, 'That's all very well, but can that view be supported by
authority?'. Since the answer is likely to be 'No' (for otherwise you would
presumably have cited the relevant case instead) you then simply find
yourself back at square one with nothing on which to base your submission.

The way to circumvent this problem is simply to plagiarise like mad! Read
all the secondary literature you can, since it will often explain the law in a far
more digestible form than the cases themselves do. If any particularly good
arguments strike you, then by all means make use of them, but present them
to the court as though they were your own views. This also has the advantage
of saving time since you will not have to take several minutes directing the
judge to particular passages in an article, and this method will also enable
you to develop your argument more clearly without your flow being
interrupted.

This advice should not, however, be taken as suggesting that you should
not make a note of where you took your preferred argument from. On the
contrary, it is imperative that you make a note of the author, the title of the
publication and the page and year references to which you can refer during
your speech. This is important because if the judge then wishes to probe
more deeply into the argument that you are making, you can then refer to
the article, casenote, textbook or whatever as though it were authority. This
tactic makes you look very well prepared and also has the ironic effect of
giving added weight to the journal article, whereas if you had cited it straight
off the views expressed therein would probably have been dismissed out of
hand.

Five

GUIDELINES ON MOOT COURT ETIQUETTE

SELECTING AUTHORITIES

You will be required to exchange authorities with opposing counsel (with a copy to the clerk of the moot) at a given time (usually one to three days) before the moot. (Sometimes you may also be required to supply a copy of the main propositions of your intended submission for exchange with opposing counsel and for the reference of the judge but you can assume that this is not required unless told otherwise. See the section entitled 'A few days before the competition' (above) for guidance as to the preparation and structure of skeleton arguments.) It is vital for the smooth running of the moot (and good manners towards the other side, the clerk and the judge) that you ensure that your citations are completely accurate. Once you have submitted your authorities, you are not compelled to use any or all of them, but you cannot cite another case which is not on your list unless it is on the list given to you by the other side. Surprise citations of cases would cause havoc in the moot court room and are emphatically prohibited.

You should also, however, ensure that you continue to use the law report whose citation you gave to the other side and to the clerk. Quite often, unnecessary problems arise in a moot simply because a mooter gives opponents and the clerk (say) the All England Reports citation, but then attempts during the moot to refer everyone to passages quoted from the Weekly Law Reports. Of course the passages will be reported somewhere in the report through which the judge is frantically leafing, but since mooter and judge are now referring to entirely different publications, it is inevitable that the mooter's carefully prepared page and section numbers will be misleading and therefore useless. It need hardly be said that it is not a good idea to demonstrate to the judge that you are incompetent, so when you have chosen a citation: stick to it.

It is sometimes said that there is a hierarchy of law reports, so that those at the top of the tree should be cited in preference to all other reports, and those with greater standing should be cited in preference to those whose standing is somewhat lesser. On this basis the 'official' reports are consider-ed 'best', which for English law means the Law Reports themselves (i.e., the Appeal Cases, Queen's Bench, Chancery and Family reports), followed by the Weekly Law Reports and the All England Reports. For European judgments the European Court Reports are official and are therefore supposed to take precedence.

The reader will probably have noticed that we are not exactly sympathetic to this view. It is our experience that mooters are never penalised for using what, on this view, would amount to an 'inferior' law report. It is also our experience that judges in a real court are not at all bothered as to which report they are asked to refer to. What matters is that the report is germane to the issue in question and (if supplied as a photocopy) is perfectly legible. Indeed, there are some courtrooms where the only readily available law reports are the All England Reports.

Our advice, therefore, is generally to use whichever report is most convenient for you, although we do wish to enter two reservations. First, there is no point in using an incomplete law report when a full report is available elsewhere. This simply demonstrates sloppy research and is clearly bad practice, so do not rely on a law report in a newspaper, for instance, unless you have checked that there is no report of the case in a more 'traditional' publication. Secondly, there is also little point in making use of a clearly inferior law report of one case when a different case would make the same point just as well and can be found in a traditional law report. This second statement is particularly applicable when you are thinking of using a LEXIS transcript. These are notoriously difficult both to read to oneself and to follow when being directed to various passages by counsel, and are therefore best avoided if the cases which you have found on LEXIS say nothing that is not said equally well elsewhere. Certainly the Court of Appeal, in particular, has warned against an over-exuberant use of LEXIS in court, so our advice is to use such transcripts only when they reveal either a decision or some process of reasoning which cannot be found in other sources.

Once you have selected the cases to which you wish to refer during the moot, you should ensure that all these references are marked — either by yourself or by the clerk — by using a strip of paper or a post-it note as though it were a bookmark with the citation written at the top of the marker where it sticks out from the top of the law report. This will assist the judge in finding the passages to which you will want to direct his or her attention. (*Never* write in or on a law report itself unless it is a photocopy: your librarian will never speak to you again.) Some mooters find it useful to use a marker which fits exactly the size of the page of the particular text, so that the exact location of each quotation can be indicated on the marker itself for easy reference.

ADDRESSING THE COURT

Nerves often consume the inexperienced mooter just as they are about to get to their feet, and this loss of composure, however momentary, can lead to an embarrassing episode of tongue-tied mumbling. In order to combat this, it can be useful to memorise some sort of opening formula for your speech, which can be practised until uttering it becomes almost second nature. The relaxing effect of opening your speech with something so familiar can be considerable, so we suggest that you employ one or more of the verbal formulae set out in this chapter.

As in a real court, a case in a moot will be opened by leading counsel for the appellant or plaintiff. The usual formula for opening a case goes along the lines of:

'May it please your Lordships, I am appearing with Mr/Ms A for the appellant (plaintiff) X, and my learned friends Mr/Ms B and Mr/Ms C are appearing for the respondent (defendant) Y.'

Unless the judge indicates that he or she considers it unnecessary, it is also customary in this opening for leading counsel to state the salient facts of the moot case, which can be introduced with a verbal formula such as:

'The case before you today concerns ...'

Once these facts have been recited, counsel can then introduce the legal issues at stake by saying something like:

'The claim/charge is ...'

There is clearly no need for the other mooters to repeat the established facts of the case, so the openings to their speeches will be somewhat simpler. (Nevertheless, *all* the mooters should be sufficiently familiar with the facts of the case to be able to reiterate them at any point during the moot should they be requested to do so.) Leading counsel for the respondent could therefore say something like:

'If it pleases your Lordships, my name is B and I represent the respondent Y, together with my learned junior, Mr/Ms C.'

Junior counsel need say only:

'If it pleases your Lordships, my name is X and I am continuing the case for the appellant (respondent).'

An eagle-eyed reader will have spotted that the terms of address directed towards the Bench which are suggested here have so far been in the plural throughout. This is because most moots are heard as appeals in which at least two judges would be expected to sit. In practice, your moots are likely to be heard on most occasions by just one judge, but mooting etiquette demands that you should still address the Bench in the plural unless dealing with a question asked by an individual judge, in which case the singular form of address will be more appropriate (as, indeed, it would in a real court).

Once underway, you can make use of the abbreviated forms of address, which are 'My Lords' or 'My Ladies' when addressing the Bench directly; and 'Your Lordships' or 'Your Ladyships' when addressing the judge(s) indirectly. If you are confronted with a panel of both male and female judges, the correct form of address (as established since the elevation of Butler-Sloss LJ to the Court of Appeal) remains, for the sake of brevity as much as anything, 'Your Lordships'. As before, the singular method of address should, however, be used when one particular judge interjects or asks a question.

The etiquette relating to the mode of address for your fellow mooters is also modelled upon that adopted in court. Thus fellow counsel should be addressed as 'My learned Leader' or 'My learned Junior', as appropriate, whilst opposing Counsel should be addressed as 'My Learned Friend (or Friends)'. Again, just as in court, appellants, respondents, plaintiffs and defendants should always be referred to as such. Never say 'My client' because, even if you really were in court, such a statement would be inaccurate since, strictly speaking, you would take your instructions from solicitors and not from the actual party in the case whom you are seeking to represent.

BEST PRACTICE WHEN ON YOUR FEET

The purpose of your speech is to communicate information and ideas to the judge. It is thus essential that the judge can hear and understand you. You must therefore speak clearly, varying your tone of voice to give expression to your words, and use short, concise sentences wherever possible. You only have a limited time in which to make the best impact you can, so you must also avoid the twin temptations of digressing in any way from the main point at issue and of waffling about nothing in particular. These are simply ways of trying the judge's patience.

But the most important thing to remember above all is to take your time. Speed can be disastrous, so do not gabble. In fact, a moot speech, like a speech in court or indeed any form of public speaking, should be made at a pace far slower than is usual in ordinary conversation. You must therefore cultivate the habit of speaking slowly in public. If you are naturally inclined to gabble or to get rather enthusiastic about things when talking, you may find speaking slowly to be the hardest aspect of a moot because your mind will have a tendency to race ahead of where your mouth has got to, leaving yourself — and everyone else — totally confused as to what you were talking about.

If you do find speaking slowly really difficult, the best advice is to model yourself on a lawyer or politician you have seen or heard on television or radio. You will notice that when a member of either of these groups of people is interviewed, their replies are almost always very slow and measured. This enables them both to think ahead and to choose their words with care and to best effect, whilst at the same time avoiding any pregnant pauses where they might feel the need to say 'um' or 'er'. Of course, you may detest most lawyers and politicians, but it is their style of speaking that you need to adopt when giving a moot speech, not their point of view.

Another technique to adopt in a moot, and which is again favoured by both practising lawyers and politicians, is that of giving your arguments an air of weight and authority even though the point you wish to make may be entirely of your own creation. Thus you should never commence a proposition of law by saying 'In my opinion' or 'I think' because this sounds far too personal and suggests that correspondingly little weight can be attached to the proposition advanced. Instead, open each proposition by using such expressions as:

'It is submitted that . . .' or 'It will be argued (or contended) that . . .'

This is particularly important at the beginning of your moot speech, since after you have introduced yourself, it is vital that you state in order the various propositions of law which form the body of your submission to the court. Thus you should say something like:

'It will be submitted that the appeal should be allowed/dismissed on the grounds that . . . This submission relies on three propositions, which I shall deal with in turn. They are, first, that . . .; second, that . . .; and finally, that . . .'

An opening like this has the added advantage that the judge will know which issues you are intending to leave until later in your speech, and will therefore be correspondingly less likely to interrupt you to ask about one of those issues until you have reached the point in your speech where you are prepared to deal with the matter.

Finally, we have some advice of the 'Motherhood and Apple Pie' variety. When speaking, stand still and do not shuffle about or pull at your clothing. You will need your hands to keep your place in your notes and, perhaps, for the odd, expressive gesture (though you should not overdo this) so keep them away from your pockets. To avoid annoying the judge (and the audience), please do not exceed the time limit for your speech. The ability to present your argument within the time allotted indicates efficiency and good preparation. If you are really unsure how long it is likely to take to deliver the speech, practise (at the appropriate pace) in front of a mirror. You may also find it a good idea to memorise the concluding sentence of your submission, even if it is only:

'My Lords, I submit that this appeal should be allowed/dismissed.'

This should give you added confidence as you know that at any moment you can resume your seat without any loss of dignity.

DEALING WITH JUDICIAL INTERVENTIONS

If asked by the judge to explain precisely what you mean or wish to argue, then a little more 'subjectivism' is permissible because you are now having to justify yourself, but phrases such as:

'My argument is . . .' or 'I am suggesting . . .'

are still preferable to the rather bald claim 'I think'.

If the judge takes issue with any argument and you consider that objection to be valid, concede by saying, for example:

'I am obliged to your Lordship.'

However, if you feel that you have a valid argument, then continue with it by using such words as:

> 'With (great) respect, my Lord . . .'; or 'I can see the force of your Lordship's argument, but it is nevertheless my (respectful) submission that . . .'

The words in parenthesis suggest greater deference, but there is in fact no need to be deferential to the judge. Etiquette demands that your obligations to the court and to the party whom you represent are best resolved by your being polite but firm. Often the judge will put a point to you because he or she wants to test it out, not because they think it is right and you are wrong. If you simply cave in you will certainly be marked down. The only times when you should stop arguing with the judge are when he or she appears satisfied with what you have said, or when they have clearly dismissed the point you are making out of hand. You cannot force a judge to change their mind, so just move on to your next point, otherwise you will simply be wasting your time.

Also do not be afraid to pause for thought. This may be particularly useful if the judge asks a question which you are unable to answer on the spur of the moment. If, after a moment or two for thought, you are still unable to answer, ask for leave to confer with your Leader/Junior. This is what would happen in real life and is usually perfectly permissible. Of course, this option is really only of use if both mooters on the same side are aware of each other's arguments. It is therefore a good idea to go through each other's submissions some time before the moot, perhaps the night before. If you are the leading counsel for the appellants, it is possible you will be granted a right of reply to the arguments of the respondents, in which case you will need to be familiar with both grounds of the appeal in any event.

One further point about dealing with interventions by the judge should perhaps be made. Some mooters get so carried away with delivering their prepared speech that they become almost oblivious of the behaviour of the judge. It is essential to look up at the judge as much as possible in order to gauge reaction to your arguments. If the judge screws up their face in anguish, it should be obvious that they are unhappy about something you have said, so ask the judge what is concerning him or her with a question such as:

> 'Is your Lordship (or Ladyship) unhappy about this contention?' or
> 'Your Lordship (or Ladyship) appears (You appear, my Lord (or Lady), to be) concerned about something. (Is it something I have said?) Perhaps I could be of some assistance?'

Conversely, if the judge keeps nodding and looking reasonably content, then you can be reasonably happy that all is going well.

There are, however, two things which you must never do. The first is that you must never interrupt the judge when he or she is speaking. It is *their* court, not yours, even if you may be distinctly unimpressed with their handling of the case. Secondly, you must allow the judge to interrupt you! It is the judge whom you are trying to persuade of the correctness of your argument, so you should be only too happy to assist them if they are still unclear about some point. It is no good trying just to keep on speaking and hoping that the judge will give up attempting to 'butt in'. We have seen mooters do this many times but they always end up looking foolish — and the judge always manages to ask his or her question in the end.

REFERRING TO LAW REPORTS

In a moot speech it is usual practice to cite law reports in full, and not by the abbreviated form commonly adopted in a citation. Although you may, of course, write down the abbreviated citation in your own notes or speech, you must remember to read it in full by stating the volume, name and year of the report. It is also a good idea to indicate at the outset which court heard the case to which you wish to refer, although this can sometimes be omitted if the case is so well known that it appears unnecessary to tell the judge which court decided it. Thus *Hedley Byrne & Co. Ltd* v *Heller & Partners Ltd* [1963] 2 All ER 575 becomes:

'The (House of Lords) case of *Hedley Byrne and Company Limited* against (or and) *Heller and Partners*, as reported in volume two of the All England Reports for 1963 at page 575.'

Criminal cases follow a similar pattern, so that *R* v *Caldwell* [1982] AC 341 should be read as:

'The (House of Lords) case of the *Crown* (or *Regina*) against *Caldwell*, as reported in the Appeal Cases Reports for 1982 at page 341.'

When introducing a case, it is considered courteous to ask the judge if any elucidation of the facts of the case is required. This avoids boring the judge silly by reciting the facts of cases with which he or she is very familiar. It also allows the judge to show off if they turn out to be familiar with the less well-known cases on which you wish to rely; and if the judge feels their failure to recall the case which you are about to cite is somewhat embarrassing they can always simply request that you 'refresh my memory'. But the most important reason for asking if the judge requires you to explain the facts of a case is that, if they do not, it will save you precious time and allow you to make the most of the period allotted for your speech by concentrating on the points of law you wish to make. After giving the (full) citation for the case in question, you should therefore ask simply:

'Are Your Lordships (or Ladyships) familiar with the facts of this case?'

Again, of course, the singular form of address should be adopted when you are citing a case in order to enable you to deal with a judicial question.

You must, of course, be ready to handle either reply with equal dexterity. We therefore suggest that you put the facts of each case on a card or sheet of paper separate from the rest of the body of your speech, so that you can turn straight to it if a recitation of the facts is called for; or alternatively, you can simply turn it over, face down, on the desk or table in front of you if the judge indicates that no reminder of what happened in the case is needed. This way, you will not have to search through several lines or pages wondering where you can once again pick up the threads of your speech.

Once you have run through the facts of a case (if required to do so), you will wish to refer to a particular passage in one or more of the judgments (or 'speeches' if in the House of Lords; 'opinions' if in the Privy Council) given. (If you do not, there is no point in your referring to the case in the first place.) Just as you should give the name and citation of a case in full, so too must you give each judge their full title when referring to one of their judgments. Smith J, for example, should therefore be read 'Mr (or Mrs) Justice Smith'. Under present convention, when referring to a female High Court Judge — Smith J would become Mrs Justice Smith (not Miss or Ms even if this would normally be appropriate). If he has since been promoted to the Court of Appeal or House of Lords, you should refer to him as 'Mr (or Mrs) Justice Smith, as he (or she) then was'.

When referring to a particular line or passage in a law report, the best way of communicating to the judge exactly where you wish him or her to look is to complete the citation by stating the relevant line or section reference (usually a letter) given in the report itself, for example:

'. . . at page 606 halfway between the letters e and f'.

If there are no such letters or markings to help indicate where the quoted passage is to be found, then you must simply state the location as clearly as possible, for example:

'. . ., 5 lines from the top of the page', or '. . ., halfway down the page'

and so on. A full reference to the passage in a judgment by Lord Justice Smith to which you wish to refer the moot judge can therefore be rendered as:

'In the Court of Appeal case of . . . as reported in . . . at page . . . at the beginning of section . . ., where Lord Justice Smith said: "...".'

In fact, the biggest problem which arises over the citation of cases in a moot is that frequently the judge is unable to find the passage in the case to which the mooter wishes to refer. An embarrassing episode while everyone shuffles pieces of paper in a desperate attempt to find the elusive passage can, however, always be avoided if certain other, simple precautions are also taken. First, make a photocopy of every case on which you wish to rely. This will be much more convenient than having to refer to the reports or books themselves during your speech. The expense of doing this will also make you think twice about citing irrelevant material; and the practice of providing the judge(s) with photocopies rather than having them raid the library is, in any case, usually insisted upon when the moot is being hosted by one of the Inns of Court. Secondly, highlight every passage you wish to quote to the judge. Thirdly, write the citation for each highlighted passage (including the section letter or number, if any) in the margin of the photocopy. This will stop you getting mixed up between different passages taken from the same case, and also overcomes the problems which often arise because the page numbers and letters get omitted from the pages on the photocopy due to the fact that the pages in the original law report are slightly bigger than the A4 size commonly used in photocopiers.

Finally, if the passage is so significant as to warrant your calling the judge's attention to it, please pause to allow the judge time to read it (if they wish to do so). If the judge does read the passage, do not continue with your submission until the judge indicates that you may do so. The judge may actually want to think about it for a few moments first.

REFERRING TO OTHER MATERIALS

As with the law reports, it is important that you give as full a citation as possible. When quoting from a textbook, state the title of the book, the author, the edition, the year, the page and line reference. When quoting from a journal state the title of the journal, the author of the article, the year, the volume and the page and any line reference. But our advice is generally to refrain from using articles and textbooks unless they put an entirely novel point not found in the case law, for otherwise there is always a strong and often irresistible temptation for the judge to argue that the author was writing in an entirely academic way and appears to have no knowledge of the 'real world'. If you do decide to quote such material nevertheless, prepare your response to this favourite judicial intervention well in advance.

KNOW THE RULES

You are mooting like a lawyer, so behave like one and ensure you know the rules of the competition before you begin. That way you will avoid embarrassing everyone — not least yourself — by claiming something to which you are not entitled. The dress code, for example, is very important for this reason: you do not wish to be the only person in jeans when everyone else is more formally attired and with a gown, or vice versa. Similarly, you should bear in mind that you must never interrupt opposing counsel, no matter how strongly you disagree with their argument, although you can rise to your feet, if they make misleading statements of fact, in order to indicate such an error. And remember: if you are nervous, think positively. Nerves can often be an advantage!

Six

HOW TO JUDGE A MOOT

MUST THE JUDGE SPECIALISE IN THIS AREA OF LAW?

Since you are expected to intervene from time to time during the moot, it is obviously important that you are *au fait* with the rudiments of the topic being mooted. However, it is rarely necessary for you to be a specialist in the area since at no stage will you be expected to provide a textbook account of the whole subject. Since the moot will be restricted typically to two issues of law, and since your primary function is to be able to decide who mooted best, you should have little difficulty in following the mooters' arguments so long as you are aware of the basic principles of the subject.

IN WHICH COURT IS THE MOOT BEING HELD?

In fact, the first rule for anyone judging a moot is to remember in which court you are sitting. Most moots are written on the basis that they will be argued before an imaginary Court of Appeal (of either Division) or the House of Lords, but some demand, for example, that the moot court be situated in the High Court or Employment Appeal Tribunal. The position of the specified court in the judicial hierarchy is all-important, since it affects the degree of importance which you must attach to authorities cited to you by the mooters.

If you are sitting, for example, in the Court of Appeal as a Lord Justice of Appeal (or, perhaps, the Master of the Rolls or Lord Chief Justice), then you must remember that you are bound by previous decisions of both the House of Lords and the Court of Appeal itself however much you may detest them. Whilst you may lambast such decisions with the full force of your invective outside the moot court, it is unfair on the mooters to behave in this way during the moot itself. You must remember that the purpose of the moot is to allow the mooters to display *their* competence and ability: everyone assumes that you already have these qualities in abundance or else you would not have been invited to judge the moot in the first place.

Of course, if you feel so strongly that a decision cited to you is wrong, there is nothing to stop you making the point to counsel that you appear to be bound by this particular case while wondering aloud whether it may not be possible to distinguish it on some basis. If all else fails, you may care to suggest to counsel that although a strict application of the doctrine of *stare decisis* suggests that you must follow the case cited, it may be overdoing things on this occasion because the case is so old and out of date.

It is, of course, to be hoped that the mooters themselves will already have anticipated these arguments. But if they have not, there is no reason why you should not 'push' them in the right direction, as indeed a judge would do in reality, although you may need to be rather gentler with less experienced mooters than would a judge in open court dealing with what he perceives to be the inadequacies of counsel.

If you are to consider yourself a Law Lord, however, your powers increase considerably since you are now bound by no case law other than that laid down by the European Court of Justice. This does not enable you, however, to dismiss with disdain any case cited to you whose *ratio* you dislike.

There is sometimes a tendency on the part of a few practitioners who act as moot judges to dismiss out of hand a previous decision of the Court of Appeal or House of Lords apparently on the basis that the leading judgment was given by a judge whose views they personally hold in low regard. But you would be doing the mooters a severe discourtesy to behave like that, since it is highly unlikely that they will have had any opportunity to learn of the esteem in which you hold particular judges or judgments; and the whole tenor of the mooters' submissions will be based on the not unreasonable assumption that all judgments of a particular court are, in principle, to be given the same weight unless a particular case has been subjected to public criticism either in other cases or in a learned journal.

You are therefore under a duty, even as a putative Law Lord, to consider the *ratio* of past cases with some degree of seriousness, although you retain the twin rights of refusing to follow a particular case or even of claiming to overrule a whole line of authority if you feel the need. Just don't let this short-lived experience of power go to your head!

Moreover, since you are free to disregard virtually any case when sitting in the House of Lords, it is important to realise that any thought of using such power — whether prompted by the submissions of one or more mooters, or by your own views on the subject — also brings with it a further obligation. For it will now be absolutely essential to hear some argument from counsel as to the policy implications of changing the law in whatever way is proposed. You must therefore ensure that the mooters address this issue in some detail and some degree of 'pushing' may again be necessary for those mooters who have not anticipated this requirement.

HANDLING CASES CITED BY THE MOOTERS

Most of each mooter's submission is likely to consist of a discussion of several cases. Whenever a mooter wishes to turn to a new case, he or she should be able to tell you the exact page in the appropriate volume of the law reports to which they wish to refer. Your clerk will then find the reference for you and pass you the relevant report.

Since the mooter's ability to indicate clearly where the reference can be found is one of the factors which you should take into account when judging a moot, it is important that you make a note of how successful each mooter is in achieving this task. The normal formulation is something like:

> 'If I may refer your Lordships to the case of *Carlill* and *The Carbolic Smoke Ball Company*, reported in volume one of the Queen's Bench Reports for 1893 at page 256, . . .'

Mooters who have no idea of where the case they wish to cite is to be found should therefore be judged accordingly.

Similarly, there is no point in a mooter citing to you an endless stream of cases. Since the mooter will be speaking under a time limit of, probably, fifteen or twenty minutes, it will be incredibly difficult for them to do justice to more than three or four cases at the outside. A mooter should really only cite you a case when he or she wishes to refer you to a particular passage. It is therefore incumbent upon you, if the mooter does not initially make it clear, to ask the following two questions:

(i)   What is the rule or principle of law for which the mooter claims that this case is authority?

(ii)   Where in the case is there a passage which the mooter believes either substantiates or summarises this rule or principle?

If the mooter does not have ready answers to these questions, this should be reflected in your adjudication on performance. Lack of an answer may also suggest either that there is nothing of importance in the case at all, or else that the relevant *dictum* or *ratio* is replicated in at least one other case (to which the mooter probably intends to refer anyway).

If, however, there is an important passage in the case to which you are referred, then you should ensure that the mooter allows you sufficient time for you to read it at your own pace. You are the judge — you can therefore control the pace of the proceedings. It is also important that you take time to read the passages which immediately precede and succeed that which has been cited to you, since many mooters (particularly the inexperienced) may attempt to put a gloss on the words which they bring to your attention which is quite clearly unwarranted by the context in which the passage is to be found.

ASKING QUESTIONS

One of the skills of experienced counsel is that of being able both to anticipate and to deal comfortably with any intervention from the Bench, particularly in the appellate courts. Since most moots are staged as if in such courts, it follows that the practice of judicial intervention must be replicated in a moot. Thus you, as the moot court judge, are expected to interrupt each mooter in turn at least once during their submission in order to ask a question. Such questions may simply request clarification on some point or other, or they may demand, for example, some consideration of the doctrine of precedent or of policy issues.

The mooters' ability to deal with your interventions is one of the factors which you will be expected to bear in mind when you are giving judgment at the end of the moot. Any intervention by you that can be dealt with by the mooter answering with a simple 'Yes' or 'No' is, obviously, insufficient as a basis for you to assess the mooter's capabilities in this area, and at least one further intervention on a more substantive point will therefore be required. Indeed, most experienced mooters look forward to the judge's interventions since it is then that the adrenalin really starts to pump and they can really shine. Mooters who come across a judge who hardly says anything during the moot are invariably disappointed since they feel they got no feedback and might as well have been talking to a brick wall.

It should also be remembered that the clock is 'stopped' while counsel is either listening to your intervention or making their reply. Whatever length of time it takes to deal with any points you may raise, this time is *always in addition* to the time initially allotted to the mooter to make their speech. Your interventions do not, therefore, have the effect of curtailing a mooter's speech unduly early and you will not be harming a mooter's prospects of success in the competition by interrupting. On the contrary, you are giving mooters their best chance to show just how much they really know about the subject.

It is always a matter of judgment as to how far you should pursue a particular point with moot counsel. A 'secondary' question to follow up the initial intervention is nearly always a good idea, but if the matter is dealt with quite shortly, there is no point in flogging a dead horse. Similarly, if the mooter clearly does not have a clue as to what you are talking about, it may be better to cut your losses and simply urge them to resume their prepared submission in order to spare them complete humiliation. The audience will also be spared what could otherwise be acute embarrassment. On the other hand, if counsel appears to be enjoying dealing with your questions and is, in fact, making some cogent points while so doing, you may well feel that some further intervention of your own is merited.

WATCHING THE TIME

Interventions by you may also be required if it appears that a mooter is likely to run out of time before getting to an essential part of the submission. At the start, the mooter should have set out briefly each step of the argument they wish to make before actually proceeding to explain each element in turn. You should therefore already be aware of what the mooter was hoping to be able to cover. If you feel that you have heard enough on an earlier point in the submission and are concerned lest insufficient time has been left to deal adequately with later points, then it may be a good idea to ask the mooter to move on to the next point.

A word of warning must nevertheless be sounded here. As it is likely that you will know substantially more about the law in this area than the mooter does, do not be too quick to demand that counsel get on to their next argument. It may be that the purpose of the moot question was precisely to have the mooters go through this particular area of law with a fine tooth comb. It may be true to say that the law is pretty clear when viewed from the standpoint of an experienced practitioner or academic, but it may be anything but clear for the mooters who are expected to make submissions for you to consider. Before asking a mooter to move on to the next point, therefore, consider whether there can be much of substance in the matters which the mooter has yet to tackle.

OTHER ASPECTS OF JUDICIAL BEHAVIOUR

Moot judges must, therefore, display a certain degree of tact and discretion. Please do not be tempted to try to turn the moot into 'your show' by humiliating the mooters, asking esoteric questions or regaling the audience with long stories of your days as a student or at the junior Bar. If you have some entertaining anecdotes you would like to share with the audience, save them for your judgment at the end or, better still, reserve them for when the mooting formalities are completely over and the atmosphere has become a little more relaxed. Until then it seems more than a trifle discourteous to the mooters, who will typically have put in many hours of research prior to the moot, to reduce them to 'bit-part' players rather than the stars of the show.

This does not mean, of course, that a touch of levity is always out of place in a moot. Humour is often a good means by which you can put the mooters at their ease, for now they will realise that although you are acting as a judge, and therefore will be adjudicating on their performance, you are nevertheless human too and not the terrifying monster they may initially have feared! Moreover, a touch of appropriate humour during the course of the moot can frequently lighten the atmosphere if the moot has become perhaps a little too serious and even a little tense. This may well be of some relief to both participants and audience alike. And, of course, some advocates may also flourish when they realise that they too can crack the odd joke during their submissions.

Nevertheless, you should not get carried away. Too much levity can overwhelm the subject matter (and any inexperienced mooters) and a little restraint may therefore be necessary at times. It is therefore obvious that the most important quality required of a moot judge is ... judgment, in all its forms and guises.

ASSESSING THE MOOTERS

As stated above, your primary function as a moot judge is to be able to judge the mooters' performance. It is, of course, perfectly possible for a good performer to have been presenting a case which you consider to be in error (or, perhaps, to have been presenting a case which you simply consider to have less merit than that of the other side).

It is for this reason that, at the end of all the mooters' submissions, you will be expected to make two decisions. First, you must give a judgment as to what you consider to be the legal position in relation to the points in the case(s) argued before you. On most occasions this decision should be relatively brief since it is not really the point of the moot exercise. Moreover, it may well be that in certain moots it is fairly clear that one side will win on the law and so there will be little point in taking too long spelling out what everyone already knows.

The second function of the judge is to decide which of the mooters has won. It may be that you have been asked to judge a competition in which the mooters are to be assessed as individuals, in which case you will be expected to nominate one mooter as the winner. In other competitions, such as many of the contests organised at the Inns of Court, mooting is treated as a team game and you will therefore be expected to nominate a team as a winner.

The organisers of each competition may offer you some 'in-house' guidelines on how the moot should be assessed. If not, we recommend that four broad factors be taken into account, namely:

(i)   the content of each mooter's legal argument;
(ii)   their presentation of that argument;
(iii) their flexibility and skill in handling your interventions and answering your questions; and
(iv)   the overall impression they created when on their feet.

We prefer to mark each mooter out of 100 and to allocate 30 marks to each of the first two categories; and 20 marks to each of the latter two. But this is personal preference born at least partly out of habit. There is nothing sacrosanct about the particular way that you score each mooter provided you do have some idea of what it is that you are looking for and therefore some idea of how to judge the mooters who appear in front of you.

There is some advantage in adopting a standardised format (whether or not it is the one suggested above) because it enables mooters to compare their performance against mooters taking part in other rounds within the same competition. This is particularly useful for large competitions organised for the students of a university law school, and also enables the organisers of such competitions to reserve places in the next round of such a competition for 'highest losers', which is not really possible if there is no standard marking scheme.

Another significant advantage of standardising the marking is that it enables each mooter to compare their own performance from one moot to another, and so be able to see whether and where they are improving and, perhaps more importantly, the areas in which it is necessary to improve.

Judges too, can benefit from a standardised marking scheme, since new moot judges can get a 'feel' of the sort of range of marks that is commonly awarded and all judges will soon be able to tell whether they are unduly severe or ridiculously optimistic in their marking. And, of course, where mooting becomes part of the academic curriculum, then a standardised marking plan will be absolutely essential as a key factor in ensuring objectivity of assessment.

Whether you choose to comment directly on the mooters' performance is generally largely up to you. Some judges are reluctant to comment orally as part of their judgment lest those comments be a source of upset or embarrassment for any of the participants, but are prepared to make brief, written comments for the eyes of each mooter in private so that they can learn from their mistakes and capitalise on their virtues.

We feel, however, that both mooters and audience expect at least some comment on the mooters' performance beyond the inevitable platitude that 'You all did very well'. After all, a typical moot takes well over an hour and it seems odd just to name a winner without any real explanation. You may feel that you just simply have insufficient time to prepare a speech in which you can make some well thought-out comments as to each mooter's performance. In this case, the problem can usually be rectified by your announcing a short adjournment for you to gather your thoughts.

A CHECK-LIST OF DOS AND DON'TS

Please do:

(i)   listen carefully to the submissions;

(ii)   make notes as an *aide-mémoire*;

(iii) read not only the passages from cases cited to you, but also the passages which immediately precede and succeed them in order to verify the context;

(iv)   look at the mooter addressing you (unless taking notes or reading passages to which you have been referred);

(v)   ask questions;

(vi)   note your views on each mooter's performance as you go along.

Please don't:

(i)   treat the moot as an opportunity to show off: that's for the mooters to do;

(ii)   ask questions which the mooter could not possibly be expected to answer;

(iii) be rude;

(iv)   ask a mooter to sit down before they have finished unless their time is up.

Part Two

A WORKED EXAMPLE OF A MOOT

Seven

A SPECIMEN MOOT PROBLEM

The following moot was argued before Deputy District Judge Adamson in the University of Birmingham in March 1995 by the four first year law students whose names appear at the foot of each of their submissions reproduced in the following four chapters.

★   ★   ★   ★   ★

Contract — terms — Sale of Goods Act 1979, s. 14 —
meaning of 'satisfactory quality' —
Unfair Contract Terms Act 1977, s. 11 —
meaning of 'unreasonableness' —
Unfair Terms in Consumer Contracts Regulations 1994 —
meaning of 'unfair term'

IN THE COURT OF APPEAL (CIVIL DIVISION)

SUGAR v *SPICE SUPERSTORES LTD*

On 4th January 1995 Angelica Sugar bought a brand new refrigerator from Spice Superstores. The fridge was manufactured by Joseph Edgar plc but was part of a range which was being discontinued and it was therefore advertised for sale by Spice Superstores at half the normal price. Mrs Sugar therefore paid £100 for the fridge instead of the usual price of £200. She also signed a form presented to her by Spice's salesman, on which she also specified the address to which Spice were to deliver the fridge. Mrs Sugar says that she saw that there was 'a lot of writing' on the form but she did not bother to read it.

The fridge duly arrived two days later and was installed in Mrs Sugar's brand new fitted kitchen. A week after installation, however, Mrs Sugar noticed a big scratch on the door. She says that, having spotted the scratch, she notices it all the time now and, since the purpose of the fridge in her brand new kitchen was not simply to keep food cool but also to look suitably decorative in keeping with the fitted units which she has also had recently installed, the fridge is not of satisfactory quality. She has therefore asked Spice Superstores to replace the fridge, refund the purchase price or pay for the cost of repair (which can only be done by replacing the whole door at an estimated cost of £85).

Spice accept that the fridge was scratched before delivery to Mrs Sugar but have refused to accede to any of her requests on the following grounds:

(i)   The model is now obsolete and, since Mrs Sugar was aware of this, it would be unreasonable to expect Spice to replace the fridge with a new model.

(ii)   The fridge had already been reduced in price by 50 per cent and it would be unreasonable to expect any further reduction or refund for a scratch, or to expect that Spice would pay for a new door, particularly since the fridge's cooling ability remained unimpaired;

(iii)   Mrs Sugar had signed a form in the shop on the back of which was stated:

'Any defect discovered in the goods supplied must be reported to the shop from where it was bought within seven days of purchase. Failure to do so will mean that Spice Superstores Ltd will unfortunately be unable to accept any liability for any defects.'

Since Mrs Sugar had reported the scratch two days after this period of seven days had expired, she had no right to claim any compensation.

In the Birmingham county court, Her Honour Judge Fairinuff found for the defendant Spice on the following grounds:

(i)   The scratch was clearly both a 'minor defect' within the meaning of section 14(2B)(c), and a matter relating to 'finish and appearance' within the meaning of section 14(2B)(b), of the Sale of Goods Act 1979 (as amended). Nevertheless, section 14(2A) and (2B) together require that 'all the relevant circumstances' including the price and description of the goods are taken into account in determining whether the goods supplied were of satisfactory quality. Since the fridge was still able to perform its primary purpose of keeping food cool, and since the fridge had been bought so cheaply as a discontinued model, the scratch did not amount to a breach by Spice Superstores Ltd of section 14(2) of the Sale of Goods Act 1979.

(ii)   The clause which purported to restrict Mrs Sugar's rights to defects specifically notified to Spice Superstores within seven days of purchase would, by virtue of section 6(2)(a) of the Unfair Contract Terms Act 1977, be of no effect if the scratch had amounted to a breach of the implied term in section 14(2) of the Sale of Goods Act 1979 that the goods supplied would be of satisfactory quality. Since, however, she had already held that section 14(2) had not been breached, Judge Fairinuff held that Mrs Sugar's failure to report the scratch to Spice Superstores within the specified seven day period precluded any remaining right which she may otherwise have had to claim damages for the cost of repairing the door.

Mrs Sugar nevertheless continues to seek a full refund of the purchase price and now appeals to the Court of Appeal on the following grounds:

(1)   the learned judge had not taken due account of the fact that the fridge purchased was installed in a new fitted kitchen, where its appearance was as important a factor as its ability to keep food cool. If this factor was accorded equal importance, then it was clear that there had, indeed, been a breach by Spice Superstores of section 14(2) of the Sale of Goods Act 1979 and, accordingly, Mrs Sugar was entitled to a full refund of the purchase price; and

(2)   Spice Superstores should not be allowed to rely on the clause requiring purchasers to inform them of defects in goods supplied within seven days of purchase since this is effectively either:

(a)   an unreasonable exclusion clause within the meaning of sections 3(2)(a) and 11(1) of the Unfair Contract Terms Act 1977; or

(b)   an 'unfair term' within the meaning of the Unfair Terms in Consumer Contracts Regulations 1994;

and is therefore ineffective. Thus Mrs Sugar should still be able, even if (1) above fails, to claim the cost of having the door replaced.

Eight

LEADING COUNSEL FOR THE APPELLANT

INTRODUCTION

May it please your Lordships, I am appearing with my learned junior Miss Griffin for the Appellant, and my learned friends Mr Najib and Miss Cope are for the Respondents.

The claim is as follows. On the 4th January 1995, the appellant, Mrs Angelica Sugar, bought a brand new refrigerator from the respondents, Spice Superstores. The refrigerator was manufactured by Joseph Edgar plc but was part of a range which was being discontinued and it was therefore advertised for sale by Spice Superstores at half the normal price. Mrs Sugar therefore paid £100 for the refrigerator instead of the usual price of £200. She also signed a form presented to her by Spice's salesman, on which she also specified the address to which Spice were to deliver the refrigerator. Mrs Sugar says that she saw that there was 'a lot of writing' on the form but she did not read it.

The refrigerator duly arrived two days later and was installed in Mrs Sugar's brand new fitted kitchen. A week after installation, however, Mrs Sugar noticed a big scratch on the door. She says that, having spotted the scratch, she notices it all the time and, since the purpose of the refrigerator in her brand new kitchen was not simply to keep food cool but also to look suitably decorative in keeping with the fitted units which she has also had recently installed, the refrigerator is not of satisfactory quality. She therefore asked Spice Superstores to replace the fridge, refund the purchase price or pay for the cost of repair — estimated at £85.

Spice accepted that the refrigerator was scratched before delivery to Mrs Sugar but refused to accede to any of her requests on the following grounds:

(i)   Firstly, the model is now obsolete and, since Mrs Sugar was aware of this, it would be unreasonable to expect the respondents to replace the refrigerator with a new model.

(ii)   Secondly, Spice Superstores state it would be unreasonable to expect any further reduction for the scratch, or to expect them to pay the cost of a new door as the model has already been reduced in price by 50% and its cooling ability remains unimpaired.

(iii)   Finally, Mrs Sugar signed a form in the shop on the back of which it stated:

'any defect discovered in the goods supplied must be reported to the shop from where it was bought within seven days of purchase. Failure to do so will mean that Spice Superstores Ltd will be unable to accept any liability for any defects.'

Since Mrs Sugar had reported the scratch two days after this period of seven days had expired, she had no right to claim any compensation.

In the Birmingham county court, Her Honour Judge Fairinuff found for the respondents on the following grounds. Firstly, even though the scratch was clearly a minor defect and a matter relating to finish and appearance under section 14(2B)(c) and (b) of the Sale of Goods Act 1979 (as amended), considering 'all relevant circumstances' the scratch did not amount to a breach. This was due to the price of the refrigerator and the fact that it was still able to perform its primary purpose of keeping food cool.

Secondly, the clause which purported to restrict Mrs Sugar's rights to defects specifically noted to Spice Superstores within seven days of purchase would, by virtue of section 6(2)(a) of the Unfair Contract Terms Act 1977, be of no effect if the scratch had amounted to a breach of the implied term in section 14(2) of the Sale of Goods Act 1979 that the goods supplied would be of satisfactory quality. Since, however, it had already been held that this had not been breached, Judge Fairinuff held that Mrs Sugar's failure to report the scratch to Spice Superstores within the specified seven day period precluded any remaining right which she may otherwise have had to claim damages for the cost of repairing the door.

On behalf of the appellant we now appeal on two alternative grounds, submitting to your Lordships the following two arguments:

(i)   The learned judge had not taken due account of the fact that the refrigerator was installed in a new fitted kitchen, where its appearance is as important a factor as its ability to keep food cool. If this factor is accorded equal importance, then it is clear that there has, indeed, been a breach by Spice Superstores of section 14(2) of the Sale of Goods Act 1979 and, accordingly, Mrs Sugar was entitled to a full refund of the purchase price.

(ii)   Spice Superstores should not be allowed to rely on the clause requiring purchasers to inform them of defects in goods supplied within seven days of purchase since this is effectively either (a) an unreasonable exclusion clause within the meaning of sections 3(2)(a) and 11(1) of the Unfair Contract Terms Act 1977, or (b) an 'unfair term' within the meaning of the Unfair Terms in Consumer Contracts Regulations 1994 and is therefore ineffective.

Thus Mrs Sugar should still be able, even if the former argument fails, to claim the cost of having the door replaced.

I myself will concentrate on the former point concerning the breach of the implied condition of satisfactory quality, whilst my learned junior Miss Griffin will explain why the clause on the back of the contract should not, and cannot, be relied on by the respondents.

ARGUMENT

My argument is based on the following submissions:

(1)   The contract formed between Mrs Sugar and Spice Superstores is governed by the Sale of Goods Act 1979.

(2)   The quality of the refrigerator was rendered unsatisfactory by the scratch under section 14(2) of the Sale of Goods Act 1979 (as amended) with particular reference to subsection 2B(b) appearance and finish and (c) freedom from minor defects.

(3)   There are no other relevant circumstances to be taken into account which could affect the outcome of this case, so that Mrs Sugar is entitled to a full refund of the purchase price paid for the refrigerator.

SUBMISSION 1

In order to assess the case before us, we must first establish whether or not the contract between Mrs Sugar and Spice Superstores for the sale of the refrigerator is governed by the Sale of Goods Act 1979. If we turn to section 1(1) of the 1979 Act it states:

This Act applies to contracts of sale of goods made on or after (but not to those made before) 1st January 1894.

May I now refer your lordships to section 2(1) of the same Act, where we see contracts of sale of goods defined. The section states:

A contract of sale of goods is a contract by which the contract seller transfers or agrees to transfer the property in goods to the buyer for a money consideration, called the price.

We can quite clearly see that the consumer contract in question complies with this definition and thus is governed by the Sale of Goods Act.

SUBMISSION 2

May I now move on to my second submission that the scratch does in fact constitute a breach of the implied condition for satisfactory quality as set out in section 14(2) of the Sale of Goods Act 1979 (as amended). This amendment changed the requirement of 'merchantable quality' to one of 'satisfactory quality'. This is defined in section 1(2A) of the 1994 Sale and Supply of Goods Act. It reads:

For the purpose of this Act, goods are of satisfactory quality if they meet the standard that a reasonable person would regard as satisfactory, taking account of any description of the goods, the price (if relevant) and all other relevant circumstances.

As this change only came into effect on 3rd January, earlier this year (1995), as yet there is no authority on how the definition is to be interpreted or applied. In order to interpret 'satisfactory quality' in the light of the present case it may be useful to look back to the definition of 'merchantable quality' and to the reasons for the change. By looking to the intentions and the aims hoped to have been achieved by the amendment we may assess how the requirement of 'satisfactory quality' should differ from that of 'merchantable quality' and thus how it should be interpreted in this case.

The original 1893 Act did not give any definition of the requirement of merchantable quality. Thus the courts took two main approaches when assessing this factor. These were the 'acceptability test' and the 'usability test'. The 1979 definition attempted to strike a balance between these two tests by holding on the one hand that it would be unreasonable to require that the goods must be fit for *all* the purposes intended by the buyer in order for them to be merchantable; whilst on the other declaring that it would be unsatisfactory to find goods to be of merchantable quality merely because they are fit for some purpose, since even extremely low quality goods can usually be used for something. The 1979 Act introduced a test of 'merchantable quality', but this tended to favour the seller as in many cases goods were held to be merchantable merely because they were fit for *a* purpose rather than *the* purpose for which they were purchased.

Cases such as *Rogers* v *Parish (Scarborough) Ltd*, as reported in the Queen's Bench Reports for 1987 at page 933, attempted to remedy this problem. Are your Lordships familiar with the facts of the case? The plaintiffs purchased a Range Rover sold as new from the defendants under a conditional sale agreement. This was found to be defective in a number of respects and, with the agreement of all the parties, another Range Rover was substituted for it on the same terms. Upon delivery the engine, gearbox and bodywork of the replacement vehicle were substantially defective and oil seals at vital junctions were unsound, causing significant quantities of oil to escape. In the first six months following delivery, a number of attempts were made to rectify the defects. However, the engine was still misfiring at all road speeds, excessive noise was being emitted from the gearbox and substantial defects remained in the bodywork. The plaintiffs rejected the vehicle claiming a breach of section 14(2) of the Sale of Goods Act 1979. This originally failed because the defects did not render the car unroadworthy. However, on appeal the plaintiffs succeeded as the courts took into account other purposes for which the vehicle was bought.

May I refer your Lordships in particular to the judgment of Lord Justice Mustill (as was) at page 944, paragraph D. He states:

> Starting with the purpose for which goods of that kind are commonly bought one would include in respect of any passenger vehicle not merely the buyer's purpose of driving the car from one place to another but of doing so with the appropriate degree of comfort, ease of handling and reliability and, one might add, of pride in the vehicle's outward and interior appearance.

This case takes steps to include not only the main purpose of the car, but other purposes such as pride in appearance when assessing what was then merchantable quality.

Despite this decision, the exact extent to which a minor defect and defects of finish and appearance fall within the definition remains unclear. May I refer your Lordships to Report 160 of the Law Commission, published in

1987, in particular Part 3 which concentrates on recommendations on the
implied term as to quality. At page 26, paragraph 3.24 reads:

> The new definition of quality should make this clear by not concentrating
> to the same extent as the present one on the fitness of goods for their
> common purposes. We intend that this shift in emphasis will make it
> clearer that other types of defect are breaches of contract, including minor
> or cosmetic imperfections which are not functional in that they do not
> impede the main use of the goods in question. The 'reasonable person'
> would not, in general, find the standard of goods to be 'acceptable' if they
> had minor or cosmetic defects . . .

This change in the focus of the law was achieved by the inclusion of
section 1(2B) in the Sale and Supply of Goods Act 1994. Here we are
presented with a shortlist highlighting the key aspects to be assessed when
determining satisfactory quality. These include:

> (a)   fitness for all purposes for which goods of the kind in question are
> commonly supplied,
> (b)   appearance and finish,
> (c)   freedom from minor defects,
> (d)   safety, and
> (e)   durability.

It is sections (b) and (c), concerning appearance and finish and freedom
from minor defects, which are important in this particular case.

Such express provisions were included in the Act to make it easier for
courts to reach a different conclusion on the facts of a case such as the
Scottish case of *Millars of Falkirk Ltd* v *Turpil* as reported in the Scottish Law
Times for 1976 at page 66. Are your Lordships familiar with the facts of the
case? Here the defendant bought a new Ford Granada motor car in
exchange for his Zodiac motor car and an agreed sum. When he did not pay
this sum the plaintiffs began an action against him. In his defence the
defendant stated that he had rejected the car as it was not of merchantable
quality. After returning home after purchasing the vehicle an oil leakage was
noted from the power assisted steering wheel. This, along with a minor
defect on the bonnet catch was repaired by the plaintiffs and the car was
returned. However, the leakage persisted and the defendant attempted to
reject the car claiming a breach of the implied condition of merchantable
quality. The court held there had not been a breach, one of the reasons being
because the defect was a minor one. Thus the defendant was left with no
remedy at all.

It does not seem fair that a buyer should have to put up with even minor
defects without a remedy which is the reason for the insertion of subsection
(2B). As stated by the Law Commission at page 30, paragraph 3.43:

> In our view the references to appearance and finish and to minor defects
> should help to emphasise that the requirement of quality does not depend
> entirely on fitness for purpose.

Taking this into account it seems quite clear that the intention behind the change to satisfactory quality was to include minor defects and matters relating to finish and appearance, so that the scratch on the refrigerator would render the model supplied unsatisfactory.

Whether this conclusion is, indeed, the correct outcome to be reached brings me on to my third and final submission.

SUBMISSION 3

It is my respectful submission that the circumstances in this case are not sufficient to conclude that the fridge was in fact of satisfactory quality. In order to justify this decision it may help to work through any possible factors which could affect the outcome already reached, and explain why, in the case before us, they are not applicable.

First, it may be argued that the refrigerator is still able to perform its primary purpose of keeping food cool thus it is still of satisfactory quality. However, this is the primary purpose stated by Spice Superstores and not the appellant, Mrs Sugar. If we look back to the Sale and Supply of Goods Act 1994, section 1(2B)(a) states that the quality of goods must be fit 'for all the purposes for which goods of the kind in question are commonly supplied'. Therefore we must apply the test of the 'reasonable person' to assess what the common purposes are. It is my submission that it is reasonable to expect that a person buying a brand new fridge to be installed in a brand new fitted kitchen would view the appearance of the exterior as being as important a factor as the ability to keep food cool.

To find to the contrary would be to ignore the reasons for which the law was changed. As I have stated previously, the new definition as to quality is an attempt to move away from stressing fitness for purpose to the exclusion of everything else. Fitness for purpose is certainly an important aspect of quality but only one among others, hence the inclusion of the list of factors such as appearance and finish in section 1(2B) of the 1994 amendment.

Under the old law and the requirement of merchantable quality, the vagueness of this definition may have permitted a scratch on the exterior of the goods without rendering them unmerchantable. However, the new definition is more precise in that it expressly states which factors must be taken into account when assessing what is satisfactory. To comply with this the effect of the scratch itself must be assessed, and it is submitted that in this case it renders the refrigerator unsatisfactory. The fact that it is still able to keep food cool is irrelevant if it is not able to comply with its other purpose concerning its appearance in a brand new kitchen.

Secondly, it may be argued that because the refrigerator was substantially reduced in price it should still be held to be satisfactory even if it is scratched. It is my respectful submission here that the price reduction is irrelevant. The reduction was made because the refrigerator was of a discontinued line. It was therefore of benefit to the respondents to sell the remaining models. They reduced the refrigerator to half price and advertised the model for sale at £100 stating clearly the reason for the reduction. If we again apply the test of the reasonable person it is logical to presume that a person purchasing the refrigerator would still expect it to be in perfect condition. Because the model is described as being of a discontinued line it is reasonable to infer that its quality and condition remains unimpaired. The reduction is merely to encourage the sale of a model no longer being made. If the refrigerator had been reduced to half price without any accompanying explanation, then it may have been reasonable to find it of satisfactory quality even with the scratch, as this would seem to justify the price reduction. However, in the present case, the reduction is already justified and this does in no way suggest a possibility of any defect with the refrigerator. Thus the existence of any defect would render it unsatisfactory.

Thirdly, it may be questioned whether the appellant should have in fact examined the refrigerator before purchase and thus should have noticed the scratch. In response may I refer your Lordships to the exact wording in section 1(2C)(b) of the 1994 Sale and Supply of Goods Act. This section states that a term implied by section 2 does not extend to any matter making the quality of goods unsatisfactory 'where the buyer examines the goods before the contract is made, which that examination ought to reveal'. This would apply if Mrs Sugar had examined the goods or had reasonable chance to examine the goods and therefore notice the scratch. However, it is my submission that she was not given this reasonable chance. The examination must be conducted before the contract is concluded, so that we must ask where in this case is the contract concluded. The contract is concluded in the superstore when Mrs Sugar paid her £100 and signed the document. Thus she must have had reasonable chance to examine the refrigerator before this. I submit that it is reasonable to presume that any examination she did conduct would have been on the model on display which would be unlikely to be the model she actually received. As the respondents are Spice Superstores Ltd, it is reasonable to infer that this is a large company dealing with a large proportion of the market. It is therefore logical that they would have many of the same type of model. Thus Mrs Sugar would have received an unseen model from the warehouse rather than the one on show. It may be argued that as this model is a discontinued line it may be possible that the refrigerator on display was in fact the last one. However, I would contend that if this was so there would have been no price reduction. The refrigerator was reduced for being part of a discontinued line: thus the company were attempting to sell their final models in stock. If they had only one left they would not be faced with the problem of disposing of a whole batch thus it would not be in their interest to reduce the price when they could sell the one remaining model easily.

The final factor which may affect whether the scratch renders the refrigerator unsatisfactory is the fact that it took Mrs Sugar a week to notice the scratch. First, may I emphasise that she has just had a whole new kitchen installed thus her whole attention and emphasis would not be on the refrigerator. In addition, there may be numerous reasons for her delay such as she may be short sighted or ill in bed for the week and thus not been in the kitchen. However, I submit that the fact that the scratch went unnoticed for a week is irrelevant. Spice Superstores included a clause in the contract stating Mrs Sugar had a period of seven days in which she was able to report any defect to the shop. Thus it was not their intention that she must notice the scratch immediately, but that she noticed the scratch and acted upon it immediately within a reasonable time. It is my submission that the appellant did in fact comply with this, so that she should be entitled to a full refund. I will leave it to my learned junior Miss Griffin, however, to discuss the clause in question in more detail.

CONCLUSION

To conclude, may I emphasise that there is no authority on this point because of the recent change in the law. It is submitted, however, that it must be the test of the reasonable person which is to be used when assessing how exactly the amended section 14(2) of the Sale of Goods Act 1979 should be applied.

May I also strongly emphasise the intensions behind the change to 'satisfactory quality' to include minor defects and matters of finish and appearance. Failure to categorise the scratch under these headings would be contrary to the aims thought to have been achieved by the 1994 Act by the inclusion of factors other than fitness for purpose set out in section 1(2B) of the 1994 Act. As regards fitness for purpose itself, it is my submission that the appearance of the refrigerator was as important a factor as its cooling ability and that this would be a reasonable assumption to expect to have been made by any seller selling a brand new refrigerator. Thus the scratch resulted also in a breach of section 1(2B) of the 1994 Act as subsection (a) requires the quality of goods to be fit 'for all purposes for which goods of the kind in question are commonly supplied'.

Finally, when taking into account all other relevant circumstances it is my respectful submission that the conclusion as to finding the refrigerator unsatisfactory could not be changed for the reasons I have already explained. Thus the scratch on the refrigerator door did constitute a breach of section 14(2) of the Sale of Goods Act 1979 (as amended) and therefore Mrs Sugar should be entitled to a full refund of the purchase price paid.

My Lords, I submit that this appeal should therefore be allowed.

Jane Bresnahan
Law Student
University of Birmingham

Nine

JUNIOR COUNSEL FOR THE APPELLANT

INTRODUCTION

May it please your Lordships, I now intend to deal with the question of the clause on the back of the contract which the appellant signed. My contention is that this clause does not affect the appellant's right to claim the cost of having the fridge door replaced. I will base this on two submissions:

(i)   applying sections 3 and 11 of the 1977 Unfair Contract Terms Act, this is an unreasonable exclusion clause and so is ineffective; and

(ii)   if not unreasonable then this is an 'unfair term' according to the EC Directive on Unfair Terms in Consumer Contracts as implemented by the Unfair Terms in Consumer Contracts Regulations 1994.

INCORPORATION OF THE CLAUSE INTO THE CONTRACT

The first question facing the Court is:

Is the clause on the back of the form actually incorporated into the contract?

We do not contest this point. The clause was set out on the form which Mrs Sugar signed. It has long been held that when the contract is signed such a clause will be incorporated even though the consumer fails to read it. Nevertheless, despite working from this basis, I submit that the term was ineffective.

UNFAIR CONTRACT TERMS ACT 1977, SECTION 3

We must now look to the 1977 Unfair Contract Terms Act to see if we can apply it. In particular, we must refer to section 3. It applies as between contracting parties where:

(a)   one of them deals as a consumer, or
(b)   one of them deals on the other's written standard terms of business.

Mrs Sugar is clearly a consumer, as defined by section 12: she did not make the contract in the course of business while Spice Superstores clearly did. Also, though not necessary as an additional requirement, the parties are dealing on standard terms of business since Mrs Sugar signed a printed form in the shop. Therefore we can apply section 3.

UNFAIR CONTRACT TERMS ACT 1977, SECTION 3(2)(a)

Section 3(2)(a) of the Unfair Contract Terms Act 1977 says:

> As against the consumer, the other party cannot by reference to any contract term —
>
> (a)   When himself in breach of contract, exclude or restrict any liability of his in respect of the breach ... except in so far as ... the contract term satisfies the requirement of reasonableness.

We therefore need to ascertain whether the clause is an attempt to exclude or restrict liability.

The answer is that it is. If we look at the clause itself, we read that:

> Any defect discovered in the goods supplied must be reported to the shop where it was bought within 7 days of purchase. Failure to do so will mean that Spice Superstores will unfortunately be unable to accept any liability for any defects.

The respondents are thus attempting to exclude liability in relation to the quality of the goods unless the defect is reported within the specified time limit. Therefore this *is* an exclusion clause and is subject to the requirement of reasonableness.

UNFAIR CONTRACT TERMS ACT 1977, SECTION 11:
'REASONABLENESS'

One of the main purposes of the Act was to protect the consumer. Therefore, section 11(5) provides that it is for those claiming that a contract term or notice satisfies the requirement of reasonableness to show that it does. The burden is *on the respondents* to show that the term is reasonable, *not* on Mrs Sugar to prove that it is unreasonable.

The matter of whether this clause is reasonable or not is ultimately for Your Lordships' discretion. However, the Act does provide some assistance. Under section 11(1), the Court must decide if:

> ... the term shall have been a fair and reasonable one to be included having regard to the circumstances which were, or ought reasonably to have been, known to or in the contemplation of the parties *when the contract was made*.

The material time is the time of contract formation. It is my submission that in this respect the clause does not satisfy the requirement of reasonableness.

TIME LIMIT

If we look again at the clause itself, we shall see that if the defect is not reported to the shop from where it was bought within seven days of *purchase*, Spice Superstores will be unable to accept *any liability for any defects*. Is seven days from the day of *purchase* a reasonable time limit for the reporting of *any* defect? I submit that it is not. Guidance is provided by the case of *RW Green* and *Cade Brothers Farm*, as reported in volume one of Lloyd's Reports for 1978 at page 602.

This case involved the application of the 1893 Sale of Goods Act, but it is useful in that the question of the reasonableness of a term is discussed. The contract there concerned the sale of potatoes by seed merchants to farmers. The agreement was on the basis of a written standard terms agreement which included a clause limiting liability to a refund of the price. It so happened that the potatoes were infected with a virus which could only be detected at harvest time. There was also a clause which required notice of any rejection claim to be given within three days of delivery.

This clause was held by Mr Justice Griffiths not to be fair and reasonable. He decided this on the basis that at the time the contract was made, no one would have expected it to have been practicable for the farmer to complain of the virus within three days of delivery. This was because the farmer would not then have known of its presence.

I accept that there are significant differences between that case and this case but, nevertheless, it is possible to extract relevant considerations from it. In particular, the central question would seem to be:

At the time the contract was made, would anyone have expected it to have been practicable for the buyer to complain within the specified time limit?

Let us turn to the facts in the case before you today. On 4th January Mrs Sugar purchased the fridge. On 6th January the fridge was installed. On 13th January she reported the defect. This means that she reported the defect within nine days of purchase, *but* within seven days of installation.

I submit that the clause was unreasonable because she wrote the address the fridge was to be delivered to on the form in the shop, so that the salesman would have known how long it would be until delivery and installation (here, an important two days). She would only have noticed any defect *after* installation. Thus it is not reasonable to make the time limit seven days from the day of *purchase* — the clause is unreasonable. The sellers could not reasonably have expected it to have been practicable for Mrs Sugar to complain within the specified time limit.

AN ONEROUS TERM

Perhaps it could be said that had Mrs Sugar read the terms properly, then she would have been able to comply. In relation to this, I would like to turn to the case of *Interfoto Picture Library* and *Stiletto Visual Programmes* as reported in volume one of the All England Reports for 1988 at page 348.

The facts were that the plaintiffs ran a library of photographic transparencies. They delivered a bag of 47 transparencies on request to the defendant. They included a note with conditions clearly set out. Condition 2 read:

All transparencies to be returned within fourteen days from date of delivery — holding fee of £5 plus VAT to be charged for each transparency per day after that.

The defendants forgot about the transparencies until long after the fourteen days had elapsed. The plaintiffs claimed the sum of £3,783.50 in holding charges.

Lord Justice Dillon said, at page 352, paragraph f:

If one condition in a set of printed conditions is *particularly onerous or unusual*, the party seeking to enforce it must show that *that particular condition* was *fairly brought to the attention* of the other party.

This was reiterated by Lord Justice Bingham, (as was), at the bottom of page 357:

The defendants are not to be relieved ... because they did not read the condition ... they are to be relieved because the plaintiffs did not do what was necessary to bring this *unreasonable and extortionable* clause fairly to their attention.

As I hope I have demonstrated, the clause here was an onerous term since the time limit was so short. It would have been a seven day limit even in the event of *serious* damage. There was nothing done by the salesman to bring this particular term to the notice of Mrs Sugar. Therefore it is not a reasonable term and is rendered ineffective under the Unfair Contract Terms Act 1977.

UNFAIR TERMS IN CONSUMER CONTRACTS REGULATIONS 1994

If the arguments so far presented do not satisfy Your Lordships that this term is unreasonable, then I would like to look to the most recent provisions in the law. In this context, I would like to apply the Unfair Terms in Consumer Contracts Regulations 1994.

It is important to note that these regulations do not come into force until 1st July 1995, however they *should* have come into force by 1st *January* 1995. The regulations are to implement the 1993 EC Directive on Unfair Terms in Consumer Contracts. Article 10 of the Directive stipulates that these provisions shall be applicable to all contracts concluded after 31 December 1994. So the Minister is acting *ultra vires* in delaying the implementation of the Directive. I therefore submit that in this area we should be able to apply the regulations.

At the very least we should be able to interpret the 1977 Act in the light of the 1993 Directive. The Directive does not have direct effect as against private parties. But the *Marleasing* case, as reported in volume 1 of the

Common Market Law Reports for 1992 at page 305, states that national courts must as far as possible interpret national law in the light of the wording and purpose of the Directive in order to achieve the result pursued by the Directive. This obligation applies whether the relevant national provisions in question were adopted before or after the Directive.

Regulation 4(1) of the Unfair Terms in Consumer Contracts Regulations 1994 says that 'unfair term' means 'any term which *contrary to the requirement of good faith* causes a *significant imbalance* in the parties' rights and obligations under the contract *to the detriment of the consumer*'. We can extract three relevant questions from this:

Question 1: Is this term contrary to the requirement of good faith?
Answer: Yes. It was an onerous term not brought to the appellant's attention.
Question 2: Does it cause a significant imbalance to the parties' rights and obligations?
Answer: Yes. It puts the consumer at a disadvantage in that she has to act very quickly.
Question 3: Is this to the detriment of the consumer?
Answer: Yes. It puts the seller in a superior position.

This is therefore an unfair term under regulation 5(1) and as such it is not binding on Mrs Sugar.

CLOSE

It is my submission that this clause is ineffective. It can be said either that it is:

(i)   'unreasonable' under the Unfair Contract Terms Act 1977; or
(ii)   'unfair' under the Unfair Terms in Consumer Contracts Regulations 1994.

Either way the respondents should not be allowed to rely on the clause and should meet the cost of having the door replaced.

Lucy Griffin
Law Student
University of Birmingham

Ten

LEADING COUNSEL FOR THE RESPONDENTS

MAIN SUBMISSIONS

(i)   There is no implied term of satisfactory quality under the Sale and Supply of Goods Act 1994. Section 14(2C)(b) of the Sale of Goods Act 1979 (as amended by the Sale and Supply of Goods Act 1994) provides an exemption.

(ii)   Even if there is an implied term of satisfactory quality under section 14(2) then the fridge satisfied the test under section 14(2B) and therefore Spice Superstores Ltd are free from any liability.

ARGUMENT

The Sale and Supply of Goods Act 1994 was designed to protect consumers when buying goods, but an exemption was given to sellers under what is now section 14(2C)(b) of the Sale of Goods Act 1979 in that if the buyer examined the goods before the contract and the examination ought to reveal certain defects, then the implied term of 'satisfactory quality' does not apply to the goods in relation to those defects.

It is our position that the appellant went into the store, saw the fridge and examined it. Thus if the scratch is as big as claimed it should have been visible and ought to have been revealed; therefore there can be no implied terms with respect to section 14.

It is reasonable to assume that she saw and examined the fridge because she had a whole new kitchen installed and it is reasonable that any person would specifically examine the goods before buying. With respect to any argument that the fridge examined could have been a different fridge from that delivered, I would submit that, because it was a discontinued model and offered at half price, this was the only fridge left and so she must have seen and examined it.

If the court finds that the situation does not fall within the section 14(2C)(b) exemption then I would submit that the fridge meets the requirements of satisfactory quality as laid down in section 14(2B) and thus the fridge is of satisfactory quality under section 14(2).

Because the Act is very new, there has been no judicial interpretation of 'satisfactory quality' yet. Therefore, we must establish a meaning to use. The Law Commission Report which preceded the 1994 Act said in paragraph 3.24 that the test of satisfactory quality would be similar to that approach used by Dixon J in the case of *Australian Knitting Mills Ltd* v *Grant* (1933) 50 CLR 387, where he describes the meaning of merchantable quality at page 408, paragraph 2 in the following terms:

> The condition that goods are of merchantable quality requires that they should be in such an actual state that a buyer fully acquainted with the facts and knowing what hidden defects exist and not being limited to their apparent condition would buy them without abatement of the price obtainable for such goods if in reasonably sound order and condition and without special terms.

However, Lord Denning in *The Hansa Nord* [1975] 3 All ER 739, referring to the Supply of Goods (Implied Terms) Act 1973, said that the best definition is that which the statute offers (at page 748 at paragraphs g-h, and at page 749 at paragraph b). There he says that in establishing the result of a breach we must look to the various matters mentioned in the statutory definition: I would submit we must follow the statutory factors and establish the guidelines for the use of the term of satisfactory quality.

Section 14(2A) says that the test is one of reasonableness, i.e., the goods must meet the standard a reasonable person would regard as satisfactory and we must take into consideration price and description, as well as other relevant circumstances. Section 14(2B) lays down various aspects of quality and, for our purposes, (a), (b) and (c) are very important, i.e., (a) fitness for purpose; (b) appearance and finish; and (c) freedom from defects.

FINISH AND APPEARANCE

The Law Commission report at paragraph 3.40 says that when looking at appearance and finish and deciding 'whether or not any particular defect or blemish is a breach of contract will depend on the *facts of the case*'. We must therefore turn to the established facts. Although we are told that it is a 'big' scratch, I would submit this is rather ambiguous because after all she has not noticed the scratch for one whole week. It is reasonable to assume that anyone taking such pride in a brand new kitchen would have examined the finished room. Clearly the scratch was not very noticeable. In fact Mrs Sugar admits it is because she has seen it, that the scratch now stands out further. This is a personal problem of hers for which Spice Superstores should not be liable.

Mrs Sugar knows the fridge she is buying is a discontinued model and that parts would be hard to find to replace, and any reasonable person would accept that a discontinued fridge at half the price could have a scratch or two and this would still make the reasonable person believe it is of satisfactory quality as stated in section 14(2A).

In addition to these factors it seems that the appellant's expectations were too high. She bought a discontinued model at half the price and expected it to be perfect (like a new full price model). In *Rogers* v *Parish* [1987] QB 933 Mustill LJ (as he then was) says (at page 944, paragraph f), 'the description "Range Rover" would conjure up a particular set of expectations, not the same as those relating to an ordinary saloon car'. On the basis of this analogy, then if one buys a full priced new range fridge one has a certain set of expectations: any reasonable person would not expect the same from a discontinued, half-price model, i.e., an 'ordinary saloon car'.

In *Bernstein* v *Pamson Motors Ltd* [1987] 2 All ER 220, Rougier J says (at page 228), 'No buyer of a brand new Rolls-Royce Corniche would tolerate the slightest blemish on its exterior paintwork; the purchaser of a motor car very much at the humbler end of the range might be less fastidious'. This reinforces the first point again, i.e., how Mrs Sugar's expectations are not those of a reasonable person, and any reasonable person would find such a scratch such a minor blemish that a reasonable person would still find it of satisfactory quality, particularly taking into account both that it is a discontinued model and that she has not seen the scratch for one whole week.

RELEVANT CIRCUMSTANCES

The fact both that the fridge is a discontinued model, and that the scratch is minor have already been discussed, so let me turn now, if I may, to a consideration of the price. The Law Commission Report said (at page 26, towards the end of paragraph 3.24) that 'a lower standard could reasonably be demanded — for example, where the goods were second-hand, or "seconds" sold at a *suitably low price*'. I would submit that 50 per cent off is suitably low and hence one could reasonably expect a slight blemish (although the price was reduced because of the discontinuation). I would also submit that, all factors considered, a 50 per cent price reduction would merit the expectation of a minor scratch — even a big scratch.

In *Rogers* v *Parish* Mustill LJ says, at page 944 at paragraph f:

The factor of price was also significant. At more than £14,000 ... the buyer was entitled to value for his money.

Whereas in the *Hansa Nord* Lord Denning says (at page 749, paragraph e):

If they are sold at a 'cut' price or 'bargain' price, or a lower price, he would have to put up with something less. He would not be entitled to reject them simply because they were not perfect.

This sums up the respondents' position perfectly.

I would submit a 50 per cent reduction is quite substantial and it would be unreasonable to expect a 'perfect', flawless fridge. Under the merchantable quality test the issue of price often centred around resale price, although this is no longer a real requirement if we were to use the test as a further example of reasonableness. It would seem that it is fair to assume that the appellant would sell the fridge at the price she bought it and perhaps even at a higher price. Clearly she has not made a bad bargain and, taking into consideration the drop of 50 per cent in price and the fact that it is a discontinued model, her expectations are too high and a reasonable person would find the fridge of satisfactory quality. See *BS Brown & Sons Ltd* v *Craick Ltd* [1970] 1 All ER 823 at page 828, paragraphs g to h, where Lord Guest says:

> If the difference in price is substantial so as to indicate that the goods would only be sold at a 'throw-away-price', then that may indicate that the goods were not of merchantable quality.

PURPOSE

Section 14(2B)(a) says that an aspect of quality is fitness for all purposes for which the goods are commonly supplied. In the old cases the judicial attitude was that as long as the goods supplied were fit for their main purpose this was sufficient for establishing merchantable quality. In the Law Commission Report (at paragraph 3.34) the Commission said that in the old cases the goods could serve various purposes, and that as long as they served some it was sufficient. The judges felt it unfair and unreasonable to expect the goods to be fit for all purposes.

However the Commission said (at paragraph 3.35) that, on policy grounds, goods should be fit for all purposes for which they are commonly supplied — this was established in section 14(2B)(a). Therefore the question for the court is whether the fridge's common purpose is to cool or to decorate.

The appellant contends both. She argues that a fridge is commonly supplied to be decorative as well as to cool food. I submit that the only purpose for which a fridge is *commonly* supplied is to cool food, and that is its primary purpose. If one person uses the goods in a different way that does not mean it should be fit for that purpose. Under the Act it must *commonly* be used (i.e., by most people) for that purpose. If we ask any reasonable person (and, for that matter, any unreasonable person) what the common purpose of a fridge was, they would definitely say to 'cool food'.

Indeed, if we apply the relevant circumstances, i.e., price and discontinuation, it seems unlikely that decoration was a common purpose. For if someone went in to buy a fridge — a discontinued, half-price model — the reasonable person would assume the primary purpose was just to cool food, and not really decoration or quality.

But in our case the opposite was done. The appellant impliedly made the sellers believe that cooling was the only purpose because, as I said before, if a person buys a discontinued, half-price model, the reasonable person would not think of decoration. Therefore because her purpose was not one for which a fridge is commonly supplied, Mrs Sugar falls within section 14(3)(a) because she did not tell Spice Superstores of her intended purpose. There is no implied term as to fitness for purpose.

It was for just such a situation that section 14(3)(a) was enacted in that if a purchaser has a 'special' purpose or a 'particular' purpose in mind, he could tell the seller and a term is then automatically implied under section 14(2).

CONCLUSION

(i)   There is no implied term of satisfactory quality because Mrs Sugar had the chance to examine, and ought to have examined, the fridge.

(ii)   Even if there is an implied term of satisfactory quality, then indeed it is fulfilled because the scratch was not seen for one week and thus cannot be too significant; and also because the price was reduced by half; and also because it was a discontinued model. Taking all these factors into consideration a reasonable person would find the fridge of satisfactory quality.

(iii)   The common purpose of a fridge is to cool and, because the appellant did not tell Spice Superstores of her intended purpose, section 14(3) does not apply and therefore there is no implied term as to fitness for purpose.

Mohammed Najib
Law Student
University of Birmingham

Eleven

JUNIOR COUNSEL FOR THE RESPONDENT

INTRODUCTION

May it please your Lordships, my learned senior has outlined his submission contending that there has been no breach of section 14 subsection (2) of the Sale of Goods Act 1979, and as such, Mrs Sugar is not entitled to a full refund of the purchase price of the fridge. It therefore remains my task to discuss the exemption clause which purports to exclude Spice Superstores' liability for any goods bought after the expiration of a certain length of time from the date of purchase.

This will be done in three stages. First, the position under the common law regime. Secondly, the situation under statute as governed by the Unfair Contract Terms Act 1977. And finally, the effect of the European Directive on Unfair Terms in Consumer Contracts, as implemented in the UK by the Unfair Terms in Consumer Contracts Regulations 1994.

Before considering these three regimes, it is vital to examine the actual wording of the exclusion clause as relied upon by Spice Superstores Limited. The clause stated:

> Any defect discovered in the goods supplied must be reported to the shop from where it was bought within seven days of purchase. Failure to do so will mean that Spice Superstores Limited will unfortunately be unable to accept any liability for any defects.

THE COMMON LAW

Examining the situation at common law, the first point to consider is whether the clause was incorporated into the contract. The document relied on as containing notice of the excluding term must have been intended as a contractual document. If, as in this case, the document is signed, its contractual nature is apparent. It is submitted that a person is bound by a writing to which he has put his signature, citing in support of this contention the case of *L'Estrange* versus *Graucob*, as reported in volume two of the King's Bench Division Law Reports for 1934 at page 394.

Are your Lordships familiar with the facts of the case? The buyer of an automatic slot machine signed and handed to the sellers an order form containing in ordinary print and writing the essential terms of the contract, and in small print certain special terms one of which was:

any express or implied condition, statement, or warranty, statutory or otherwise not stated herein is hereby excluded.

The machine was delivered by the sellers to the buyer, who paid to the sellers an instalment of the price. The machine did not work satisfactorily, and the buyer brought an action against the sellers claiming (inter alia) damages for breach of an implied warranty that the machine was fit for the purpose for which it was sold. The sellers pleaded (inter alia) that the contract expressly provided for the exclusion of all implied warranties. The buyer replied that at the time when she signed the order form, she had not read it, and knew nothing of its contents, and that the clause excluding warranties could not easily be read owing to the smallness of the print. There was no evidence of any misrepresentation by the sellers to the buyer as to the terms of the contract.

The Divisional Court found for the defendants, with Lord Justice Scrutton expressing the law on this point in detail. He states at page 403, near the end of the first paragraph:

When a document containing contractual terms is signed, then, in the absence of fraud, or, I will add, misrepresentation, the party signing it is bound, and it is wholly immaterial whether he has read the document or not.

It is therefore submitted that Mrs Sugar, under the law stated in *L'Estrange* versus *Graucob*, is bound by the exclusion clause.

It could be argued that because this exemption clause was printed on the back of the form, insufficient steps were taken by Spice Superstores Limited to bring the clause to Mrs Sugar's attention. This question of reasonable notice was discussed in the case of *Parker* v *The South Eastern Railway Company*, as reported in volume two of the Common Pleas Division Law Reports for 1877 at page 416.

Are your Lordships familiar with the facts of the case? The plaintiff, on depositing a bag in the cloak-room at the defendant's station received a ticket with a number, the date, and the words 'See back' on the front of it. On the back were printed several clauses, including one which stated, 'The company will not be responsible for any package exceeding the value of £10.' The plaintiff did not read the cloakroom ticket, and his bag, valued at £24 and 10 shillings, was lost.

In determining liability, the question to be answered was whether the defendants did what was reasonably sufficient to give the plaintiff notice of the term. Lord Justice Mellish, in considering this issue, states at page 423, five lines down from the top of the page:

> The railway company ... must be entitled to make some assumptions
> respecting the person who deposits luggage with them ... they are entitled
> to assume that he can read, and that he understands the English language,
> and that he pays such attention to what he is about as may be reasonably
> expected from a person in such a transaction ...

It therefore follows that Spice Superstores Limited are entitled to make
similar assumptions about their customers. It seems unreasonable that if a
plaintiff signs a contract, without reading its terms, that they can then force
upon the defendants a different contract by asking for a certain clause to be
struck out.

In a business transaction of this kind, a reasonable customer would expect
that a form requiring their signature, and details of a delivery address would
indeed constitute a contract. From this, it is submitted that the reasonable
customer would also expect such a contract to contain various terms and
conditions.

Mrs Sugar herself admits that there was 'a lot of writing' on the form.
What did she believe this writing to be? Indeed, what would the reasonable
customer take this writing to be? Such writing, must, in the mind of the
reasonable customer, be associated in some way with the contract, otherwise
why would the writing be on the form in the first place?

Mrs Sugar does not pretend that she thought the writing was an
advertisement or some other matter unconnected with the business in hand.
Her statement can be summarised as that she did not think, or thinking, did
not care about what the writing actually said. She now attempts to sue Spice
Superstores Limited, and to have the benefit of her own indifference. Is this
fair and reasonable?

Lord Justice Mellish comments on such a situation in *Parker* v *The South
Eastern Railway Company*, which I think your Lordships already have before
you. He states at page 427, approximately half way down the page:

> Is it even allowed to a man to 'think', 'judge', 'guess', 'chance' a matter,
> without informing himself when he can, and then when his 'thought',
> 'judgment', 'guess', or 'chance' turns out wrong or unsuccessful, claim to
> impose a burden or duty on another, which he could not have done had
> he informed himself as he might?

Based on the common law regime of exclusion clauses, it is submitted that
Mrs Sugar is bound by the exemption clause as she signed the contract
presented to her by the salesman of Spice Superstores Limited. It is also
submitted that Spice Superstores Limited did indeed take reasonable steps
to bring this clause to Mrs Sugar's attention. Reinforcing this last submission, I once again cite the case of *Parker* v *The South Eastern Railway
Company*. At page 427, eight lines up from the bottom of the page, Lord
Justice Mellish states:

> Why is there printing on the paper, except that it may be read? The
> putting of it into their hands was equivalent to saying 'Read that'. Could
> the defendants practically do no more than they did? Had they not a right
> to suppose either that the plaintiffs knew the conditions, or that they were
> content to take on trust whatever is printed?

THE UNFAIR CONTRACT TERMS ACT 1977

The second situation to consider is the position under statute, as governed by the Unfair Contract Terms Act 1977. The section which governs this case is section 3 subsection (2)(a), as previously mentioned by my learned friend Miss Griffin. This applies as between contracting parties where one of them deals as a consumer or on the other's written standard terms of business. Subsection (2)(a) states:

As against that party, the other cannot by reference to any contract term when himself in breach of contract, exclude or restrict any liability of his in respect of the breach; except in so far as ... the contract term satisfies the requirement of reasonableness.

The question to be asked, therefore, is, what actually constitutes reasonableness? Section 11, subsection (1) of the same Act provides some clues. It states:

In relation to a contract term, the requirement of reasonableness for the purposes of this Part of the Act ... is that the term shall have been a fair and reasonable one to be included having regard to the circumstances which were, or ought reasonably to have been, known to, or in the contemplation of the parties when the contract was made.

As my learned friend Miss Griffin has already drawn to your Lordships' attention, the burden of proof falls on Spice Superstores Limited to show that the exclusion clause is reasonable as, under section 11 subsection (5) of the Unfair Contract Terms Act 1977, it is for those claiming that a contract term satisfies the requirement of reasonableness to show that it does. In order to do this, it is important to look once again at the wording of the exclusion clause. It states:

Any defect discovered in the goods supplied must be reported to the shop from where it was bought within seven days of purchase. Failure to do so will mean that Spice Superstores Limited will unfortunately be unable to accept liability for any defects.

It is contended that such a clause is reasonable. Spice Superstores Limited are not so unreasonable as to exclude liability for their goods altogether. They allow Mrs Sugar a period of seven days from the purchase date to find any defects before they exclude liability. The issue can therefore be reduced to whether or not the period of seven days is a reasonable length of time in which to discover any faults.

THE UNFAIR TERMS IN CONSUMER CONTRACTS REGULATIONS 1994

It is submitted that Schedule 2 of the Unfair Contract Terms Act 1977 is not strictly applicable to this situation and therefore, at this point, it is necessary to be guided by the effect of the Unfair Terms in Consumer Contracts Regulations 1994. Schedule 2 of these regulations gives details of items to be taken into consideration when making an assessment of good faith or reasonableness:

    (a) the strength of the bargaining positions of the parties;
    (b) whether the consumer had an inducement to agree to the term;
    (c) whether the goods or services were sold or supplied to the special order of the consumer; and
    (d) the extent to which the seller or supplier has dealt fairly and equitably with the consumer.

It is contended that although the parties' bargaining position was originally unequal, Mrs Sugar did have the opportunity at the end of the day not to enter into the contract with Spice Superstores Limited. As your Lordships mentioned to my learned friend Miss Griffin, such inequality in bargaining power was balanced by Spice Superstores' reduction in the price of the fridge. The second item points in favour of the clause being reasonable as Mrs Sugar did receive a substantial reduction off the price of the fridge, and therefore had an inducement to agree to the term. The third item is irrelevant, as the fridge was not sold to the special order of Mrs Sugar. It is submitted that the fourth item has been met by Spice Superstores Limited, as they have dealt with Mrs Sugar in a fair and equitable manner. They freely admit that the fridge was scratched before purchase. A less honest firm may well have contested such an issue, laying the blame for such a defect on Mrs Sugar's own negligence. With two of the four items meeting the standard of reasonableness, and a third being irrelevant, it is submitted that under these regulations, the exclusion clause is reasonable.

Another factor supporting the reasonableness of Spice Superstores' exclusion clause is found in Schedule 3 of the Unfair Terms in Consumer Contracts Regulations 1994. This gives an indicative and illustrative list of terms which may be regarded as unfair. Although not an exhaustive list by any means, it is an important factor that the draughtsmen of the regulations did not accord a purported exclusion of liability for lack of timely complaint as being unreasonable enough to warrant mention in this list.

As regards the fairness of the length of time given to Mrs Sugar to report any defects, guidance can be sought from common law examples. The case of *RW Green Limited* v *Cade Brothers Farm*, reported in volume one of Lloyd's Reports for 1978 at page 602, sets out some guidelines regarding reasonable time limits. The facts of the case provide that the plaintiffs were seed potato merchants who had had regular dealings for several years with the defendants who were farmers. The contracts involved were for the sale of seed potatoes, and contained conditions which provided, amongst other things, that:

Notification of rejection, claim, or complaint must be made to the seller ... within three days ... after the arrival of the seed at its destination.

In respect of one contract for the sale of 20 tons of King Edward potatoes, it later appeared that they were affected by potato virus Y, which could not be detected by inspection of the seed potatoes at the time of delivery. The plaintiffs sued for the price of the potatoes and the defendants counterclaimed for the loss of profits.

In considering the reasonableness of the exempting provision, Mr Justice Griffiths held that the purported exclusion of liability for lack of timely complaint was unreasonable. This decision overruled the plaintiff's contention that the time limit was fair in that potatoes are a perishable commodity, and may therefore deteriorate after delivery, especially if badly stored. Mr Justice Griffiths agreed with this argument in relation to defects discoverable by reason of inspection, but held that this reasoning did not hold true for defects like virus Y, which was not discoverable by inspection.

It is therefore submitted that Spice Superstores' purported exclusion of liability for Mrs Sugar's lack of timely complaint is reasonable, based on Mr Justice Griffiths's reasoning. The scratch on the fridge was definitely a 'defect discoverable by reason of inspection' and therefore seven days was an ample time limit in which to discover its existence.

My Lords, it is my respectful submission that this appeal should be dismissed. It is submitted that on the arguments already presented to your Lordships, the reasonableness of the exclusion clause has been established under all three regimes, namely common law, statute and the European Directive, and accordingly, this appeal should be dismissed.

Leah Cope
Law Student
University of Birmingham

Twelve

COMMENTARY

INTRODUCTION

The moot and submissions published here as Chapters 7 to 11 inclusive are based on the problem set and the speeches given at the Final of the Freshers' Mooting Cup competition in the Faculty of Law at the University of Birmingham on 16th March 1995, which was judged by a partner from the Birmingham solicitors Buller Jeffries, Mr Derek Adamson, who is also a part-time District Judge. Accordingly, the submissions reproduced in Chapters 8 to 11 were all written by students in their first year of mooting competition.

It should also be borne in mind that while the submissions of Jane Bresnahan (Chapter 8) and Leah Cope (Chapter 11) are reproduced here more or less *verbatim*, Lucy Griffin's original submission did not rely on a full, written speech but was based on a rather shorter series of notes, and Mohammed Najib's method was to have just a few words jotted onto each of two or three sheets of paper. The latter two contributors have kindly expanded their notes at our request for reproduction here (in Chapters 9 and 10 respectively) in order to make them more intelligible to other readers! Since the result of the moot itself was a very close-run thing — though we shall not embarrass anyone by revealing who won — this variety of approaches demonstrates that there is no such thing as the correct way to prepare or write a moot speech and that it is for each individual mooter to find a suitable style of working.

It is also important to remember that success in a moot depends at least as much (and often more) on courtroom manner, method of presentation and the ability to answer the judge's questions as it does on the substance of the mooter's argument. The submissions reproduced above do not attempt to take account of, or to mimic, either the judge's questions or the mooter's answers, and cannot therefore really be expected to do justice to the flavour of the full mooting experience, particularly in the case of Mohammed Najib (see Chapter 10), whose success in mooting is due primarily to his ability to think on his feet when required to answer questions posed by the judge. Furthermore, the tone of voice of the speaker and the way in which points are stressed, or eye contact maintained with the judge can never be rendered successfully on the written page except by means of the most thorough stage directions.

We also wish to draw attention to the fact that three out of the four mooters in the final of this competition were female. This does not appear to us to be a mere accident or quirk of fate. It is our experience that women as a group tend to out-perform their male counterparts in mooting competitions; and we therefore trust that this talent will be properly exploited by a very substantial growth, for the foreseeable future at least, in the numbers of female advocates recruited into the professions.

DISSECTING THE MOOT

The moot in Chapter 7 demonstrates, as we argued in Chapter 3, how important it is to read the grounds of the appeal with care. The second ground, for example, relies on section 3(2)(a) of the Unfair Contract Terms Act 1977 rather than on section 6(2)(a). (For those pondering as to why, it is because the judge at first instance had already found for the plaintiff on section 6(2)(a).) This means that it is impermissible for the mooter to plead section 6(2)(a) in argument (though he or she should be aware of it in case the judge asks a question about it). It is important to stick to the grounds of appeal specified because that is what would be expected in a real courtroom, and also because otherwise counsel on the other side have no way of predicting the sort of arguments which might be advanced. A moot is not about surprising the opposition, but is about handling the law more skilfully and with greater clarity than your opponent.

Another fact illustrated by this moot is that, like a good recipe, it is not always necessary to reproduce slavishly the exact scenario set out in any of the moots printed in this book when deciding on the particular moot problems to be used in competition. Thus the person in charge of mooting can choose to vary the facts slightly as required in order to change the focus and emphasis of the moot, provided that all the participants (i.e., mooters, clerk and judge) are made aware from the outset of the changes that have been made. So, for example, the scratch on the fridge door in the moot problem in Chapter 7 could be a small scratch rather than the big scratch stated. (This might have implications for the applicability of section 14(2) of the Sale of Goods Act 1979.) Alternatively, the date of the purchase could be amended to 4th July 1995 so as to avoid both the question about the indirect effect of an EC Directive and the question of whether the Secretary of State acted *ultra vires* in delaying implementation of that Directive. Alternatively, the clause requiring that any defects be reported to Spice Superstores within seven days of purchase could be amended to (say) reporting within three months, or indeed to any other length of time that may be felt appropriate; or the time could run from the date of delivery.

But perhaps the most important fact demonstrated by the specimen moot is that it serves to refute the oft-heard contention that a moot is workable only if the answer to the legal questions raised is genuinely uncertain. If this view had any substance, it would be very difficult ever to get a competition off the ground because the law is, in many of its core areas at least (and, since all students study them, it is they which form the basis of most moots), relatively well established unless some very unlikely factual scenarios are conceived by the author of the moot. In fact, many excellent moots can also be conducted even when the law clearly favours one side rather than the other, provided that there is no recent, explicit, authoritative court decision or legislative provision which makes one side's case completely unarguable.

The moot reproduced in Chapter 7 itself illustrates how a good competition can be based both on questions of law which are relatively evenly balanced as between the two parties, and on points of law which strongly favour one party rather than the other. Thus the law relating to the second ground of appeal in *Sugar* v *Spice Superstores Ltd* strongly favours the appellant, whereas the first ground of the appeal is more evenly balanced and the outcome on this point may well depend on the precise interpretation of the given facts.

Different skills are required when dealing with these different types of moots. Where the law appears quite finely balanced, the object of each mooter will be simply to try to persuade the judge of the merit of their case. Where the law seems to be tilted in favour of one party rather than the other, however, the ability to persuade the judge will not be so important since the judge will be likely to decide in that party's favour no matter how good (or bad!) the quality of the argument advanced turns out to be. Instead, more credit is likely to be gained by putting the case before the court into its wider legal or social context, for example, or by addressing major policy issues that are raised by the case, or by the ease with which the mooter handles the judge's questions, or simply by putting the case with particular clarity. It is evident that as junior counsel for the appellant, Lucy Griffin chose to opt for the clarity route and, as a consequence, the reproduction of her speech in Chapter 9 is probably the easiest of all the mooters' speeches to follow. The mooter who appears to have correspondingly less chance of success, on the other hand, will be rewarded principally according to the degree of ingenuity shown in the line of argument presented to the moot court. In particular, credit will be given for any novel or original points which have not hitherto been explored in the law reports. Perhaps this too might include a resort to policy or contextual issues, or perhaps it could involve an argument based on the law of a foreign jurisdiction, or the *ratio decidendi* of an old or long-forgotten case. Such an argument might not be appropriate when a more finely balanced legal issue is at stake since it may not be the most persuasive argument available, but in a case where the odds are stacked against you, you often get a much better chance to show off. Mooters, like good 'real-life' advocates, must of necessity be very resourceful.

We should, however, point out that it is all too easy for a mooter, particularly an inexperienced mooter, to assume that the outcome on the law of any particular moot is utterly predictable when, in fact, nothing could be further from the truth. Most of the moots reproduced in this book have been mooted on more than one occasion either within the Faculty of Law of the University of Birmingham and/or in competitions involving teams from the Faculty. We are therefore witnesses to the fact that the judgments given by a variety of judges (including not only academics but also practitioners and part- and full-time judges) can and do go either way on the law on a large majority of these moots. Surely what this demonstrates above all is that the art of advocacy is not dead and that judges can be, and are, actually persuaded as to what the state of the law is by the quality of the submissions advanced by counsel. A better justification for mooting in vocational terms would be hard to find.

The moral of this tale for all mooters is that you should not be put off if at first it seems that you have drawn the short straw. Some mooters actually prefer to be allocated to the side whose prospects of success on the legal front seem unfavourable, on the grounds that this gives them considerably more scope to display the full range of their talents than is available to the other side. Others, on the other hand, prefer to be on the side with the correspondingly greater chance of success because they find it reassuring that their arguments on the law are likely to be well founded. And a third group prefer the more finely balanced moot because there is then a realistic prospect of actually managing to persuade the judge of the plausibility of their submission. But, as our remark about the unpredictability of moot judgments shows, it is not always possible to know in advance into which group of moots the problem set actually falls!

DISSECTING THE SUBMISSIONS

If the submissions in Chapters 8 to 11 are compared with each other, perhaps the first thing to strike the reader is the length of time that must sometimes be taken up by the leader for the appellant in simply reciting the facts of the case for the benefit of the judge. In a case where the facts are brief or uncomplicated this does not really present a problem, but where (as here) there is a certain amount of necessary detail to be explained, this can mean that the opening speaker in the moot is at a severe disadvantage in that several minutes of the allotted time can be taken up in such an endeavour even before the presentation of the legal argument 'proper' can begin. In some competitions this disadvantage can be balanced out to some extent by giving leading counsel for the appellant a right of reply when all the other mooters have finished speaking. But in moots which are not 'team' events as such but are competitions where each mooter competes against every other participant, this can sometimes be a rather 'rough and ready' solution. In such cases it is worth considering granting the leader for the appellant an extra amount of time (say five minutes) in order to compensate for having to run through the facts of the case at the outset. Alternatively, it may be thought better simply not to start the clock until this initial phase of the speech has been completed, a strategy that has a particular advantage on those occasions where the judge indicates a sufficient awareness of the facts not to need their repetition.

The second point to note about the speeches is that they all attempt to set out as early as possible precisely what steps their argument will proceed along. It is also noteworthy that, having set out these steps as clearly and briefly as they can, each mooter then proceeds immediately to the first of these points. No time is taken up in presenting some general overview either of the law or of the practice of retailing. On the contrary, each mooter simply plunges into the first point. This is essential not only for the obvious reasons of not wasting any of their precious time or of running the risk of boring the judge, but also because they have just told the Bench the steps involved in their forthcoming submissions, so that it would be quite illogical to start anywhere other than at the first of these very points.

REVIEWING CHAPTER EIGHT

Jane Bresnahan's case is based largely on the provisions of the Sale of Goods Act 1979 as amended by the Sale and Supply of Goods Act 1994. Since the amending legislation was passed too recently for there to be any significant interpretations of the new law already in the law reports, she is left with a choice of presenting her case by putting forward her own interpretations of the relevant provisions or of looking to other sources for guidance as to the meaning of these provisions. Since her own views, if unsupported, would carry limited weight, she turns in the section entitled 'Argument' on p. 56, to the report of the Law Commission which recommended the changes to the law which have now been enacted. Of course the views expressed there, whilst highly persuasive, are not binding upon the court and so Jane seeks in the same section to give the Commission's views added authority by tracing briefly the history of the law on the sale of goods as far as their acceptability for use is concerned. This helps to establish not only what the law was in the past but also, by implication, what it must have become if parliament has decided to intervene by amending the pre-existing law through the 1994 Act.

Jane's third submission, however, is of a quite different character (see the section entitled 'Submission 3' on p. 59), for this involves a continual comparison of the law with the facts of the moot in order for her to relate the one to the other. The ability to do this with great facility is not only essential to the success of every mooter, but is also an important skill for every successful practitioner; and is as important on paper as in court. It involves being able to pick out those facts which are legally relevant from those which are not, and also requires that you do so in an order (or, if you prefer, on the basis of a method) entirely intelligible to others.

REVIEWING CHAPTER NINE

Lucy Griffin's submission takes a slightly different approach. Her contentions are all based either on the provisions of a well-known statute (the Unfair Contract Terms Act 1977, or UCTA) or on those of an EC Directive (and on the Regulations which purport to implement it) whose content and style is so new as to gain little interpretative assistance from the former English common law.

The main body of Lucy's submission is therefore taken up with a close examination of the words employed in the relevant provisions of the legislative instruments. Whereas Jane had to show (in the section on p. 59) that she could relate the facts to the law with precision, Lucy's principal task is to accomplish this whilst at the same time linking together successfully and in a sensible order all the relevant statutory law. Thus she must start at the right point, section 3 of UCTA, pick out the appropriate subsection, move on to the next appropriate section (section 11), and pick out the appropriate subsections there whilst at the same time explaining how each provision relates to the given facts. She adopts a similar, though briefer, approach to the Unfair Terms in Consumer Contracts Regulations 1994 in the section on p. 65.

REVIEWING CHAPTER TEN

Mohammed Najib's approach is different again. The substance of his case is that a proper interpretation of the new provisions enacted by the Sale and Supply of Goods Act 1994 depends, in the words of the Law Commission itself, on the facts of each case. Taken at face value, this statement would leave him with literally nothing to say to the court, since the latter would simply have to make up its own mind as to how to interpret the given facts. Clearly this would not be very good advocacy and so Mohammed adopts the classic advocate's tactic of going through a number of past cases to show how the courts in the past have interpreted certain words and phrases in order to draw analogies between these cases and the one before the court.

In a sense, this tactic seems to undermine the implicit assertion in the initial claim that the facts of each case are different. It also demonstrates that the art of advocacy is not necessarily one that depends to any great degree on one's command of logic, since the 1994 Act is so recent that there are no significant reported cases on its meaning and the cases that Mohammed cites were all decided under the previous law. Yet it is nonetheless true that Mohammed's is a very persuasive line of reasoning since judges are rightly concerned to ensure that the law maintains a certain degree of consistency and does not become so arbitrary as to be entirely unpredictable.

REVIEWING CHAPTER ELEVEN

In the course of her submission, Leah Cope also lays great emphasis on the common law position prior to the passage of an Act of Parliament (in her case it is the Unfair Contract Terms Act 1977). However, Leah's reason for so doing is not so much to find support for her contentions about the most appropriate way to interpret that statute, but is directed rather at trying to diminish the importance of any changes brought into force by that Act. After all, some statutes are enacted more to codify the law than to change it, and a prime example of this was actually the original Sale of Goods Act passed in 1893.

In the section on p. 76 Leah does seek to interpret in detail the intricacies of a legislative provision, namely the Unfair Terms in Consumer Contracts Regulations 1994. At first, she does this in much the same way as Jane Bresnahan, by seeking to relate the facts of the case to each limb of Schedule 2 of the Regulations. But then she moves on to an entirely different argument, which relies on the *omission* from the Regulations of anything in the very detailed provisions of Schedule 3 which could be said to cover the facts of the case at hand. In other words, statutory interpretation is as much about noticing what is *not* written as about the explication of what is.

CONCLUSION

The submissions reproduced in Chapters 8 to 11 and discussed here are not presented as definitive. Indeed, it is fundamental to a proper understanding of mooting (and advocacy in general) to realise that there is no such thing as the definitive moot speech. It is therefore quite possible that, had you been presented with the problem in Chapter 7, you would have wished to tackle it in a rather different way from that chosen by the contributors to this book. It is also obvious that as the Sale and Supply of Goods Act 1994 and the Unfair Terms in Consumer Contracts Regulations 1994 become more familiar and generate their own jurisprudence, some of the arguments reproduced here will become redundant as new ones emerge.

Nevertheless, we have found that many people new to mooting feel that it is easier to find their feet if they have access to the speeches of more experienced mooters in order to gain a 'feel' for what is required in the moot court. These speeches are therefore reproduced here in the belief that they will serve to put flesh on the bones of our suggestions in Part I as to how to prepare for and conduct a moot. Of course, the best way to learn is simply to take part, but there is everything to be said for being as well prepared as possible before you enter your first competition. We believe that the moot speeches reproduced here are excellent models of their kind and demonstrate a wide variety of mooting techniques for you to draw on as you wish. Indeed, we hope that as these techniques become more familiar to you, some of the suggestions we made in Part I will soon become so much like second nature that you will be able to carry out many of the tasks in a rather less mechanical way than our advice might sometimes be taken to suggest. After all, each of the mooters whose speeches are published here had never even heard of mooting six months before the competition for which their speeches were prepared.

Part Three

MOOTING PROBLEMS

Conflict of laws — contract — jurisdiction — want of prosecution

ARBITRATION

Islamic Kingdom of Datahara v *Walseswell Associates*

In 1975 the Islamic Kingdom of Datahara (Datahara) entered into a contract with Walseswell Associates, a firm of architects based in Streatham, in which Walseswell Associates agreed to design and supervise the construction of a £100m tourist village and golf complex on the coast of Datahara. The complex was large and prestigious and took six years to build. It was envisaged that it would put Datahara on the international map not only for tourism but also for business purposes, and create growth and stability for the ruling family. Construction commenced in 1976 and the complex was handed over to the government on 4th December 1982.

The Government was to pay Walseswell Associates' fees by Lazards London transferring money to Walseswell Associates' Guernsey account at Morgans, the English merchant bank. The complex was financed by a loan agreement between Datahara and Sachs International, an American bank. That loan agreement had an express choice of law clause saying that English was the proper law. Walseswell Associates were unaware of the agreement until 1982 when it was disclosed to them after disputes broke out between Datahara and Walseswell. The construction contract was between a UK company and a Datahara company of limited liability owned 50 per cent by the Government's Ministry of Tourism and 50 per cent by the famous US Hotel Group Hillsnob Inns and Parks. That contract, at the insistence of Walseswell Associates, chose English law as its proper law.

In terms of man-hours, 70 per cent of Walseswell Associates' architectural work was done in Datahara and 30 per cent in Streatham. Prior to the contract the Datahara Minister of Tourism hoped that 60 per cent would be done in Datahara and expected more than 50 per cent to be done in Datahara. Walseswell Associates' senior partner thought that the percentages would be reversed; i.e., 60 per cent of the work in terms of man-hours would be done in Streatham. It was accepted that the senior brainpower for design was Streatham based, but it was also known that much supervision would need to be done in Datahara which would weight the man-hours content in favour of Datahara where local and expatriate labour could be used. Walseswell Associates estimated their fee recovery to be 50 per cent design and largely performed in Streatham, whilst supervision would take up the other 50 per cent of fee recovery which would be Datahara based.

The contract between Datahara and Walseswell Associates was in Arabic but based upon the RIBA terms of engagement. It was signed in the Datahara Embassy in London by Walseswell Associates' senior partner and the Datahara Minister of Tourism. Walseswell Associates had done business in Datahara before. They had entered into four prior contracts, each larger than the one before and each important to Datahara. The first two were expressed to be subject to English law, the last two had no choice of law clause. Each was in the English language. This contract was twice the size of the previous one.

In 1982 disputes broke out. Datahara complained of a design defect to the foundations of the main hotel which, in 1983, they spent £5m rectifying. They therefore did not pay the final instalment of fees in the sum of £750,000.

There was an Arbitration clause, which stated that in default of agreement the Arbitrator was to be appointed by the 'President of the RIBA, London'. The parties agreed upon an English QC in 1982, Datahara having preferred a Dataharan lawyer and Walseswell Associates an English lawyer as their first choice.

Points of Claim were delivered in 1983 by Datahara alleging breach of contract and a claim in tort. Points of Defence and Counterclaim (for fees) were delivered by Walseswell Associates in 1984. The King of Datahara died in 1985 and was succeeded as King by his son, the Crown Prince, six months later. (The army staged a coup, declared a Republic, dissolved the Government and was overthrown in the period January to June 1985.) Nothing was done in the Arbitration until 3rd December 1991 when the Government wrote to the Arbitrator asking that he issue further directions. In the meantime the Chief Foundation Designer for Walseswell Associates, who was responsible for the foundation design, had died. Datahara cannot explain the delay.

There is a nine-year contractual prescription period in Datahara; no limit applied in tort. Walseswell Associates contended that the proper law of the contract was English law, that the action was statute barred and should be dismissed for want of prosecution. Datahara contended that the proper law was Dataharan, that the action was not statute barred and that there was no power to dismiss for want of prosecution.

The facts contained in the above narrative were agreed between solicitors to be the evidence admitted on the application so that Affidavits could be dispensed with.

On 25th December 1991 the Arbitrator was made a High Court Judge. On 1st January 1992 the Arbitrator wrote to the parties saying he had leave from the Lord Chancellor to hear the application to dismiss and that he would hear the case on the first day of the legal term in Chambers at the Courts in The Strand following which he would deliver an *extempore* Award/Decision on the application. He said that he was particularly interested in hearing submissions on proper law and the power to dismiss for want of prosecution.

Richard Wilmot-Smith QC, *39 Essex Street, Temple*
Middle Temple Annual Mooting Competition

Conflict of laws — contract — acceptance by post — damages

IN THE COURT OF APPEAL (CIVIL DIVISION)

Plover v *German Travelwell Ltd*

Geoff Plover read a holiday brochure of German Travelwell Ltd (GTL) and decided to book a 'mobile home' holiday with the company. He therefore filled in a booking form and sent it to the company's offices in Bonn. GTL sent a letter of acceptance back by return.

While on holiday Plover tripped over and gashed his leg when the steps up into the mobile home gave way. The manager of the site called a doctor, who examined the wound, inserted six stitches and prescribed various antibiotics which the site manager then purchased from a pharmacist. The doctor's bill, when converted to sterling, was £300. The antibiotics cost a further £40.

Plover did not have holiday insurance and sought to recover the £340 from GTL in both contract and the tort of negligence. In addition he sought damages of £360, being the price of the holiday, and damages of a further £200 as compensation for his disappointment and loss of expectation caused by the injury ruining his holiday. GTL denied that they were liable and argued, moreover, that any court action should be taken in Germany since:

(a)   under the English postal acceptance rule, the contract between the parties was concluded in Bonn; and

(b)   any alleged tort must have taken place in Germany.

District Judge Smith took judicial notice of the fact that German contract law considers a contract to be concluded when an acceptance by post is received, and held that it was therefore appropriate for Plover to sue in an English court for the breach of an implied term in the contract to provide a reasonably safe mobile home. He refused, however, to award Plover damages of more than £340.

GTL appeal to the Court of Appeal on the grounds that the county court had no jurisdiction to hear the case. Plover cross-appeals on the grounds that his damages should be assessed at £900.

Conflict of laws — carriage of goods by sea — damage — *res judicata*
- Civil Jurisdiction and Judgments Act 1982, s. 34

IN THE HOUSE OF LORDS

The Government of Emirate v Crafty Shipping plc

The Government of Emirate engaged Crafty Shipping plc to carry 77 Cruise missiles and 101 tonnes of butter from London to Cochin, Emirates, on *The Safety First.*

After the voyage began a fire was discovered on board ship, caused by the negligence of a Crafty employee, and the Master immediately discarded the Cruise missiles and headed for a safe port. The ship radioed the loss of the missiles to its headquarters and Crafty immediately informed the Government. The Government immediately issued proceedings in the Emirates' courts for $100m for the loss of the missiles.

The ship arrived at Cochin harbour 14 days after the fire and 10 days after the issue of the Emirate's proceedings. Upon arrival the butter was discovered to have gone rancid because the refrigeration equipment had failed. This failure was established, by an official enquiry of the Emirates Department of Agriculture, to be as a result of the fire.

The Government applied to amend its claim in the Emirate's court to add its claim for the loss of the butter. Before the application was heard the court, of its own motion, granted the Government summary judgment for $100m for the loss of the missiles. Crafty agreed not to appeal the judgment provided the Government made its claim in the English courts in respect of the claim for the loss of the butter. In Emirates law the claim for the loss of the butter would involve a different cause of action from that relating to the missiles.

The Government issued a writ claiming £3m for the loss of the butter. Crafty admitted negligence in their defence but relied upon section 34 of the Civil Jurisdiction and Judgments Act 1982 as providing an absolute defence ousting the jurisdiction of the court. The section provides:

> No proceedings may be brought by a person in England . . . on a cause of action in respect of which a judgment has been given in his favour between the same parties . . . in a court of an overseas country, unless that judgment is not enforceable or entitled to recognition in England . . .

It is common ground that Emirate's judgments are enforceable and entitled to recognition in England.

The trial judge and the Court of Appeal upheld Crafty's plea. The Government appealed to the House of Lords on the grounds that:

(1)   the causes of action in respect of the missiles and the butter were separate; and
(2)   section 34 was a procedural provision which was waived.

Richard Wilmot-Smith QC, *39 Essex Street, Temple*
Middle Temple Annual Mooting Competition

Contract — passing of title — mistake — misrepresentation — conversion

IN THE COURT OF APPEAL (CIVIL DIVISION)

Aroma Supplies v Sally Gullible Trading as Natureworks

Carol Hughes runs a successful beauty salon. Aroma Supplies is a company which supplies a wide range of products suitable for a beauty salon. Caroline used to work with Carol and had left because of disagreements over money and clients. Caroline, unknown to Carol, had kept a key to the salon and, knowing that Carol was away on holiday, went to the salon with the intention of getting her own back on Carol. Caroline found in the salon a card from a representative of Aroma Supplies. The representative had met Carol once. Caroline faxed Aroma Supplies and said she urgently needed a substantial quantity of products. Aroma Supplies were persuaded to send the order immediately and arranged for a representative to call three days later. The products were delivered the same day and a different representative from Aroma Supplies called three days later. Caroline spoke to the representative who always referred to her as Carol. Caroline then persuaded the representative to leave a very expensive piece of equipment in return for a cheque which Caroline had found in a drawer and which she signed as Carol Hughes.

Caroline has now vanished. The products and equipment were sold to Sally Gullible whose business is known as Natureworks and who sells beauty products to the public. Sally had responded to an advertisement placed by Caroline in the local paper.

Aroma Supplies sued Sally for either the return of the products and equipment or their value. The county court judge held that the order had not led to the making of a contract with Caroline since it was placed by fax and had not involved a contract being made between parties face to face. Accordingly Sally was not the owner of the products and was liable to Aroma Supplies. As to the equipment, it was held that this was a contract made face to face and that, therefore, Sally was the owner and was not liable.

Sally appeals to the Court of Appeal on the ground that there was a valid contract between Aroma Supplies and Caroline such that Sally could obtain good title to the products.

Aroma Supplies cross-appeals on the ground that there was no contract between themselves and Caroline since they always intended to contract with Carol and that title in the equipment never passed to Caroline and therefore did not pass to Sally.

David Chalk, *Anglia Polytechnic University*

Contract — tort — negligence — damages — contribution — Civil
Liability Contribution Act 1978, s. 1

IN THE COURT OF APPEAL (CIVIL DIVISION)

The British Bank v Wigzell, Yates & Hart and Churchill Property Development Company Limited

In June 1989 the British Bank entered into an agreement ('the Agreement') with the Churchill Property Development Company ('Churchill') whereby it agreed to provide 90 per cent of the costs of development of a sports and leisure complex in Scarborough.

By Clause 3.1 of the Agreement the British Bank agreed to pay 90 per cent of the development costs as defined in Schedule 1 of the Agreement.

Clause 3.1.7 of the Agreement provided that the British Bank would pay the sums due to Churchill in respect of the development upon receipt of an Architect's certificate or other proper evidence of expenditure approved by the British Bank's consultants as to the amount due.

In September 1989 the British Bank appointed Wigzell, Yates & Hart as its development consultant.

Work on the development commenced in 1990 and progressed according to programme. As the project progressed Churchill made various applications for payment of the development costs. The sums applied for included notional interest. The applications were all checked and approved by Wigzell, Yates & Hart and the British Bank paid Churchill the sums claimed in full.

In January 1993 the British Bank realized for the first time that the sums which it had paid to Churchill included notional interest and concluded that Churchill was not entitled to notional interest as part of the development costs under the Agreement. By this stage £2.3 million had been paid by way of notional interest. By letter dated 15th February 1993 the British Bank demanded repayment of £2.3 million. Churchill refused to repay the sum.

In May 1993 the British Bank issued proceedings against Wigzell, Yates & Hart alleging that the consultants were negligent and in breach of their retainer in failing to consider whether notional interest was properly payable under the Agreement and in approving Churchill's application for payment in full. The British Bank claimed loss and damage resulting from Wigzell, Yates & Hart's negligence and/or breach of contract in the sum of £2.3 million.

Wigzell, Yates & Hart issued a Third Party Notice against Churchill claiming a contribution under the Civil Liability (Contribution) Act 1978. The Third Party Notice alleged that the notional interest had been paid by the British Bank under a mistake of fact and that Churchill held the money on trust for the British Bank and so was liable to repay the sum.

It was agreed by all parties that on the true construction of the Agreement notional interest was not payable as part of the development costs, though it was arguable on a literal construction that it was. It was also agreed that notional interest had not in fact been expended by Churchill.

Churchill issued a summons to strike out the Third Party Notice against it as disclosing no reasonable cause of action and under the inherent jurisdiction of the Court. The summons was heard by Hawksmoor J. At the hearing Churchill argued that:

(1)   a liability to repay money paid under a mistake of fact did not constitute a liability in respect of any damage suffered by the British Bank and so did not fall within section 1(1) of the Civil Liability (Contribution) Act 1978; and

(2)   the money was paid under a mistake of law, not fact, and that accordingly Churchill was under no obligation to repay it.

The British Bank took no part in the hearing.

Hawksmoor J struck out the Third Party Notice as disclosing no reasonable cause of action. He concluded that:

Section 1(1) of the 1978 Act provides that a contribution is payable by a person only if he is liable in respect of damage suffered by another person. Section 6(1) of the Act defines liability in respect of damage in terms of an entitlement to compensation. The Act envisages, in my opinion, that a contribution is recoverable only where a person is responsible for damage. The restitution of money paid under a mistake of fact is not compensation nor can it be said that Churchill has caused the British Bank to suffer damage through its acts or defaults. Accordingly I consider that it is plain and obvious that Wigzell, Yates & Hart have no cause of action under the Civil Liability (Contribution) Act 1978 and the Third Party Notice should be struck out in its entirety. There is, therefore, no need for me to consider in full the question of whether the money was paid under a mistake of law as Churchill claims or a mistake of fact as argued by Wigzell, Yates & Hart. However, it is my view that the money was paid under a mistake of law as to the true construction of the Agreement.

Wigzell, Yates & Hart now appeal to the Court of Appeal against Hawksmoor J's decision to strike out the Third Party Notice on the grounds that:

(1)   the learned Judge erred in concluding that there was no right to a contribution from Churchill under the Civil Liability (Contribution) Act 1978; and

(2)   the learned Judge erred in concluding on the limited material available to him that the money was paid under a mistake of law not fact.

Richard Wilmot-Smith QC, *39 Essex Street, Temple*
Middle Temple Annual Mooting Competition

Contract — passing of title — mistake — conversion

IN THE COURT OF APPEAL (CIVIL DIVISION)

Chorlton Ltd v *Smith*

Chorlton Ltd received an order by letter for 200 boxes of Christmas crackers. The order was written on headed paper; the heading being Gunton & Co. Ltd. The address given was 65 Longwire Street, Chelmsford. Unknown to Chorlton Ltd, there was an established firm of grocers, H Gunton Ltd, whose place of business was 112 Longwire Street, Chelmsford. The order was accompanied by a letter purporting to come from a local bank supporting the creditworthiness of Gunton & Co. Ltd. This letter was a forgery. Chorlton despatched the crackers which were delivered to 65 Longwire Street, Chelmsford.

Three days later a man called at Chorltons and claimed to be Mr Gunton the proprietor of Gunton & Co. Ltd. He thanked Chorltons for the delivery of crackers and then asked for 150 sets of Christmas tree lights which he wanted to take with him. The order clerk at Chorltons telephoned the number which was on the headed paper on which the order for crackers had been made. The clerk obtained confirmation that Mr Gunton was calling at Chorltons for lights and also obtained an order number from the person who had answered the telephone. The man left with 150 sets of lights.

It was later discovered that no business was being conducted at 65 Longwire Street, Chelmsford and that the man calling himself Mr Gunton cannot be found. Chorlton Ltd has never been paid for the crackers or the lights which were later purchased in good faith by Smith.

Chorlton sued Smith for damages. The trial judge held that:

(1)   there was a contract between Chorlton and the writer of the letter. Under that contract title in the crackers had passed to the writer of the letter and ultimately was obtained by Smith; and

(2)   Chorlton made a contract for the sale of the lights with the man who called at their premises and title to the lights passed to him and ultimately to Smith.

Chorlton Ltd now appeal on two grounds:

(i)   following *Cundy* v *Lindsay* no contract was made with the writer of the letter; and

(ii)   the identity of the contracting party was crucial to the sale of the lights and no contract was intended to be made with the man who had called at Chorlton's premises.

David Chalk, *Anglia Polytechnic University*

Contract law — insurance — terms — environmental damage

IN THE COURT OF APPEAL (CIVIL DIVISION)

Environ Insurance Company v Pollutalot

Pollutalot is a chemical company operating on the banks of the river Thames. Owing to the nature of its operations and the high probability of consequential river pollution, the company obtained a comprehensive general liability insurance policy from the Environ Insurance Company. The policy was occurrence based, meaning that coverage was provided for matters which occurred during the policy period. The policy expired two years ago. Coverage extended to pollution damage subject to the following contractual exclusion:

> This insurance does not apply to bodily injury or property damage arising out of the discharge, dispersal, release or escape of smoke, vapours, soot, fumes, acids, alkalis, toxic chemicals, liquids or gases, waste materials or other irritants, contaminants or pollutants into or upon land, the atmosphere or any water course or body of water; but this exclusion does not apply if such discharge, dispersal, release or escape is sudden and accidental.

There was also a personal injury endorsement in the policy which provided cover for personal injury, but it is unclear as to whether the endorsement covered both sudden/accidental *and* gradual pollution.

Last year, local Thames residents began suffering from severe chest infections. Scientists and medical experts explained that these ailments were a result of inhaling fumes which had risen when Pollutalot's waste products mixed with river water. The injured parties claimed against Pollutalot for compensation. Pollutalot, in turn, claimed under its insurance policy.

During proceedings in the High Court, Pollutalot claimed that they had not on this occasion anticipated any damaging effects from their chemical processes. They had taken particular care to ensure that no pollution damage should result from their waste disposal methods. Expert witnesses gave evidence showing that the discharge of waste into the Thames had been a gradual process, which began five years ago, and that no single abrupt and sudden accident could account for the resulting damage. Waters J said that Environ were liable to cover Pollutalot's claim under the insurance policy because:

> (1) an 'occurrence-based' policy covers damage which may be completely unexpected and unintended despite the waste discharge itself being intentional; and
> (2) the terms 'sudden and accidental' have no temporal element and hence gradual pollution is covered.

Environ appeals on both grounds.

Salma Khan, *Pinsent Curtis*
London and Birmingham

Contract — terms — breach
Tort — negligence — duty of care — economic loss

IN THE HIGH COURT

Flim Limited v *Estates Limited and Champion plc*

Flim are lessees of factory premises; their landlord is Estates. Under the
lease there is the following covenant:

The tenant shall have the right of quiet enjoyment of the premises.

Flim are manufacturers of compact discs, a delicate process which requires
clean conditions inside the factory; and twice a day for a period of one hour
there must be no vibration of any kind to the factory floor. If dust gets into
the factory then there is a danger that the £10m machinery will be damaged.
Such a risk is so unacceptable to Flim that their standard procedure on such
occasions is to stop production and clean the premises. A cleaning operation
such as this will normally take half a day costing £30,000 in lost profits.

The compact discs are made in two daily batches, morning and afternoon.
By a secret patented process the production run for the morning or
afternoon is placed in a special kiln-like laser charger which subjects the
discs to a process that prevents the disc, when played, from suffering any
detriment in the quality of the reproduced sound should fingerprints stray
onto the silver area of the disc. Vibration of the factory floor, when this
two-minute process is applied, damages the machine. Production is then
halted for one week while the patented machinery is repaired and this costs
a further £600,000 in lost profits.

Estates was aware at the time the lease was entered into of the potential of
damage caused by dust but did not become aware of the secret laser process
until the day before the events complained of. On 1st April 1990 Champion
were engaged by Estates to carry out demolition work to the adjoining
factory premises to that occupied by Flim. Champion knew that there was
delicate machinery in the factory but did not know the detail outlined above.
The work went swiftly, but some operations alarmed Flim's Production
Director who, on 30th April 1990, telephoned Estates' Managing Director
and told him of the need for care and outlined the dangers described above.
The Managing Director of Estates never got round to telling Champion of
the things he had been told of the production process.

On 1st May 1990 a workman in the employ of Champion carelessly
caused damage to the wall of the factory unit, panicked and allowed the
demolition ball to drop to the floor. This drop caused no physical damage to
the premises but it did cause the factory floor to vibrate at exactly the wrong
time with catastrophic consequences to the machine, though the batch of
discs being processed survived. The damage to the wall allowed a small
amount of dust into the premises, which brought about the standard
cleaning procedure. Flim sued Estates for breach of covenant and Champion in negligence and nuisance. Estates third-partied Champion, pleading
an indemnity under the contract and Champion then agreed to take over
Estates' defence and indemnify against any liability they might have to Flim.

The Master, on the application of the defendants, struck out the statement of claim on the grounds that the pleadings did not disclose a cause of action against Estates who, having employed reputable contractors, were not in breach of covenant; nor against Champion, since the claim involved pure economic loss. The plaintiffs appeal to the Judge in Chambers.

Richard Wilmot-Smith QC, *39 Essex Street, Temple*
Middle Temple Annual Mooting Competition

Contract — incorporation of terms — misrepresentation

IN THE COURT OF APPEAL (CIVIL DIVISION)

Fratchitt v *Bodger*

In July 1990, the plaintiff, Albert Fratchitt, decided to take out a maintenance contract for his solid fuel central heating boiler. He entered the defendant's shop, having noticed a sign on the door which read:

ARCH

MEMBER OF ASSOCIATION OF REPAIRERS OF CENTRAL HEATING

The defendant, Alfred Bodger, agreed to service Mr Fratchitt's central heating system on payment of an annual feel of £60. He told Mr Fratchitt that this fee covered routine servicing, but the cost of replacing major parts and attending 'breakdowns' would be charged separately. Mr Fratchitt was asked to sign a form headed 'Central Heating Service Contract' and he handed over a cheque for the first year's service. He was given a copy of the form, but it merely contained his name and address, that of the defendant's shop, the make and model of Mr Fratchitt's boiler and the date of the agreement.

Within a week the defendant called to service Mr Fratchitt's central heating system. He spent some time with the boiler, and then said, 'You'll be all right till the next time, now'.

During the night of 28th February 1991, the temperature was extremely low. The fuel hopper feed mechanism had jammed due to accumulation of dirt. It had never been cleaned. In consequence the fire went out and the pipes for the heating system froze and later burst and the boiler was badly damaged. The cost of repairs, which were carried out by another firm, amounted to £1,220, and the plaintiff was without central heating for ten days.

The ARCH Code of Practice contains certain minimum standards for service contracts for solid fuel central heating boilers. Three clauses are relevant.

(1) The first visit under a new service agreement must include a thorough inspection of the boiler. A written evaluation must be presented to the customer within a week of the visit. The written evaluation must include recommendations for any work required that is not covered by the service contract.

(2) Normal service visits must be carried out at intervals of not more than six months.

(3) Normal service visits must include the following work ... *Hopper feeds* ... Where these are fitted, they should be inspected, cleaned and tested to ensure smooth delivery of fuel to firebox.

The plaintiff obtained a copy of the Code after 28th February 1991. When he pointed out the relevant provisions to the defendant, the latter replied, 'I don't know about that — I always use my own judgment!'. Bodger did admit that he had not inspected the hopper feed at all because they 'never really go wrong'. He also admitted that seven months had elapsed since his first visit.

The plaintiff brought an action against Bodger alleging:

(i)   breach of contract, on the grounds that the ARCH Code of Practice was incorporated into the service agreement by means of the notice on the door of the shop, and the provisions of the Code therefore became terms of the contract; or, alternatively

(ii)   the notice on the door of the shop constituted a misrepresentation that service agreements would be performed according to the ARCH Code of Practice when Bodger in fact used his own standards.

In the Firth Street County Court Judge Naylor held:

(1)   the action in breach of contract must fail on the ground that the notice could not, in these circumstances, lead to the incorporation of provisions from the Code of Practice into an individual contract between the trader and a customer; and

(ii)   similarly, the content of the notice was not sufficiently precise to constitute a representation about the performance of the plaintiff's service contract.

The plaintiff now appeals against the judgment in the county court on the grounds that:

(1)   There is no reason in law why, on the facts of the present case, the notice could not lead to the incorporation of provisions from the Code of Practice into the contract between the plaintiff and the defendant.

(2)   The content of the notice was sufficiently precise to constitute a misrepresentation by the defendant about the manner in which he conducted his business.

M B Murphy, *University of Huddersfield*

Contract — consideration — promissory estoppel

IN THE HOUSE OF LORDS

Greedbank plc v *Poorstudent*

Ms Poorstudent borrowed £3,000 from Greedbank plc to finance her Entomology studies at the University of Britannia. The loan agreement provided that she would repay the principal and interest by making twenty monthly instalments of £200, beginning sixteen months after the completion of her third year examinations. After making ten payments, Ms Poorstudent was made redundant by her employer. She sent a letter to Greedbank plc in which she explained her situation, advised them that she was unsure when she would be able to resume making payments, and asked whether they would be willing to accept her redundancy payment of £500 as a final payment on her loan. Greedbank plc responded with a letter in which they agreed to accept the £500 (together with her earlier payments of £2,000) in full satisfaction of her debt of £4,000 under the loan agreement. Ms Poorstudent then sent a cheque for £500 to Greedbank plc. Six months later, after a change in the management of their Student Loans Department, Greedbank plc brought an action against Ms Poorstudent seeking to recover the £1,500 that remained outstanding under the original terms of the loan agreement.

The trial judge, Cautious J, held that:

(1)   Ms Poorstudent could not argue that the doctrine of promissory estoppel prevented Greedbank plc from recovering the £1,500 because (a) she had suffered no detriment in relying on their acceptance of her payment of £500 as satisfaction of her debt, and (b) promissory estoppel would at most suspend her obligation to pay the balance of £1,500 until Greedbank plc gave her reasonable notice that they were returning to the original terms of the loan agreement, which they had done by bringing this action; and

(2)   Ms Poorstudent could not rely on *Williams* v *Roffey* because (a) she had conferred no benefit on Greedbank plc by making the £500 payment, and (b) the Court of Appeal had held in *In re Selectmove Ltd* [1994] BCC 349, that *Foakes* v *Beer* precludes the application of *Williams* v *Roffey* to cases of part payment of a debt.

Ms Poorstudent's appeal to the Court of Appeal was dismissed. She now appeals to the House of Lords.

Robert Wintemute, King's College, London

Contract — offer and acceptance — consideration — promissory estoppel — economic duress

IN THE COURT OF APPEAL (CIVIL DIVISION)

Hardup Construction v *University of the West Midlands*

In 1990 the University of the West Midlands (UWM) decided to open what it hoped would be a highly prestigious Institute for Space Research. The Institute was to be housed in purpose-built accommodation to be built by Hardup Construction Ltd (HCL), who had submitted a tender for the work in which the price was stated to be £400,000. No other tender submitted to UWM had indicated a price of less than £600,000. The construction work was due to be completed by March 1992 in order that the new Institute could be opened at a grand ceremony by Her Majesty the Queen.

By April 1991, however, it had become clear to HCL that the contract price was too low and that it would be unable to complete the work for that price. HCL therefore approached UWM to ask for an additional payment of £300,000 on top of the original contract price. UWM reluctantly agreed because it realised the Institute would otherwise not be ready by March 1992 for the grand opening by the Queen.

Construction work was completed in February 1992, but UWM refused to pay HCL more than the £400,000 originally agreed. HCL sued UWM in the High Court for the extra £300,000 agreed in April 1991.

Brickson-Mortar J found the following facts:

(1)   The original contract price of £400,000 was too low since no contractor could have done the work at that price.

(2)   UWM should have realised that the price was too low.

(3)   The additional £300,000 requested by HCL in April 1991 was not unreasonable.

(4)   UWM would not have agreed to pay the extra £300,000 if it had not been for the impending visit of the Queen.

(5)   HCL knew that the Queen would be opening the Institute, and therefore knew the importance of completing the construction work on time.

Brickson-Mortar J found for the defendant UWM on the following grounds:

(1)   HCL had provided no consideration for the promise by UWM of an extra payment of £300,000, since HCL had already undertaken to complete construction work before the Queen's visit; and

(2)   HCL could not rely on promissory estoppel because it had used the fact of the Queen's visit as a means of coercing UWM into agreeing to pay the extra £300,000, and therefore HCL had not 'come with clean hands'.

HCL now appeals to the Court of Appeal on the following grounds:

(1)   HCL had provided consideration for the extra payment of £300,000 since HCL had conferred a benefit on UWM by ensuring that the Institute was completed on time for the Queen's visit; and

(2)   HCL could claim the benefit of promissory estoppel since the extra £300,000 for which it had asked represented no more than a reasonable sum in the circumstances and HCL had accordingly behaved equitably through-out, relying on the reasoning of Robert Goff J (as he then was) in *Amalgamated Investment and Property Co. Ltd* v *Texas Commerce International Bank Ltd* [1982] QB 84.

Contract — offer and acceptance — revocation — implied terms at common law

IN THE COURT OF APPEAL (CIVIL DIVISION)

Hastie v Puff & Bragg plc

On 2nd January 1990, at 9.15 p.m. an advertisement appeared on West TV, a regional, independent television station. The advertisement announced that the annual January sale would commence at Puff & Bragg's store on the Greenfield Trading Estate the following day. Over a map of the area showing the location of the store a voice announced that all prices would be reduced by at least 25 per cent. The advertisement ended with a photograph of a three piece suite of furniture covered with 'antique finish' leather accompanied by a voice that proclaimed, 'The first person through the door tomorrow morning can have this luxurious leather suite, worth £1,750, for only £500! Be there early! Doors open at 9.30 a.m.'

Jessica Hastie saw the advertisement and persuaded her husband Oliver to attempt to buy the suite. Oliver set off at 10.45 p.m. to drive the 35 miles to the Greenfield Trading Estate. He was delighted to find that he was the only would-be customer outside Puff & Bragg's store. The night watchman allowed him to park his car outside the entrance to the store, and he settled down for the night.

The following morning Mr Hastie was at the front of the queue when Puff & Bragg's doors were opened. He entered the store when the doors were opened and asked the first employee of Puff & Bragg that he saw for the leather suite that had been advertised on television. He was told that the suite had been withdrawn from sale. Mr Hastie brought an action in the county court for damages for breach of contract.

In the Westfaster county court Judge Onions (who has since retired) found the following facts:

(1)   The edition of the local television news programme *Gone West* broadcast on 2nd January on West TV, at about 10.43 p.m., a brief item indicating that the offer by Puff & Bragg plc to sell the leather suite had been withdrawn; and

(2)   The suite had been sold to the assistant manageress of the store who had entered the store on 3rd January before Mr Hastie.

Judge Onions therefore decided that the plaintiff's claim should fail on the grounds that:

(1)   The advertisement was not an offer to sell the suite in question to any specific person.

(2)   Even if the advertisement did constitute such an offer, it had been withdrawn before acceptance via the television programme *Gone West*.

(3)   Despite the first two grounds, the company had sold the suite to someone who had entered the store before the plaintiff, so there could be no breach of contract even if the aforementioned ground was wrong.

The plaintiff now appeals to the Court of Appeal on the following grounds:

(1)   An advertisement of the type broadcast on behalf of Puff & Bragg plc on 2nd January was a contractual offer.

(2)   Such an offer cannot be withdrawn after a legitimate offeree has begun to accept, and any revocation of such an offer must be communicated reasonably in the circumstances, which was not so in the instant case.

(3)   An offer such as that broadcast on behalf of Puff & Bragg plc on 2nd January is subject to an implied term that it is open only to *bona fide* customers and not to employees of the advertising company.

M B Murphy, *University of Huddersfield*

Contract — terms — incorporation — Unfair Contract Terms Act 1977 — reasonableness

IN THE COURT OF APPEAL (CIVIL DIVISION)

Massinger v *Wax*

Demi Massinger, a well known model, used 'The Beauty Box' salon from December 1993 until October 1994 when Sally Wax left the salon. Sally had always attended to Demi's needs. Demi regularly had her eyelashes tinted a special colour which she had made part of her now well-known appearance. At the salon Sally used a form on which the client's name and treatment would be written. A carbon copy of the form was then given to the client. On the reverse of the copy was printed the following statement:

> All staff are professionally qualified and will take every care over your treatment. In the unlikely event of complaint we will refund the cost of your treatment and provide another treatment of your choice free of charge. We cannot accept liability for any losses arising from any treatment.

Sally had mentioned this form to Demi on her first visit to the salon saying it was to keep prices down but that clients were not to worry because they were fully insured for injuries. Sally and Demi had joked about clients losing eyes and being scarred for life.

In November 1994 Demi had an introduction to an internationally renowned film director who offered her an audition for a part in a new James Bond film. Demi was concerned to ensure that her appearance was perfect for the audition and had not yet found a new salon. Although she knew that Sally had given up such work she pleaded with her to prepare her for the audition. The eyelash tint reacted badly and Demi's usual colour was not achieved — worse still a spot of dye had stained her forehead and could not be removed except by washing over several days. As a result Demi was distraught and, being convinced that she would fail the audition, she decided not to attend. The part was given to another actress.

Demi sued Sally for substantial damages for losing the audition opportunity. Sally had not renewed her insurance cover but in any event the policy only covered personal injury. The trial judge found:

(1) Sally was in breach of contract;
(2) the contract was made on the same terms as in the salon; and
(3) the clause excluding liability for loss consequent upon a breach was reasonable.

Demi now appeals to the Court of Appeal on the following grounds:

(1) the clause on the salon form was not incorporated into the contract; and
(2) in any event, applying the test of reasonableness in the Unfair Contract Terms Act 1977, the clause was invalid.

David Chalk, *Anglia Polytechnic University*

Contract — formation — statutory relationship — Unfair Terms in Consumer Contracts Regulations 1994

IN THE COURT OF APPEAL (CIVIL DIVISION)

Midlands Water plc v *Thirsty*

During the summer of 1995, Midlands Water (MW) became concerned at the high demand for water from its domestic consumers at a time of unusually high temperatures and unusually little rainfall. MW therefore banned such customers from using hosepipes as from 1st August 1995 in accordance with its power under section 76 of the Water Industry Act 1991.

One domestic customer, Plantagenet Thirsty, whose water supply was not metered and who had moved into the area on 1st July 1995, then wrote to MW asking for a rebate from his water charge on the grounds that he was not able to use his supply entirely as he wished for domestic purposes, so that MW was in partial breach of contract. MW refused to pay any rebate.

Thirsty therefore sued MW in the Birmingham County Court for a rebate of £20. MW defended the action on the grounds that the relationship between MW and Thirsty was not contractual at all but a purely statutory relationship, and that statute had made no provision for the payment of a rebate in these circumstances.

In the county court the District Judge held that there was a contract between MW and Thirsty. He further held that since this contract had been made on 1st July 1995, it was subject to the Unfair Terms in Consumer Contracts Regulations 1994. In his view, these Regulations, particularly paragraph 1(o) of Schedule 3, meant that MW was bound to pay Thirsty a rebate, which he assessed at £20.

MW now appeals against the findings of the District Judge.

Contract — limitation clause — incorporation — coverage — reasonableness

IN THE COURT OF APPEAL (CIVIL DIVISION)

Mugg Ltd v Potts Ltd

Mugg Ltd manufacture dinner services and other pottery. Potts Ltd supply Mugg Ltd with the clay required for the manufacturing process under a contract which includes the following clause:

> Any liability of Potts Ltd for the supply of defective clay is hereby limited to the price of such clay.

One consignment of clay supplied by Potts Ltd to Mugg Ltd during October 1993 was not suitable for Mugg's purposes because it was of a type intended for the production of bathroom suites. This error was not, however, apparent until Mugg had put the clay through the firing process, which rendered it entirely useless for any purpose whatsoever.

Mugg sued Potts for £20,000 damages, which sum included:

(i)   the price of the clay at £1,000;
(ii)   the cost of wasted materials and labour at £12,000; and
(iii) loss of profit on the dinner services assessed at £7,000.

Potts paid £1,000 into court but resisted claims (ii) and (iii) on the ground that Mugg's claim was covered by the limitation clause quoted above. Doulton J agreed, but Mugg Ltd now appeal to the Court of Appeal on the following grounds:

(1)   the loss suffered by Mugg was not covered by the limitation clause since this concerned only defective clay, whereas the problem with the clay was that it was simply of the wrong type; or, alternatively

(2)   the limitation clause, if applicable, was unreasonable in the circumstances.

Contract — agreement — mistake

IN THE COURT OF APPEAL (CIVIL DIVISION)

Simpson v *Excessive*

Stephen Simpson made a claim on his buildings insurance. The insurance company, Excessive Ltd, wrote back claiming that Simpson was partially to blame and offering to pay a proportion of Simpson's claim. In this typed letter the figure '50 per cent' had been typed but then, it appeared, an 'X' in blue biro had been written over the top of the '50' and the proportion '25 per cent' had been written alongside in the margin in apparently the same blue biro. The letter was signed in black ink. Excessive has conceded that the signature and the purported amendment were written by two different employees.

The figure 50 per cent had remained perfectly visible and when Simpson replied to 'accept Excessive's offer' he said in evidence that he had the '50' figure in mind. He further stated that he thought the '25 per cent' figure in the margin could safely be disregarded since if a large company like Excessive had really meant it, it would have ensured that the letter was re-typed rather than sent out with such an amendment.

When Excessive sent a cheque amounting to just 25 per cent of Simpson's original claim, Simpson sued for breach of contract. The district judge dismissed the claim on the grounds that:

(1)   there was no contract between Simpson and Excessive in relation to the claim because there was no true agreement; and

(2)   even if there were a contract, it was void for mistake.

Simpson appeals to the Court of Appeal.

Contract — privity — remoteness of damage
Tort — negligence — duty of care — remoteness of damage

IN THE COURT OF APPEAL (CIVIL DIVISION)

Smith and Executors of the Estate of Beswick v Slow & Bideawhile

David Beswick lived in his council house for 25 years, 15 as a married man and 10 as a widower. The Council asked him, by letter, in November 1991 if he wanted to buy the property at a 40 per cent discount on the market price. He received the letter shortly before the Christmas holidays and was inclined to refuse the offer. His daughter was married with three children and lived three miles away. That Christmas Day her family visited and Mr Beswick told them about the offer. His son-in-law, Mr Peter Smith, had just been made redundant. The family agreed over the Christmas turkey that David Beswick would, from his own resources, buy his house, and that the Smiths would sell their house and move in with Mr Beswick. The proceeds from the sale of the Smiths' house would pay off the Smiths' mortgage and pay for a small extension to Beswick's home.

In the new year Beswick went to his local solicitors, Slow & Bideawhile, and told them that he intended to buy the house. He handed the Council's offer letter to them and asked them to make the arrangements for the purchase. Beswick told the solicitors about his agreement with the Smiths. After a week Slow & Bideawhile asked Mr Beswick for the deposit money. Mr Beswick was in poor health and about to go into hospital for an operation so he arranged for a building society cheque for the whole of the purchase price to be paid to Slow & Bideawhile, 'So I do not have to do anything more'. Slow & Bideawhile put the money into their client account. On the day that the deposit was paid, 7th February 1992, Peter Smith instructed Slow & Bideawhile in respect of the sale of his house and told the partner concerned (a different one from the partner dealing with the Beswick purchase) of the intended arrangements with Beswick. Contracts for the sale of Peter Smith's house were exchanged on 18th February 1992; completion was to take place on 18th March 1992. Friday 6th March 1992 was the date for completion of the Beswick purchase.

David Beswick was in hospital on 6th March for an operation on his heart. Slow & Bideawhile failed to pay the balance of the purchase money to the Council. This was not unusual for Slow & Bideawhile or indeed any solicitor dealing with the Council, which tolerated a day or two's delay as a matter of course in 'right to buy' cases. The contract of sale provided that the Council need not complete and could declare the deposit forfeit in its absolute discretion if the purchase moneys were not paid on the contract date. This term had never been relied upon by the Council. Slow & Bideawhile did not contact Mr Beswick about the error. However the senior partner contacted the local authority's solicitors to inform them of the error and that they intended to complete on Monday. David Beswick died over the weekend. Slow & Bideawhile were informed of the death on Monday morning and the local authority through their solicitors informed Slow & Bideawhile that in the light of the death of Mr Beswick they would no longer complete but that the deposit would not in the circumstances be forfeit. Were Mr Beswick still alive, they would have completed, but, they said, there was no sense in the sale at a 40 per cent discount if there was no tenant in the property.

Slow & Bideawhile were responsible for Mr Beswick's will which left all his property, real and personal, to his daughter and son-in-law, who were also named executors.

In the circumstances Mr and Mrs Smith decided not to complete on their own sale and agreed damages with their purchaser in the sum of £3,000. That sum was less than the costs they would have incurred in completing the sale and arranging a fresh purchase. They then sued Slow & Bideawhile as joint plaintiffs with Mr Beswick's executors. The damages sought to be recovered were:

(i)   Mr and Mrs Smith's £3,000; and
(ii)   the value of the 40 per cent discount.

The judge held that Slow & Bideawhile owed no duty to Mr and Mrs Smith in relation either to the £3,000 or the 40 per cent discount. He also held that the loss of value of the discount was caused by the death of Mr Beswick and not by the negligence of Slow & Bideawhile. If he was wrong about that the judge held that damages did not fall within either limb of *Hadley* v *Baxendale* (1854) 9 Exch 341. In his view it was not reasonably foreseeable either that Mr Beswick would die or that completion would be prevented.

Mr and Mrs Smith appeal to the Court of Appeal on their own behalf and as executors.

Richard Wilmot-Smith QC, *39 Essex Street, Temple*
Middle Temple Annual Mooting Competition

Contract — consideration — implied term — notice

IN THE COURT OF APPEAL (CIVIL DIVISION)

Squiffy v *London Bus Company*

On 1st January 1994 at about 4 p.m. Ms Jane Squiffy was waiting for a bus at a bus stop in the centre of London. When the bus came along she got on and sat on a seat. The bus moved off. When the conductor came along she proffered her fare, but the conductor said she was drunk, refused the fare and ordered her off the bus.

As Ms Squiffy got up from her seat, she slipped and sprained her ankle. She claimed £1,000 in compensation from the London Bus Company (LBC) for breach of contract in that the company had failed to ensure that the floor of the bus was safe and not slippery.

LBC now accept that Ms Squiffy was not drunk but deny liability on the following grounds:

(1)   there was no contract between LBC and Ms Squiffy; and
(2)   there was a large notice situated by the bus's entry doors which said: 'Warning. The floor of this bus can get slippery at times. Please take care. LBC cannot accept liability for any personal injury caused by slipping on the floor.'

In the High Court Pratt J found for LBC on both points. Ms Squiffy now appeals against both findings.

Contract — breach — balance of probabilities — execution of judgment

IN THE COURT OF APPEAL (CIVIL DIVISION)

Stanley Developments Limited v *Smith*

Robert Smith was a land consultant and speculator who, on 1st July 1988, entered into a written contract with Stanley Developments Limited (Stanley) in which Smith agreed to purchase from Stanley an option to buy some waste land in Thurrock, Essex. It was a term of the agreement that Smith would apply for planning permission for the residential development of the site to allow '130 homes' to be built upon it and that the land would revert to Stanley if the option was not exercised within 24 months of the date of the agreement. The land was of sufficient size (35 acres) for the plot to take 130 detached houses. The purchase consideration for the land provided for in the option agreement was that it was to be the open market value of the land at the date of exercise of the option less one half of any increase in value of the land since the date of the option.

Smith did not apply for the permission as provided for by the terms of the agreement. His application was for three large tower blocks to be built on the land providing for 500 flats. The planning permission application went to a public inquiry and was turned down one month after the expiry of the term of the option.

Stanley sued Smith for breach of contract in not applying for the planning permission envisaged by the agreement. The evidence at the trial was that had such application been made it would have stood a much better chance of being granted and would have been dealt with by the spring of 1989, at the height of the property market. The trial judge said that the chances of success of the contractual planning application being granted were 'substantial but less than 50 per cent, probably nearer 30 per cent'. He also held that it was 'almost certain' that the application for permission in accordance with the contract would have been adjudicated upon by the local authority by the spring of 1989 because there would not have been a public inquiry.

Had the permission been granted in the Spring of 1989 then Stanley's profit upon the exercise of the option by Smith would have been very substantial and in the order of £1m. Since that time property values have collapsed and the project envisaged by the contractual permission is not viable.

The judge awarded Stanley damages of £300,000 plus interest but stayed the execution of the judgment pending appeal. The evidence before the judge at the time of the judgment was that Stanley was impecunious and had expended most of its resources on the litigation. However it had a reputable stock exchange quoted parent company which had guaranteed its debts.

Stanley appealed against the stay of execution. Smith appealed against the judgment. He conceded the breach of contract but argued that the evidence demonstrated that on a balance of probabilities the permission would not have been granted at all and therefore no loss flowed. Smith argued that nominal damages only should have been awarded.

At the time of the appeal against the stay one of the Lords Justices fell ill and the appeal was adjourned. The appeal against the stay was then re-listed to be heard at the same time as the substantive appeal.

Richard Wilmot-Smith QC, *39 Essex Street, Temple*
Middle Temple Annual Mooting Competition

Contract — invitation to treat — offer and acceptance — revocation — damages

IN THE COURT OF APPEAL (CIVIL DIVISION)

Starling v Bramble

The plaintiff, Starling, owns a junk shop in Sheffield. Early last March she displayed a painting in the shop window with this sign attached:

> For sale at the special offer price of £200. This offer stays open until the end of March.

On 20th March the defendant, Bramble, saw the painting and orally offered to buy it for £200. Starling said she would take a little time to consider his offer as she had received a similar offer from another person. Bramble considered the painting to be worth far more than £200 and was very keen to buy it, so the next day he sent a letter by first class post to Starling at the shop offering £500. The letter was delivered two days later, but Starling did not make an immediate reply.

At 10 a.m. on 1st April Starling telephoned Bramble and left a message on his answering machine. This stated, 'I am happy to accept your offer', but did not specify which offer. Bramble listened to that message at 4 p.m. that same day. However, Bramble had already changed his mind. On 31st March he had pushed a letter through the letter box at Starling's shop, stating that his offer was withdrawn. 31st March was a Saturday, and, as a notice on the shop door stated, the shop was closed on Saturdays and Sundays. Starling did not see Bramble's letter until 8 a.m. on Monday, 2nd April. Starling spoke to Bramble on 5th April and claimed that he had agreed to buy the painting for £500. Bramble replied that there was no contract between them at all. Bramble refused to accept delivery of the painting on 10th April. Expert evidence has established that the painting is worth £50. Starling brought this action in the Sheffield County Court, claiming damages of £450, being the difference between Bramble's offer price of £500 and the painting's actual value of £50.

Her Honour Judge Tremble, having found the above facts, gave judgment for the plaintiff, but assessed the damages as only £150, being the difference between Bramble's offer price of £200 and the painting's actual value of £50. She gave the following reasons:

(1)   The display of the painting in the shop window was an offer to sell and not an invitation to treat, since that was how the plaintiff had described it; it followed that the defendant's 'offer' on 20th March to buy the painting for £200 was in fact an acceptance of the plaintiff's offer, and therefore a contract was concluded on that date.

(2)   If she was wrong on the first point, Her Honour would have held that there was no contract between the parties. If the defendant on 20th March was making an offer to buy the painting for £200, that offer was never accepted, because the plaintiff's telephone message of 1st April was to be construed as referring to the defendant's second offer of £500. However, that offer had been revoked on 31st March by the defendant's letter

delivered to the plaintiff's trade premises, and was therefore incapable of being accepted.

The plaintiff appeals to the Court of Appeal, contending that there was a contract for sale at a price of £500. The defendant cross-appeals, contending that there was no contract.

Professor Graham Battersby, *University of Sheffield*

**Contract — collateral contract — guarantee — misrepresentation —
Misrepresentation Act 1967**

IN THE COURT OF APPEAL (CIVIL DIVISION)

Supercookers Ltd v *Slocombe*

In October 1993 Susan Slocombe bought a pressure cooker made by
Supercookers from a local shop at a cost of £45. The salesman had shown
her various pressure cookers made by different manufacturers, but
Slocombe had chosen one made by Supercookers because it was advertised
as having a 'five year manufacturer's guarantee'.

Slocombe used the cooker for about 15 months without any problems,
but it then became apparent that the synthetic gasket had become so
compressed that it no longer provided an effective seal when cooking under
pressure. Slocombe wrote to Supercookers asking for a new gasket, but
Supercookers replied by drawing Slocombe's attention to the user booklet
supplied with the pressure cooker. On page 3, this states that:

> The five year guarantee does not apply to the gasket, which should be
> replaced every six months in order to ensure that the cooker provides
> optimum performance.

Slocombe therefore felt that she had to purchase a new gasket at a cost of
£20. She then claimed this sum in the county court, where the registrar
decided that it raised an issue of law inappropriate for arbitration and
ordered that the case be heard in open court, where the district judge found
the following additional facts:

(i)   that every competent cook would realise that no ordinary gasket
could possibly last five years unless the cooker were hardly used during this
period;

(ii)   that Slocombe was a cook of above-average competence;

(iii)   that Slocombe had believed that this gasket was made of some
special substance which meant that it would last five years; and

(iv)   the gasket had not been defective.

The judge held that Slocombe had entered into a contract of guarantee
with Supercookers collateral to her contract with the local retailer. He
further held that the advertisement concerning the five year guarantee was
an innocent misrepresentation within the meaning of section 2(2) of the
Misrepresentation Act 1967, and gave judgment in favour of Slocombe.

Supercookers appeal to the Court of Appeal on the following grounds:

(1)   there was no collateral contract between Supercookers and
Slocombe; and

(2)   the advertisement in the shop could not, on the facts found, amount
to an innocent misrepresentation within section 2(2) of the Misrepresentation Act 1967.

Contract — bond — guarantee — variation — interest

IN THE HOUSE OF LORDS

Tinkers City Company v *Citycenter Insurance*

Tinkers City Company entered into a building contract with Speedybuild (London) (1988) Limited (Speedybuild) on 12th May 1987 for the construction of a banqueting suite and a hostel for the homeless in Threadneedle Street in the City of London. The contract sum was £7.5m and the standard of work demanded was lavish. The contract period was two years. Speedybuild undertendered considerably. The next lowest tender was for £10m. The Tinkers City Company obtained a bond dated 13th May 1987 from Citycenter Insurance in the following terms:

> We, Citycenter Insurance, in consideration of the receipt by them of £50,000, hereby bind ourselves to Speedybuild under the contract dated 12th May 1987 and unconditionally guarantee the performance of Speedybuild. Provided always that Citycenter Insurance's liability under this Bond shall not exceed £3m.

The date for commencement of Speedybuild was 1st June 1987. On that date Speedybuild were not ready to begin. They had a considerable overdraft and their bank said they would not support them unless they completed and were paid for their other large project first. The Managing Director of Speedybuild estimated that their other project would be completed on 1st August 1987 and a large payment would be made shortly thereafter. He contacted the Secretary of Tinkers City Company who agreed that the work could begin on 12th August 1987 and that the completion date would be adjusted pro rata, provided that Speedybuild used their best endeavours to make up the time. Tinkers City Company did not contact Citycenter Insurance. However at the trial their Senior Vice President, Hiriam Johnson, conceded in cross-examination that if the arrangement had been put to him he would have agreed to it. He said he thought that a consensually delayed start was frequent in his experience: he often consented to them and he did not think that it was commercially significant. Indeed in this case it was beneficial because if Speedybuild's bank had not supported them at all, Citycenter Insurance would have been immediately liable under the bond (albeit that their exposure to defective work claims might have increased); at least under this arrangement he would have felt (if it had been put to him) that Citycenter Insurance had a chance of seeing the primary obligations discharged.

Speedybuild went into liquidation on 1st August 1989; on 13th August Tinkers City Company's quantity surveyors estimated that completion by a fresh contract would cost them an extra £5m at the minimum. Through their solicitors they demanded from Citycenter Insurance the £3m under the bond. Hiriam Johnson on 17th August 1989 heard about the adjustment of the commencement date. His initial reaction was that the figure demanded was too high and that he wanted it checked. He instructed Citycenter Insurance's solicitors to reserve their rights and get more information on the figures. On 13th September 1989 Tinkers City

Company's solicitors said that they had lost patience. The next day they served a writ claiming the £3m plus interest as sums due under the bond from the date of insolvency of Speedybuild. Hiriam Johnson, on receiving a copy of the writ instructed his solicitors to defend the proceedings and ensure that the 'trigger happy critters' never got a penny.

Tinkers City Company issued Order 29 proceedings and appeared by Leading Counsel. Citycenter Insurance instructed Junior Counsel to defend them. By the hearing date it was clear that the estimate of losses of £5m from the insolvency was conservative and it looked more like £7m in view of the massive defects to the banqueting suite then coming to light. The standard of work to the hostel was impeccable, indeed the bathtaps installed in the hostel were those specified for the suite. Junior Counsel therefore argued only that the bond had been discharged by a material variation of the underlying contract in the consensual change of dates. He submitted that because there had been no indulgence clause in the bond, Tinkers City Company could recover nothing.

Hiriam Johnson flew in from New York to watch Junior Counsel's argument fail on 13th December 1989 before Merits J. The hearing took 20 minutes. Merits J said that the bond was good, the variation of the date for commencement was immaterial, the contract was not one of guarantee and that the full sum ought to be paid under Order 29. He also said that if Junior Counsel wanted to argue the point at a full trial, he could do so only after an Order 29 payment for the full sum. Hiriam Johnson ensured that the Order 29 payment was made on 25th December 1989 and said to his solicitors that he wanted a 'QC guy to get the ball back and fast'.

The trial was held on 13th December 1990. Junior Counsel appeared for the Tinkers City Company, Leading Counsel being unavailable. Leading Counsel's argument for Citycenter Insurance that the bond was discharged was accepted by Law J. He ordered that there be judgment for Citycenter Insurance and that £3m be repaid plus interest, which had then accrued in the sum of £370,000. Tinkers City Company appealed on the grounds that:

(1)   The variation of the underlying contract was *de minimis*.

(2)   The contract was not one of guarantee.

(3)   The discharge of the bondsman on the grounds of a change in the primary contracting party's obligations of the type seen in this case was old law and ought to be changed.

(4)   There was no power in the judge to order repayment of interest.

In the appeal there was particular reliance on Hiriam Johnson's evidence at trial that the variation would not have been of real concern to him. In the appeal both parties were represented by Leading and Junior Counsel. The Court of Appeal upheld the decision of Law J. Tinkers City Company now appeal to the House of Lords.

Richard Wilmot-Smith QC, *39 Essex Street, Temple*
Middle Temple Annual Mooting Competition

Contract — action for the price — consideration — economic duress

IN THE HOUSE OF LORDS

Bigshot v Tryhard plc

James Bigshot is an eccentric multimillionaire; Tryhard plc is a specialist engineering company. In 1992 Bigshot entered into an agreement to purchase, ex works Newcastle, a lifesize replica of the first aeroplane flown by the Wright brothers. Payment was agreed in the sum of £50,000 upon signature on the contract, £450,000 ex works and a further £20,000 upon assembly and completion of the first flight.

The contract provided that Bigshot would be responsible for the transport of the plane (in pieces) to his estate in Lossiemouth, Scotland and for assembly of all pieces save the electrical gear. Tryhard agreed to assemble the electrics and provide a pilot for the first flight, which would be deemed to have taken place if the plane was in the air for at least one minute and covered at least half a mile. Bigshot paid the first £50,000.

On 1st February 1993 the Managing Director of Tryhard stated that in his view the plane was ready for delivery ex works and called upon Bigshot to provide the transport. Bigshot stated that he no longer trusted Tryhard to do a good job and he wanted a maintenance manual and assembly instructions before he would send transport. The judge found that:

(i)   there were no subsisting defects to the plane then at that time;

(ii)   there was no entitlement to the manual and instructions under the contract; and

(iii)   no responsible person could believe that there was such an entitlement; but

(iv)   Bigshot genuinely believed that he had such an entitlement.

'Give me the book, and I will send the lorry. Keep it until then', said Bigshot to Tryhard. Tryhard was under pressure from its banks because it was at the limit of its banking covenants. If the £450,000 was paid to it by the end of March, then Tryhard could operate for the rest of the year within the limits of its covenants. Without that money Tryhard was in danger of insolvency. The judge could make no finding that insolvency would have taken place without payment. The Managing Director of Tryhard was desperate. His company was the subject of a hostile bid and the bank's attitude to the bid would be affected both by the cash flow situation and whether Tryhard was in dispute with a major customer.

At a meeting at the Hilton Hotel in London the Managing Director of Tryhard said that he could not provide the 'book' in the timescale required by Bigshot. Bigshot stated that he still did not trust Tryhard to perform and said that he would pay the £400,000 in seven days provided an on-demand bond was given by Tryhard to Bigshot in that amount. 'That's all you're getting for this plane, either those terms or the deal is off. I will put the thing together: I do not want you having anything to do with this plane once it has left your works.'

The Managing Director said: 'I dispute your suggestion that we cannot assemble this plane and your suggestion that you are entitled to the manuals, etc before payment. However, to settle this I will accept the £400,000 in exchange for the bond.'

The bank refused to provide the bond. Tryhard then wrote to Bigshot stating that it was entitled to the £450,000 under the original agreement and demanding payment because the plane was ready for collection ex works. Bigshot refused and relied on the Hilton Hotel agreement, stating that there would be no payment without the bond.

Tryhard wrote alleging a fundamental breach of the original contract giving Bigshot seven days to collect the plane and pay the money. Bigshot refused, stating: 'No bond, no money.' Tryhard then stated that it accepted the repudiation and sued for the price of the plane. It pleaded economic duress and lack of consideration in relation to the Hilton Hotel agreement, stating that it could therefore rely upon the original agreement which was repudiated.

The judge accepted both pleas, stating that Bigshot repudiated the original agreement and that there was no entitlement to rely upon the later agreement. The Court of Appeal reversed that finding. Tryhard appeals to the House of Lords.

Richard Wilmot-Smith QC, *39 Essex Street, Temple*
Middle Temple Annual Mooting Competition

Contract — intention to create legal relations — Supply of Goods and Services Act 1982, s. 4(2) — 'satisfactory quality'

IN THE COURT OF APPEAL (CIVIL DIVISION)

Vivien v Rowena

Vivien and Rowena are next-door neighbours who are both enthusiastic gardeners and growers of vegetables. Indeed, they have become so experienced and knowledgeable about horticulture that, in the summer (approximately April or May to September or October, depending on the weather) both grow a substantial surplus of produce in their gardens and allotments. For the last five years, they have both been selling this surplus to ordinary members of the public from their respective kitchens. Both women are in their sixties and find that the extra income generated is a useful supplement to the state pension (in Rowena's case) and to a salary earned as a part-time clerk with the local authority (in Vivien's case). For each of them, the income from typical sales per week is equivalent to about 50 per cent of their pension or salary entitlement, although sometimes they have been known to take more money in one week from their sales of produce than they receive from their pension or salary.

Every year each woman experiments with one or two new varieties of seeds. This year Rowena grew a new variety of tomato, known as 'Rose Red', whilst Vivien grew a new variety of courgette, called 'Green Velvet'. For the past three years it has been their custom to exchange some of the new vegetables and this year was no exception, for Vivien gave Rowena six 'Green Velvet' courgettes in exchange for 3lbs of 'Rose Red' tomatoes.

In fact, Rowena has never liked tomatoes and only grows them for other members of her family. She therefore never tried any of her 'Rose Red' tomatoes. Vivien, on the other hand, is very fond of tomatoes and put several of these tomatoes into a salad which she ate. The next day, she was taken seriously ill with a particularly virulent attack of food poisoning caused by the 'Rose Red' tomatoes, which appear to have become contaminated in Rowena's kitchen by a micro-organism which is very rarely found in domestic premises and against which most household cleaners are useless.

Vivien was so ill that she required a lengthy stay in hospital and a considerable period of convalescence. She was also forced to give up her job. She claimed compensation from Rowena for breach of an implied contractual term that the tomatoes were not of 'satisfactory quality' under section 4(2) of the Supply of Goods and Services Act 1982, but in the county court the district judge found for Rowena on the following grounds:

(1)   there was no intention to create legal relations between Vivien and Rowena, and thus no contract between them which Rowena could be said to have breached; and

(2)   even if there was a contract between them, section 4(2) of the Supply of Goods and Services Act 1982 did not apply because Rowena had not supplied the tomatoes in the course of a business.

Vivien now appeals to the Court of Appeal against both these findings.

Contract — agreement — mistake — misrepresentation

IN THE HOUSE OF LORDS

Waddington Walkers Ltd v *Mason*

Michelle Mason attended a sale in a local working men's club which was advertised in the local free newspaper. The advertisement stated that all goods stocked would be sold at a discount of at least 50 per cent. She bought several pairs of training shoes for her family for a total price of £100. If sold in ordinary retail outlets, these training shoes would have been worth at least £250.

The person running the sale, Albert Allen, had obtained these shoes from the manufacturer, Waddington Walkers, by agreeing to purchase them wholesale on notepaper headed 'Allen & Co.'. Allen & Co. (of which Allen had been purchasing manager) had ceased trading three years earlier, and Waddington had never dealt with it before, but Waddington's sales director had been prepared to sell it training shoes once he had checked with the Federation of Professional Wholesalers (FPW), a trade association, that Allen & Co. was a member. It now appears that the FPW's list was rather out of date. It is believed that Allen has left the country.

Waddington Walkers claim that all the purchasers at the sale are guilty of conversion of Waddington's training shoes. They sued Michelle Mason as a test case, claiming that the purported contract between them and Allen was void both for mistake and for deceit.

Her Honour Judge Farrow held in the county court that Waddington's mistake was legally of no consequence, but that the purported contract between them and Allen was void for deceit. The Court of Appeal upheld Mason's appeal that Allen's deceit was immaterial and declared that the training shoes belonged to Mason. Waddington's cross-appeal on the mistake point was rejected.

Waddington Walkers appeal to the House of Lords on both points.

Contract — unilateral — bilateral — offer and acceptance

IN THE COURT OF APPEAL (CIVIL DIVISION)

Wonderstores Ltd v *Sidebottom*

On a Friday in January 1994 Wonderstores placed the following advertisement in the local newspaper:

> Wonderful Wonderstores present their World-renowned Wonderful January Sale. Bargains galore: 3 Piece Suites £100. Panasonic Camcorders £30. Rolex Watches £80. Many more bargains inside. Must be sold on Monday. First come, first served. Please form an orderly queue in the marked area outside our main entrance.

Sidney Sidebottom was first in the queue. He arrived on Friday evening, intending to buy a Panasonic Camcorder and a Rolex Watch, and carefully arranged his deck chair and sleeping bag in the designated area. However, on the intervening Saturday, Wonderstores Ltd was taken over by another company, and its management were immediately instructed to cancel the sale. This they did by placing a new advertisement in the local newspaper that evening, but Sidebottom did not see it because he was in the queue.

When Wonderstores opened on Monday, Sidebottom attempted to buy a Panasonic Camcorder and a Rolex Watch for the prices advertised in the original advertisement, but sales staff refused to sell him the items at those prices. Sidebottom sued Wonderstores for breach of contract.

In the local county court, the district judge found that the original advertisement amounted to a unilateral offer, and that Sidebottom had begun to perform his acceptance by queuing outside the shop in the manner directed. Following the dictum of Goff LJ (as he then was) in *Daulia* v *Millbank Nominees* [1978] 2 All ER 557, the judge held that Wonderstores could not prevent Sidebottom from completing his performance and that, since they had done so, they were in breach of contract. Damages were agreed at £2,000.

Wonderstores appeal to the Court of Appeal on the following grounds:

(1)   the advertisement was an invitation to treat and not an offer; or, alternatively

(2)   if it was an offer, then it was a bilateral offer and not a unilateral offer; or, alternatively

(3)   if it was a unilateral offer, then it had not been accepted by Sidebottom by the time that it was revoked by Saturday's advertisement.

Criminal law — criminal damage — recklessness — duress

IN THE COURT OF APPEAL (CRIMINAL DIVISION)

R v Fairhead

Charlie Fairhead is the nursing manager at Holby City Hospital. At 10 p.m. on the night in question Isaiah Isaacs, the sales representative of a local manufacturer of hospital equipment, was demonstrating to Mr Fairhead an experimental model for a new type of portable X-Ray machine. As he was watching the demonstration, Mr Fairhead saw out of his office window that someone appeared to be attempting to break into his car. Instinctively he rushed out of his office door in an attempt to prevent his car from being stolen but, as he did so, he knocked over the X-Ray machine, which smashed into little pieces on the floor. Mr Isaacs was so incensed by this loss of the company's only experimental model that he reported the incident to the police, who charged Mr Fairhead with recklessly causing criminal damage contrary to section 1(1) of the Criminal Damage Act 1971. It has now been established that no one was attempting to break into Mr Fairhead's car, but that it was simply being checked by one of the hospital's own security officers.

At his trial Mr Fairhead claimed that he had given no thought to any possible risk of his breaking the X-Ray machine because he was so concerned that his car was (as he believed at the time) about to be stolen. Reeve-Jones J directed the jury that:

(a) Mr Fairhead's reason for not considering the possibility that he might damage the machine was irrelevant, and that they should convict if they believed that the risk of his so damaging the machine was obvious in the circumstances; and

(b) Mr Fairhead could not rely on a plea of duress of circumstance as a 'lawful excuse' within the meaning of section 1(1) of the Criminal Damage Act 1971 because:

(i) no one had, in fact, been attempting to steal his car; and

(ii) such a defence was inapplicable in any event when the accused was charged with committing the offence recklessly.

Fairhead was convicted, but now appeals to the Court of Appeal on the following grounds:

(1) the jury should have been directed to consider the reason for Mr Fairhead's thoughtlessness in deciding whether or not he acted recklessly; and

(2) the jury should have been allowed to consider whether the defence of duress of circumstance amounted to a 'lawful excuse' within the meaning of section 1(1) of the Criminal Damage Act 1971.

Criminal law — manslaughter — corporate *mens rea* — duty to act

IN THE HOUSE OF LORDS

R v *Flytours plc*

On 7th July 1993 the Goodluck family flew out to Lanzarote for a fortnight's holiday in the Heartbreak Hotel, which they had selected from the Flytours 'Summer 93' brochure. That evening, however, they discovered that the gas water heater in their suite (No 197) was faulty. The flue was so badly fitted that in one place there was a gap of two inches between sections, allowing potentially lethal carbon monoxide fumes to escape directly into the suite. The family complained immediately to the manager, who agreed to move them to a different suite whose water heater was correctly fitted.

On 22nd July 1993, after returning to the UK, Mrs Goodluck wrote to Mr Arthur Fly, Managing Director of Flytours, to tell him about the faulty flue in suite 197. Mr Fly passed the letter to the director in charge of hotel inspections, Mrs Linda Maybee, and wrote back to Mrs Goodluck saying that 'it was, indeed, a serious matter' and that he 'would personally ensure that steps would be taken to rectify the matter'. Mrs Maybee decided, however, that since the hotel had passed an inspection in January 1993 and that there had been no other such letters, there was no need for any immediate action and that the matter could be discussed with the hotel management at a meeting on 6th September 1993, which had already been agreed with the hotel. The two other directors of the company knew nothing about either Mrs Goodluck's letter or the Heartbreak Hotel.

On 18th August 1993 the Sweet family moved into suite 197 for their holiday. During the night they all died through carbon monoxide poisoning.

Flytours plc was prosecuted for manslaughter. No charges were brought against anyone else. At the trial Helpful J directed the jury that, in order to reach a verdict of guilty, they had to be satisfied that Flytours was under a duty to take reasonable care of all its holidaymakers and that Flytours had failed to do so. He further directed the jury that the company's 'state of mind' was independent of any one individual, and could be deduced from putting together the states of mind of all the directors. The jury returned a unanimous verdict of guilty and Flytours was fined £250,000.

Flytours appealed to the Court of Appeal on the grounds that Helpful J had misdirected the jury on both points. The Court of Appeal dismissed the appeal. It upheld the direction of Helpful J in relation to the question of Flytours' duty towards its holidaymakers, but ruled that the judge's direction on corporate *mens rea* was faulty in that it was impermissible to aggregate the states of mind of company directors in order to deduce that of the company. Nevertheless, the Court of Appeal applied the proviso, saying that, on the evidence presented to the Crown Court, Mrs Maybee had the requisite *mens rea* in any event, thus fixing Flytours with the same *mens rea*.

Having obtained leave and the necessary certification, Flytours now appeals to the House of Lords on the grounds that:

(1)   Helpful J misdirected the jury as to Flytours' duty towards its customers since, although Flytours accepted that it was under a general duty

to take reasonable care of its customers, this could not extend to the checking of every hotel appliance; and

(2)   Mrs Maybee did not have a state of mind sufficient to satisfy a jury that Flytours had the requisite *mens rea* for manslaughter, so that there had been an inappropriate use of the proviso by the Court of Appeal.

The Crown cross-appeals on the ground that the states of mind of company directors can be aggregated to determine whether or not a company has the necessary *mens rea* for manslaughter, so that the direction of Helpful J to the jury on this point should be upheld and the decision of the Court of Appeal reversed, thus rendering the use of the proviso unnecessary.

Criminal law — Food Safety Act 1990, s. 8 — 'contaminated' food

IN THE DIVISIONAL COURT OF THE QUEEN'S BENCH
DIVISION

Dredgeford Metropolitan Council v Bodger (Foods) Ltd

Case stated by the Trodfoot Justices

Bodger (Foods) Ltd is a manufacturer of sandwiches and snack foods which
are supplied to a number of shops, cafés and works canteens in the
Dredgeford area. On 4 May 1994, Miss Tipe, an office worker, bought a
prawn sandwich from a shop trading as Syd's Sarnies. The sandwich had
been made and supplied to the shop by Bodger (Foods) Ltd. It contained a
piece of sharp steel which has been identified as a part of the blade of a
stainless steel knife that had broken whilst being used in the preparation of
the sandwiches. Miss Tipe cut her mouth on the piece of metal, and it was
sore for three days. Bodger (Foods) Ltd pleaded not guilty to a charge of
selling food (namely the sandwich) which failed to comply with food safety
requirements contrary to section 8(1) of the Food Safety Act 1990 in that it
was so contaminated that it would not be reasonable to expect it to be used
for human consumption in that state as provided by section 8(2)(c).

The Justices reluctantly came to the conclusion, having heard the
arguments, that the prosecution had not made out the offence. There was
no evidence as to the cleanliness or otherwise of the fragment of steel; it
was accepted that the defendant company had a strict procedure for
ensuring that utensils, including knives, were in a hygienic state at all
times. It could not therefore be said that the food was contaminated
merely because it contained extraneous matter. The Justices felt obliged to
accept the submission made on behalf of the defendant that the prosecution
should have been brought under section 14 of the Food Safety Act and not
section 8.

The prosecution now appeals to the Divisional Court by way of case
stated on the grounds that:

(1)   to require the prosecution to produce evidence that the extraneous
matter was in an unhygienic state would be to frustrate the intention of
Parliament which had introduced section 8(2)(c) of the Food Safety Act
1990 specifically to deal with such circumstances as those in the instant case;
and

(2)   in a case where extraneous matter is likely to do harm, the
extraneous item itself is the contaminant and there is no need to do more
than rely on the ordinary meaning of the word 'contaminated'.

M B Murphy, *University of Huddersfield*

/ **Criminal law** — *mens rea* **for murder** — **defence of necessity**

IN THE COURT OF APPEAL (CRIMINAL DIVISION)

R v Fright, Chary and Windy

In 1992, Jeremy Luckless, Harry Fright, Charles Chary and Walter Windy embarked on a climbing expedition in the Andes. They made a base camp and Charles Chary remained there whilst the other three climbed up the mountain. On the third day of their climb, they were traversing a slope with Harry Fright leading and Jeremy Luckless in the middle and Walter Windy bringing up the rear. They were roped to one another. Suddenly a crevasse opened beneath them, leaving Harry Fright clinging to one side of the chasm and Walter Windy clinging to the other, with Jeremy Luckless hanging over it.

Walter Windy called to Harry Fright, 'We'll have to cut him off or we'll all go!' Fright called back, 'We'll have to do it together or one of us will go with him.'

Luckless asked them to cut only one side to allow him the chance to try to gain a hold on the other side of the crevasse. Windy said that this was not practicable in the circumstances. Windy counted to three and he and Fright cut the rope simultaneously. Luckless fell into the chasm and the other two returned to base camp.

They stayed there for three days to regain their strength. As they were preparing to leave, Luckless crawled into the camp. He had a broken leg, but miraculously he was still alive. At first the others were delighted, but then a bad storm hit the camp and Windy, Chary and Fright decided that the only hope of salvation was to descend to the foothills immediately. They all agreed that Luckless could not make the descent and that they could not manage to carry him. With great difficulty they erected a tent and wrapped him in a sleeping bag and left him with a small amount of food. They told Luckless that they were going for help and left him.

On the descent, which they thought would only take two days, the three men became lost, and it was not until a week later that they finally reached the nearest village. Assuming that Luckless was dead, they told the authorities that their expedition had suffered a casualty. They then returned to the UK.

In fact, Luckless was found alive by a local team of climbers and was rescued by them. On his return to the UK he told his story to the police and Fright and Windy were charged on two counts of attempted murder and Chary was charged on one count of attempted murder.

At the trial, Fright and Windy pleaded necessity as a defence to the first count of attempted murder by cutting the rope. To the second count of attempted murder by deserting Luckless, Fright, Windy and Chary argued that, in the circumstances, they had not formed the necessary intention for murder, and thus they could not be guilty of attempted murder. In the alternative, the defence of necessity was argued.

Hangman J ruled that necessity was not recognised by the courts of England and Wales as a defence to a charge of murder or attempted murder. In consequence he refused to allow the pleas of necessity to be put to the jury. He also directed the jurors that, if they found that the act of leaving

Luckless alone on a mountain during a severe storm would be highly likely to result in his death, then they should find Fright, Windy and Chary guilty on the second count of attempted murder. The jury returned guilty verdicts on all counts of attempted murder.

Fright, Windy and Chary now appeal against their convictions on the following grounds:

(1)   The defence of necessity should not have been withheld from the jury and it was capable of providing a defence to the charges against Fright and Windy in respect of cutting the rope, and the charges against all three men for leaving Luckless on the mountain; and

(2)   The trial judge erred in his direction to the jury on the *mens rea* required for the offence of murder and attempted murder in the circumstances of the case.

M B Murphy and L C Foxcroft, *University of Huddersfield*

Criminal law — insider trading — reckless disclosure

IN THE COURT OF APPEAL (CRIMINAL DIVISION)

R v Freelance

One Saturday afternoon, in London's most prestigious tennis club, two directors of Bank-With-Us (UK) plc were enjoying a well-deserved drink, seated at the bar. After discussing ways of improving their tennis game, they began a more serious conversation regarding recent goings-on in the bank. Apparently, the company's auditors had discovered severe discrepancies in the bank's accounts, with evidence of debts in the region of £5 million. Mr Big and Mr Know, the two directors, were musing on the seriousness of this situation and, after reiterating the findings of the auditors, concluded that there were only two solutions to the problem: either to find another bank to buy them out, or to declare the company insolvent. Mr Big concluded the conversation with a somewhat solemn and remorseful comment about the shareholders being the ones to suffer the most, whichever solution was chosen.

Despite the particularly low voices of Mr Big and Mr Know, Freelance (the barman) overheard the whole conversation. On returning home that evening, he wrote an article for the local newspaper, warning shareholders of the impending disaster at Bank-With-Us. As a freelance journalist he wrote regularly for various newspapers on items of public interest. For the past few weeks, however, he had been working on a selection of articles for one local newspaper alone, *The London Local*. Freelance was always worried about the legal implications of his work and therefore always asked his solicitor, Mr Law, to read over his articles prior to submission. With this in mind, Freelance made a note in his diary reminding him to contact Mr Law the next morning. In the meantime, he instructed his wife to post a pile of other articles to *The London Local* early the next day. Carelessly, he left the Bank-With-Us article alongside this pile, so that his wife posted it along with the others. By the time Freelance realised what had happened it was too late. *The London Local* had already included it in their lunchtime edition. As a result of the article, the shareholders of Bank-With-Us sold their shares *en masse*, hence avoiding prospective personal losses. Freelance was charged under section 52(2)(b) of the Criminal Justice Act 1993 with insider dealing.

At his trial, Freelance gave evidence, saying that he had never intended disclosing the information contained in the article without first seeking the advice of Mr Law. He added that if this had been obtained in time, then he would have realised the criminal nature of any attempt at publication and would then have destroyed the offending article. Furthermore, he asserted that it was not his fault that his wife had inadvertently collected the article and posted it along with the others. He maintained that he had instructed his wife to post only those articles which formed the pile on his desk, and no others. Finally, as to the issue of the contents of the article being inside information, Freelance argued that he did not know whether the information had been communicated to others or not, nor whether the auditors report was confidential and known only to the auditors and Messrs Big and Know. His Honour Judge Sharey directed the jury that a person could be classed as an insider even if it was not actually part of his employment function to have access to the information. He further directed that the disclosure offence could be committed by recklessness. Freelance was convicted.

Freelance now appeals against his conviction on the grounds that the learned judge erred in directing the jury both that:

(1)   insider status could be conferred on a person whose function in employment does not necessarily include having access to such information; and that

(2)   recklessness formed part of the section 52(2)(b) disclosure offence.

Salma Khan, *Pinsent Curtis*,
London and Birmingham

Criminal law — obtaining property by deception — meaning of 'property' — whether 'obtained' or 'belonging to another'

IN THE COURT OF APPEAL (CRIMINAL DIVISION)

R v Ketteridge

In order to allocate pupils to primary schools in accordance with the provisions of the Education Act 1980, Elstree City Council asks parents to indicate on a form their three preferred schools in order of preference. The same form also requires that parents state their names (and that of the child) and the address at which the child is normally resident.

Nesta Ketteridge indicated her preferences for her son, Toby, with North Cross school as first choice. However, she gave as her (and Toby's) address that of a friend who lived much nearer the school. Toby was duly allocated a place at North Cross which, as Nesta had expected, he would not have been allocated had she given the correct address. Elstree City Council, on learning of Mrs Ketteridge's dishonesty, immediately decided to admit to North Cross school the child placed highest on the waiting list.

Mrs Ketteridge was prosecuted under section 15(1) of the Theft Act 1968. The judge ruled that a school place was property capable of being stolen; and that it was for the jury to decide whether the other elements necessary for a conviction had been proved beyond reasonable doubt. Mrs Ketteridge was convicted. Mrs Ketteridge now appeals on the following grounds:

(1) a school place cannot amount to 'property' within the meaning of section 4 of the Theft Act 1968; and

(2) even if a school place can amount to 'property', it neither 'belonged to another' nor was it 'obtained' by Mrs Ketteridge and these issues should not have been left to the jury.

Criminal law — murder — provocation — diminished responsibility

IN THE COURT OF APPEAL (CRIMINAL DIVISION)

R v Samantha

Samantha has been married to Edgar for seven years. Over the last three years, Edgar has taken to going out drinking of an evening and coming back late at night the worse for drink. Samantha frequently scolds him when he returns and tells him she will leave him if he does not mend his ways. Edgar has a violent temper and, on some occasions, he has hit Samantha forcefully. On other occasions, Edgar has forced Samantha to engage in sexual intercourse with him despite her protests.

Samantha recently sought help from a counsellor who advised her to leave Edgar and move into a hostel for battered wives. The next time Edgar came home drunk, he staggered into the bedroom and Samantha told him she was leaving the next day, whereupon Edgar punched out at her several times, breaking some of her teeth, cutting her lip and badly bruising her. Eventually, Edgar went to sleep on the bed with Samantha sobbing in the corner of the room. Several hours later, in the early hours and whilst Edgar was still asleep in a drunken stupor, Samantha went downstairs and poured herself a couple of large brandies. She then went to the tool shed in the garden and took out a large hammer. She returned to the bedroom and hit Edgar several times about the head, killing him. She then calmly called the police and said: 'You had better come quickly — I have just murdered my husband.'

Samantha was arrested and questioned the next day. She made a statement to the police. In the statement, Samantha explained that she just could not take any more and that she had told the counsellor that she would kill Edgar if he ever hurt her again. Samantha was charged with murder and, despite her plea of diminished responsibility, was found guilty of murder at the Crown Court on a majority verdict. She is appealing against that verdict on the basis that the judge should also have left her alternative defence of provocation to the jury. The judge had not allowed the defence to be put to the jury because of the cooling off period of some hours.

Dr David Bainbridge, *Aston University*

Criminal law — theft — Theft Act 1968, ss. 1 and 9 — meaning of dishonesty — meaning of 'intention permanently to deprive'

COURT OF APPEAL (CRIMINAL DIVISION)

R v *Swindler*

Upon learning that an end of semester examination paper had been written, Swindler, a law student, decided that since the course had been particularly tough (due to the incompetence of the course co-ordinator) he and his fellow students needed all the assistance possible to gain good marks in order to impress potential employers in the tough economic climate. He therefore decided he would attempt to read the examination paper and then inform everyone on the course of the questions which they were expected to answer.

All the students used the Law School's General Office to channel enquiries to their tutors and they were normally allowed access to the office. During the lunch hour, and knowing the secretaries never locked the door when they went out for lunch, Swindler entered the office and rifled through the filing cabinets. Upon finding the examination paper he took notes on it and then put the exam paper back into the cabinet and left before the secretaries returned.

Swindler informed as many as possible of those who were studying the course of the contents of the paper. He was duly traced as the source of the information circulating around the Faculty and charged with burglary and theft of the exam paper contrary to sections 9(1) and 1 respectively of the Theft Act 1968. Swindler's defence argued that his actions were not dishonest within the test laid down in *Ghosh* [1982] QB 1053; and also, since he had no intention permanently to deprive, his actions could not amount to theft.

In his direction to the jury, Plodder J advised them to convict Swindler of theft if they felt his behaviour was dishonest. He continued:

> It is not my place to make any comments about his deplorable behaviour. It is up to you to be satisfied both that his behaviour was dishonest by the standards of ordinary, reasonable, honest people and not those of his fellow law students, and secondly that he realised his actions would be seen as being dishonest.

On the issue of permanent deprivation, Plodder J stated:

> The question is one of intention. Did Swindler's actions render the exam paper useless? Admittedly, it can be used for next year's tutorials and other teaching purposes but can it be used for the purpose for which it was intended? If you feel the answer to this is no, and you also believe Swindler's actions were dishonest, then you must convict him of theft.

The jury convicted Swindler on both counts. He appealed to the Court of Appeal on the grounds that the trial judge had misdirected the jury:

(1) on the meaning of 'dishonesty' in section 1 of the Theft Act; and
(2) in his direction to the jury on 'the intention permanently to deprive'.

Urfan Khaliq, *University of Southampton*

Criminal law — murder — intention — causation — *novus actus intervҽniens*

IN THE COURT OF APPEAL (CRIMINAL DIVISION)

R v Tube

In January 1993 John Tube, a plumber, was employed by Mr & Mrs Warder to upgrade the gas pipes and fittings at their large Birmingham home in preparation for its change of use into a nursing home. After five days' work, however, the Warders sacked Tube for shoddy workmanship and engaged George Blaze, another plumber, to complete the work. Blaze's work was of the appropriate standard but he did not check everything that Tube had already done.

Mrs Betty Newman, aged 73, moved into one of the newly refurbished rooms on 3rd March 1993. When she went to light her gas fire that evening there was an explosion and Mrs Newman was killed instantly.

John Tube was subsequently charged with murder. In evidence which was uncontested it was found that Tube had failed to connect the gas supply pipe to the fire itself, so that the pipe simply allowed gas to escape straight into the room. This had not been noticed before 3rd March, however, because Blaze had not checked this installation; and because the gas supply to that particular room had been turned off until Mrs Newman moved in. Mrs Newman herself, it was agreed, had lost her sense of smell.

Vapour J directed the jury that in order for them to find Tube guilty of murder they must be satisfied both that:

(i)   Mrs Newman's death was a natural consequence of Tube's poor workmanship; and that

(ii)   it would have been obvious to Tube that death or really serious injury would result from his poor workmanship.

The jury returned a unanimous verdict of guilty. Tube now appeals to the Court of Appeal on the grounds that Vapour J misdirected the jury in that:

(1)   his explanation to the jury as to what was required to satisfy the *mens rea* for murder in this case was faulty; and

(2)   he had failed to appreciate that the failure of Blaze to check Tube's work was a *novus actus interveniens* breaking the chain of causation because of regulation 33(3) of the Gas Safety (Installation and Use) Regulations 1984, which states:

Where a person installs a gas appliance in any premises at a time when gas is not being supplied to the premises, no person shall supply gas to that appliance unless he has caused such testing and examination and adjustments as are specified in paragraphs (1) and (2) above to be carried out.

/Criminal law — rape — intent — recklessness

IN THE HOUSE OF LORDS

R v Wolf

Donald Wolf spent the evening at his local public house drinking a large quantity of alcohol. Towards closing time he fell into conversation with Mandy Lamb and they went to his flat for coffee. They had not met before that evening. Ms Lamb refused to have sexual intercourse with Wolf unless he wore protection. She produced a contraceptive for him to use. He appeared to agree to her condition but had sexual intercourse with her without protection. Ms Lamb did not realise the lack of protection until after intercourse had taken place.

Wolf was charged with rape contrary to section 1(1) of the Sexual Offences (Amendment) Act 1976. The indictment alleged that Wolf had unlawful sexual intercourse with Ms Lamb, who at the time of the intercourse did not consent to it, and that at the time Wolf knew that she did not consent to the intercourse or was reckless as to whether she consented to it or not.

Wolf's defence was that Ms Lamb had given consent to sexual intercourse. On the issue of *mens rea* his defence was that he was not guilty because he was intoxicated and did not form the requisite specific intent. He further claimed that he was not reckless as to consent because as a result of his intoxication he believed Ms Lamb was consenting.

In the absence of the jury and after legal argument Modern J ruled as a matter of law that on the issue of consent there was in this day and age a fundamental difference between protected and unprotected sexual intercourse and that Ms Lamb's conditional consent could not amount in law to consent for the purposes of rape if the defendant had unprotected sexual intercourse.

Her Ladyship further ruled that reckless rape is not an offence of specific intent following the dicta of Lords Simon of Glaisdale and Russell of Killowen in *DPP* v *Majewski* [1977] AC 443 and accordingly intoxication afforded no defence to Wolf since the consumption of alcohol amounted to the requisite recklessness.

Wolf thereupon changed his plea to guilty to reckless rape, the Crown accepting his defence to the alternative of knowledge of a lack of consent. Wolf unsuccessfully appealed to the Court of Appeal which agreed with the trial judge on the issue of consent and considered itself bound by authority on the issue of intoxication.

Wolf now appeals to the House of Lords on grounds which raise the following questions:

(1)   Whether the offence of rape makes a distinction between consent to protected sexual intercourse and consent to unprotected sexual intercourse.

(2)   Whether the decision in *DPP* v *Morgan* [1976] AC 182 and section 1(2) of the Sexual Offences (Amendment) Act 1976 mean that on a charge of reckless rape the defendant's intoxication should be taken into account.

David Chalk, *Anglia Polytechnic University*

Criminal law — murder — manslaughter — attempted murder — provocation

IN THE COURT OF APPEAL (CRIMINAL DIVISION)

Yorke v *Attorney-General*

During the summer of 1994 Mr and Mrs Yorke went on a camping holiday. While she was preparing her husband's meal, Mrs Yorke remembered that her husband had beaten her severely exactly one year ago. Although he had not hit her since, she believed he might beat her again that day and so attempted to kill her husband by putting what she thought was caustic soda into his soup. In fact, the container had been wrongly labelled and what she did, in fact, put into the soup was powdered milk.

After he had eaten the soup Mrs Yorke made her husband a cup of tea. She put two tablets into the tea believing them to be saccharin. But again the bottle had been wrongly labelled and the tablets were, in fact, aspirin, to which Mr Yorke was severely allergic. He died in hospital two hours later as a result of an allergic reaction to the aspirin.

Mrs Yorke was tried for the murder of her husband and found guilty. She appeals to the Court of Appeal on the grounds that the requisite *mens rea* and *actus reus* for murder had not coincided, and that she should have been convicted either of attempted murder and/or of manslaughter on the grounds of provocation.

**Employment law — maternity leave — accrual of holiday entitle-
ment — unfair dismissal — sex discrimination**

IN THE COURT OF APPEAL (CIVIL DIVISION)

Arthur Waterprice v *Slaughter*

Jennifer Slaughter had worked as a manager at Arthur Waterprice (AW),
Management Consultants, for five years. She then became pregnant and,
having given the appropriate notification to AW, took 35 weeks' maternity
leave from 1st August 1994. She received Statutory Maternity Pay (SMP)
for the first 18 weeks' leave, but nothing thereafter.

After Slaughter had been back at work for four weeks (for which she was
duly paid), she asked Tom Cooper, the Partner at AW responsible for
personnel matters, if she could book two weeks' holiday. He replied that this
was out of the question since Slaughter had been absent from work for 35
weeks and had therefore only acquired the right to two days' holiday by
virtue of the four weeks for which she had been at work.

In fact, Slaughter's contract of employment says nothing at all about
whether holiday accrues to a woman on maternity leave. The provision to
which Cooper was referring relates to employees who join or leave AW
during a calendar year, but AW claim that it is also, by analogy, applicable to
women like Slaughter.

Slaughter, who had never been absent from work through illness, felt that
AW were victimising her for having taken maternity leave. She resigned from
AW and, after an exchange of letters had failed to produce any agreement,
she made a complaint of unfair constructive dismissal and sex discrimination to an industrial tribunal.

AW now accept that Slaughter was entitled to an accrual of annual leave
for the first 14 weeks of her maternity absence under section 33(1) of the
Employment Protection (Consolidation) Act 1978 (as amended) and have
sent Slaughter an *ex gratia* payment equivalent to seven days' pay as
compensation.

AW refuse to accept, however, that any holiday entitlement could have
accrued for the remainder of Slaughter's maternity absence. Slaughter
contends, on the other hand, that such entitlement does accrue during the
whole period of absence and that AW's failure to acknowledge it amounted
to a breach of contract and thus a constructive dismissal which was also
unfair.

Slaughter also contends (and AW accepts) that male (and female)
employees absent from work through long illnesses, or because of second-
ment to a client company, are able to enjoy the accrual of holiday
entitlement during such absence, so that she has been the victim of unlawful
sex discrimination.

The industrial tribunal found in favour of Slaughter on both her claims.
The tribunal's findings were upheld by the Employment Appeal Tribunal.
AW now appeals to the Court of Appeal.

**Employment law — employee or independent contractor —
continuity of employment**

IN THE COURT OF APPEAL (CIVIL DIVISION)

Whistle v *Flute*

Miss June Flute worked as a peripatetic music teacher. From 1st September 1984 until 7th July 1996 she had given piano lessons for three hours per week at the fee-paying Bass Drum school. During the academic year 1995-96 a new headmistress, Miss Gill Whistle, had been appointed at Bass Drum. Miss Whistle had then decided to replace Miss Flute with Miss Penny Piccolo as from 1st September 1996 on the grounds that Miss Piccolo was 'more friendly', though no one had ever complained about Miss Flute's manner before.

Miss Flute claimed that she had been unfairly dismissed. Miss Whistle and Bass Drum contended, however, that Miss Flute was self-employed and not an employee; and that even if she were an employee, each period of school holidays prevented there being the requisite continuity of employment.

The industrial tribunal found that Miss Flute was an employee on the following grounds:

(1)   the piano used belonged to Bass Drum school;

(2)   teaching took place solely on Bass Drum's premises;

(3)   the teaching times were set at the beginning of each academic year by the head teacher; and

(4)   the fact that Miss Flute also taught at other schools at other times was irrelevant.

The tribunal also found that the school holidays did not break Miss Flute's continuity of employment on the grounds that there was an implied term in her contract of employment that she should practise playing the piano during such holidays in order to maintain her abilities as a teacher.

The Employment Appeal Tribunal upheld the findings of the industrial tribunal. Miss Whistle and Bass Drum now appeal to the Court of Appeal.

Employment law — redundancy — unfair dismissal — compensatory award — damages

IN THE COURT OF APPEAL (CIVIL DIVISION)

Younger Ltd v Elder and Others

Mr Elder worked for Younger Ltd as a driver of the company's delivery lorries. The ownership of the company shares changed in 1991 and a new managing director, Mr Callas, was appointed. Callas decided after being with the company for three weeks that the labour force was too large and that a significant saving would be made by reducing the number of drivers. Callas decided that three drivers of the twelve employed should be made redundant. He decided that the drivers to be selected for redundancy should be the oldest in age irrespective of length of service. Mr Elder and two other drivers were the oldest and were given notice of redundancy. There had been no prior agreement on method of selection and no employees had previously been made redundant. There was no consultation between Younger Ltd and any employee or any union. Each employee was paid the statutory redundancy payment. Mr Elder was 58 years of age when made redundant, the other two drivers were 57 and 61. Mr Elder had been employed by the company for over 20 years. The other two drivers had been employed for 8 and 12 years respectively. None of the nine drivers retained had worked for the company for more than 10 years. None of the drivers has obtained new employment.

Only Mr Elder complained to an industrial tribunal that he had been unfairly dismissed by an employer who was subjectively prejudiced against older workers. The tribunal decided that to adopt age as the sole criterion for selection for redundancy was not unreasonable but that the lack of consultation was unreasonable and that accordingly the dismissal was unfair. The tribunal made a compensatory award.

The tribunal rejected an argument that the compensatory award should be reduced by the amount of the redundancy payment. It was said by the employer that the only argument the employee had was that consultation might have led to him not being selected for redundancy. In such a case, said the employer, the employee would have received wages whilst employed but would not at the same time be due a redundancy payment. It was argued that in a case where unfairness is due to lack of consultation, compensation should only be awarded on the basis that consultation would have made a difference. Consultation would only make a difference according to the likelihood that the employee would not have been chosen for redundancy, in which case the employee would not be due a redundancy payment. The tribunal rejected the contention that to award compensation, for a chance that the employee might not have been selected, as well as the redundancy payment, was to put the employee in a better position than he would have been had no unfairness occurred.

Mr Elder appealed to the Employment Appeal Tribunal against the decision that age was not an unreasonable criterion. The employer cross-appealed against the award of compensation. Both appeals were dismissed.

Mr Elder now appeals to the Court of Appeal on the grounds that the use of age as the sole criterion for selection for redundancy is unreasonable and no reasonable tribunal could reach the decision reached by the industrial tribunal in this case.

Younger Ltd cross-appeals to the Court of Appeal on the grounds that the award of compensation in a case of unfair dismissal should not leave the employee in a better position than he would have been had there been no unfairness, since to do so is contrary to general principles of damages which Parliament cannot have intended to exclude from the calculation of compensation under the Employment Protection (Consolidation) Act 1978.

David Chalk, *Anglia Polytechnic University*

Environmental law — judicial review — Wildlife and Countryside Act 1981 — EEC Birds Directive

IN THE HOUSE OF LORDS

Birdrights v Secretary of State

Aberarden, a remote coastal town, suffering from high unemployment and poor health (found in a report accepted as sound by the Government's Chief Medical Officer to be related to its unemployment levels), has the prospect of a £250 million Japanese investment in a lead smelter. This is expected to provide 500 jobs, reducing the unemployment rate from 25 per cent to 18 per cent.

The smelter would require a constant supply of water, necessitating a new main. The main would pass through and effectively destroy, a group of tarns used as a storm weather roosting area by migrating birds. The tarns are on the edge of, but just within, a Special Protection Area (SPA) designated under the Birds Directive (79/409 EEC). (The trial judge found as a fact that the only alternative would cost so much that the return on investment would be 2 per cent which would fall below generally accepted returns for projects of this sort of 5 per cent.) The Environment Statement (accepted by everyone as impeccable) recorded that there was some far from conclusive evidence that the loss of the tarns would have a serious effect on the rare Diomedia Judex Ecorhynchos, close to extinction (and listed in Annex I to the Birds Directive), which passed through the area on its way to breed in Greenland. Three years further study would enable the significance of the tarns to be assessed with confidence.

Pluto (Tokyo) plc have said that their investment will be made in Italy unless the British Government demonstrates a firm commitment to the project. They announced in 1994 that they would abandon the project unless a Nature Conservation Order made under section 29 of the Wildlife and Countryside Act (WCA) 1981 was amended to exclude the tarns area from its scope and to exclude from the list of potentially damaging operations 'the creation or modification of the structure of water courses, including their realignment, regrading and dredging'. An amendment to that effect has passed through the correct procedural stages. It was followed by a press release from the Secretary of State of 15th March 1994, which included the following passage:

> We will not accept European dictation. Jobs are more important than birds. The precautionary principle is a foreign concept. It should stay that way.

'Birdrights', whose standing has been conceded, have challenged the amendment under Schedule 11(7) of the WCA 1981. The Secretary of State argues that the affected area is rarely used by the birds, that there is no scientific proof of real harm to them and that it is for him to balance the issues. 'Birdrights' argue that the affected area is an integral part of the SPA, that the precautionary principle must as a matter of law be applied, and that the prospect of employment is an inadmissible consideration in European law.

The Secretary of State was successful before Ironglove J; 'Birdrights' before Warmheart and Farsight LJJ (Sharpmind LJ dissenting). The Secretary of State now appeals to the House of Lords.

Professor Colin Reid, *University of Dundee*
Robert McCracken, *2 Harcourt Buildings, Temple*
United Kingdom Environmental Law Association

Environmental law — judicial review — Town and Country Planning Act 1990

IN THE HOUSE OF LORDS

Motown MDC v ETIB

Motown MDC published the Notice of Adoption of their Unitary Development Plan on 11th May 1994. It contained the following policy in the Movement Chapter:

> M9 When levels of specified air pollutants exceed the relevant EU Directive limit values the Council will declare an Air Pollution Emergency. Non-essential motor vehicle use within specified zones will be treated as a public nuisance.
>
>   Appropriate legal remedies such as prosecutions of motorists and injunctions against car park operators will be pursued by the Council. Details of air pollutant levels, methods of measurement, definition of zones and essential vehicle use, and means of public notification are set out in Schedule 3.

The Regional Office of the Department of the Environment objected to the policy when the Plan was placed on deposit on the grounds that 'it was not a land use policy'.

The Inspector who held a local inquiry into the Deposit Plan reported that:

> Policy M9 is well founded on research into patterns of traffic movement and effects on air pollution. Schedule 3 sets out a practicable and fair scheme. I am, however, uncertain whether a UDP policy would be material in a court of law adjudicating on public nuisance. I therefore recommend that it be retained in the UDP if it is lawful so to do.

Motown MDC received three opinions from counsel. Two juniors advised that the policy was unlawful. Then Ms Prudence Greene QC advised that the policy was lawful. Her opinion emphasises that section 12(3A) of the Town and Country Planning Act 1990 imposes a duty to:

> include policies in respect of . . .

> (b)   the improvement of the physical environment; and
> (c)   the management of traffic.

The Environmental Transport Information Bureau (ETIB) (a motor industry lobby group) challenged Policy M9 of the UDP by application under section 287(1)(a) of the Town and Country Planning Act 1990 on 11th June 1994. At first instance the application was successful before Irongrove J. In the Court of Appeal Wier and Hermiston LJJ agreed that the Plan should be partially quashed as:

Policy M9 is a dangerous attempt to interfere with the freedom of the motorist. It is no more reasonable than a policy purporting to specify times when lawnmowers can be used in suburban areas without causing a nuisance. Local politicians should not seek to interfere with the discretion of the courts to decide when to exercise their powers in relation to nuisance.

Farsight MR dissented on the grounds that:

The carefully considered views of the local community expressed through the decisions of their elected representatives after full opportunities for scrutiny and debate at public inquiry ought to carry great weight with judges and magistrates who cannot because of the nature of their offices be elected. Policy M9 has the potential to make an important contribution to the common weal.

Motown appeals to the House of Lords.

Professor Colin Reid, *University of Dundee*
Robert McCracken, *2 Harcourt Buildings, Temple*
UKELA Prize Moot Final 1996, Lincoln's Inn
United Kingdom Environmental Law Association

Land law — contractual licence — constructive trusts — proprietary estoppel

IN THE COURT OF APPEAL (CIVIL DIVISION)

Green v Brown

Mr and Mrs Black owned a large house, Dunroamin, in extensive grounds. In the grounds was a small cottage known as Ivy Cottage, which had a small fenced-off garden. In 1985, Mr and Mrs Black allowed Mrs Brown to occupy Ivy Cottage rent-free on condition that she spent three hours a day on weekdays cleaning the Blacks' house. Nothing was put in writing although Mr and Mrs Black told Mrs Brown that she could remain in Ivy Cottage as long as she wished. Mrs Brown planted some shrubs in the garden and, in 1988, repaired the fence at her own expense after it had been damaged by storms. In 1990, the path to Ivy Cottage was resurfaced. Mr Black arranged the contract with a local firm of builders but Mrs Brown contributed £300 of the total cost of £450. Since moving into Ivy Cottage, Mrs Brown has organized and paid for internal decoration work as and when required.

In July 1994, Mr and Mrs Black sold and conveyed the whole of their property to Mrs Green for £215,000. It appears that this was slightly below the true market value with vacant possession of both Dunroamin and Ivy Cottage. Mrs Green agreed orally with Mr & Mrs Black to abide by the arrangement with Mrs Brown. However, Mrs Green and Mrs Brown did not get on well and Mrs Green was very critical of the standard of Mrs Brown's cleaning work. Eventually, in February 1995, Mrs Green served a notice to quit on Mrs Brown and told her not to clean the house any more.

Mrs Brown refused to leave and Mrs Green sought an order for vacant possession. This was refused at first instance. Mrs Green now appeals against that decision to the Court of Appeal.

Dr David Bainbridge, *Aston University*

Land law — resulting trust — constructive trust — strict settlement — contractual licence

IN THE HOUSE OF LORDS

Merryweather v Merryweather

In 1989 Mr and Mrs Merryweather, a couple in their eighties, conveyed ownership of their house to their son, Alfred (then 57), who had lived with them since the break-up of his marriage. Alfred furnished no consideration for this conveyance since it was executed on the common understanding that Alfred could take over the management and maintenance of the house and the paying of all bills without his parents needing to worry about them, with the further expectation that he would be spared the need to transfer ownership of the house to himself after they had died. The solicitor who drew up the conveyance has no record of whether it was envisaged that Mr and Mrs Merryweather would remain in the property for the rest of their lives or not, and the couple themselves simply cannot remember. Alfred was entered on the register as sole proprietor with absolute title.

A month after the conveyance Mr and Mrs Merryweather also executed a monthly standing order of £200 in favour of Alfred, which was designed to meet their own estimated contributions to electricity, gas, telephone and water charges and the council tax, together with any expense incurred by Alfred in purchasing items of heavy shopping (such as tins of food and potatoes) which his parents might have difficulty in carrying. Neither the idea for this standing order, nor the fact of its having been executed, appear to have been mentioned to the solicitor who drew up the conveyance; and it is unclear both as to when it was decided to execute such a standing order and as to whose idea it was.

In 1992 Alfred was diagnosed as suffering from lung cancer and he died a year later. Two payments were made into Alfred's bank account after his death in accordance with Mr and Mrs Merryweather's standing order before that standing order was revoked. In Alfred's will, which had been drawn up after he had moved back in with his parents but three months before the house was conveyed to him, he left everything:

> to be divided equally between my four children: Brian, Calum, Daphne and Eugene Merryweather.

Mr and Mrs Merryweather knew about the terms of Alfred's will but did not expect him to pre-decease them and so did not consider the terms of Alfred's will to be of particular importance. The solicitors who drew up Alfred's will were not the same as those who prepared the conveyance of the house and what evidence there is on this point (which is very little) suggests that no advice was either sought or given as to the legal ramifications of the combination of the will and conveyance. Mr and Mrs Merryweather have, however, long been alienated from all their grandchildren except Eugene and are unhappy that the grandchildren are now effectively their landlords. They therefore wish to have their home conveyed back to themselves. Eugene has expressed his willingness to comply with this request since he considers it unfair that his grandparents no longer have effective control over their own home. Brian, Calum and Daphne do not agree. They wish to charge their grandparents rent at the market rate of £600 per month.

Mr and Mrs Merryweather took court proceedings designed to obtain:

(i)   a declaration that Alfred had held the house on a resulting trust for Mr and Mrs Merryweather;

(ii)   a declaration that Alfred had therefore been unable to pass ownership of the house under his will; and

(iii)   an order that Brian, Calum and Daphne convey ownership of the house to Mr and Mrs Merryweather;

or, in the alternative to (i) to (iii) above:

(iv)   a declaration that the conveyance from Mr and Mrs Merryweather to Alfred had created a constructive trust entitling Mr and Mrs Merryweather to remain in the house rent-free for life.

The three grandchildren resist these claims and themselves seek a declaration that they are entitled to charge their grandparents a monthly rent of £600.

On Alfred's death the house was worth about £150,000 if sold freehold and with vacant possession. With the occupancy of Mr and Mrs Merryweather, who are in good health and paying no rent, it was estimated to be worth about £50,000. The vagaries of the housing market mean that the respective values of the house quoted above remain unaltered today, although if the grandparents were to pay a monthly rent of £600 while in occupation, the freehold value of the house would rise to £95,000.

At first instance Hardy J held that a resulting trust had been executed by the conveyance of the house to Alfred and that, accordingly, the house should be conveyed back to Mr and Mrs Merryweather. Hardy J therefore felt no need to rule on the other issues raised. The Court of Appeal allowed an appeal by the three grandchildren in part, holding unanimously that a constructive trust had been created with an interest in the house for life to both Mr and Mrs Merryweather, remainder to Brian, Calum and Daphne in fee simple.

Brian, Calum and Daphne now appeal to the House of Lords, whilst their grandparents cross-appeal.

Land law — ownership by finding

IN THE COURT OF APPEAL (CIVIL DIVISION)

Lord Tollbooth and Slight v *Cringe*

This is an appeal from the decision of Short J in the Queen's Bench Division, who found the following facts. Lord Tollbooth owns an extensive estate in South Yorkshire. In 1980 he granted to Cringe a 99-year lease comprising 100 acres. Cringe uses part of the land for agriculture, but the remainder is forest and moor land which Cringe uses for hunting and shooting. Cringe employs Slight as a gamekeeper. Last August, when Slight was trudging back through the forest after a hard day's work, he saw something bright glinting in the grass. On investigation, the bright object turned out to be a brooch, subsequently discovered to be an antique valued at £10,000. The following morning Slight reported his find to Cringe, who has made inquiries among the hunting and shooting fraternity; no one has claimed the brooch, which has remained in the custody of Cringe. Neither the lease nor Slight's contract of employment contains any provision relevant to the finding of the brooch.

In these proceedings the brooch is claimed by Lord Tollbooth as the freehold owner of the estate, and by Slight as the finder. Short J dismissed both actions for the following reasons:

(1) As between Lord Tollbooth and Cringe, the claim by Cringe was superior, because Cringe was in possession of the relevant land at the date of the finding (applying *London Corporation* v *Appleyard* [1963] 1 WLR 982, [1963] 2 All ER 834, and disapproving *Elwes* v *Brigg Gas Co.* (1886) 33 ChD 562).

(2) As between Slight and Cringe, the claim by Cringe was superior because although Cringe could not claim as occupier of the land, since he had not manifested an intention to exercise control over things which might be found on it, he could claim as the employer of Slight, since the finding was sufficiently connected to his employment as to be in the course of employment and not wholly incidental or collateral thereto (applying dicta of Donaldson LJ in *Parker* v *British Airways Board* [1982] QB 1004, at p. 1017).

Both plaintiffs now appeal to the Court of Appeal.

Professor Graham Battersby, *University of Sheffield*

Public law — judicial review — *locus standi* — jurisdiction

IN THE HOUSE OF LORDS

R v *Secretary of State for the Environment ex parte CARE*

Community Action to Rescue the Environment (CARE) is a pressure group which campaigns on environmental issues. It is primarily concerned with the dumping of toxic waste. In the course of 1992 CARE sought legal advice on the compatibility of the Disposal of Controlled Waste Act 1988 (which came into force on 1st May 1989) with the 1986 EC Directive on the Regulation of Waste Disposal. It was advised that the provisions contained in Part III of the 1988 Act were incompatible with the Directive. Accordingly CARE applied for judicial review, seeking a declaration that Part III of the Act was incompatible with the Directive. No other relief was sought.

Leave to move for judicial review was heard by Marshall J. He concluded that Part III of the 1988 Act was incompatible with the Directive. However, he declined to make the declaration sought by CARE on the following grounds:

> Although I have formed the view that Part III of this Act is completely incompatible with the relevant provisions of European law, I must bear in mind that this is an application for judicial review. I can only grant relief if the various procedural requirements laid down by national law are satisfied. In the present case I am not prepared to make the declaration which the applicant seeks. In the first place I do not think that CARE has the necessary *locus standi* to bring these proceedings. My attention has been drawn to the decision of the House of Lords in *R* v *Secretary of State for Employment ex parte Equal Opportunities Commission* [1994] 2 WLR 409. However that decision does not, in my view, assist the applicant. It is plain, to my mind, that the House of Lords concluded that the EOC had *locus standi* to challenge an Act of Parliament because of its statutory duty to work towards the elimination of discrimination. CARE has no such equivalent duty. It is a mere pressure group. I cannot believe that the House of Lords intended to permit such groups to challenge Acts of Parliament. In the second place an application for judicial review must be brought promptly and in any event within three months. This Act has been in force since 1989 yet proceedings were not commenced until 1993. Accordingly, and in the absence of any authority on this point, I consider that the application should be dismissed on this ground also.

CARE appealed to the Court of Appeal which upheld Marshall J's decision. CARE now appeals to the House of Lords. The Secretary of State for the Environment does not challenge Marshall J's decision (with which the Court of Appeal agreed) that Part III of the 1988 Act is incompatible with the Directive but cross-appeals on the basis that the court would, even if CARE's appeal were successful, have no jurisdiction to make the declaration because none of the prerogative orders of mandamus, prohibition or certiorari could be granted. The Secretary of State relies, inter alia, on the decision of Lord Wilberforce in *Davy* v *Spelthorne BC*

[1984] 1 AC 262 and intends to ask the House of Lords to rule that Lord Browne-Wilkinson's view in *R v Secretary of State for Employment ex parte EOC* that a declaration could be granted in such circumstances was wrong.

Richard Wilmot-Smith QC, *39 Essex Street, Temple*
Middle Temple Annual Mooting Competition

Public law — judicial review — *locus standi*— **legitimate expectation**

IN THE COURT OF APPEAL (CIVIL DIVISION)

R v *Secretary of State for the Environment ex parte 'Friends of Dingly Dell'*

Acting pursuant to the (fictitious) Gravel Extraction Act 1982, the Secretary of State for the Environment purported to alter the regulations relating to gravel extraction from quarry sites. Under the proposed scheme, instead of extracted materials having to be replaced with topsoil, each site operator would be given a choice between extracting a larger amount of material and replacing it with topsoil, or extracting a smaller amount of material and replacing it with household refuse. Hence a site operator could choose to extract less material, but adopt a cheaper system of landfill.

Dingly Dell is a well known area of outstanding natural beauty in the Surrey countryside. Nearby is a gravel extraction site, the operators of which plan to take advantage of the proposed changes in the regulations by switching to a system of replacing extracted materials with household waste. 'Friends of Dingly Dell', a pressure group comprising local residents and ramblers, fear that using household waste for landfill purposes will cause pollution, infestations of rats, have a negative visual impact, and generally destroy the quality of the surrounding area.

The Secretary of State for the Environment is also the MP for the constituency in which Dingly Dell is situated. Prior to his decision to alter the regulations, he attended a public meeting organised by Friends of Dingly Dell at which he assured the audience that local conservation was a major priority for him, and that he would not sanction the development of any policies that would have a deleterious effect on the local environment.

Friends of Dingly Dell applied for a judicial review of the minister's decision to alter the regulations on the ground that they had a legitimate expectation that the new scheme for gravel extraction would not result in increased pollution. At the hearing of the application Copout J ruled that, following *R* v *Secretary of State for the Environment ex parte Rose Theatre Trust Company* [1990] 1 All ER 754, the applicants lacked *locus standi* to challenge the minister's decision. In the event that he was wrong on this first issue (which he did not concede), he further ruled that, in any event, the applicants had suffered no unfairness since they enjoyed no legitimate expectation that the regulations would not be altered in a manner that would adversely affect their interests. In arriving at this second conclusion Copout J cited *R* v *Secretary of State for Transport ex parte Richmond-upon-Thames London Borough Council* [1994] 1 All ER 577.

The applicants now appeal against the decision at first instance on the grounds that Copout J erred in law in ruling that:

(i)   the applicants did not have *locus standi* to challenge the minister's decision; and

(ii)   the applicants did not have a legitimate expectation that the regulations would not be altered as proposed.

Michael T Molan, *South Bank University*

Public law — judicial review — *locus standi* — unreasonableness

IN THE COURT OF APPEAL (CIVIL DIVISION)

R v *Secretary of State for the Environment ex parte Frampton*

In January 1995 divers discovered the well-preserved remains of a ship off the coast of Cornwall. The remains were situated within British territorial waters. Marine archaeologists from the nearby University of Penzance, led by Professor Osbert Lyons, investigated the find and discovered that the ship was a seventeenth century Portuguese trading vessel, the *Eldorado*, which had been owned by a company of Portuguese spice merchants and had mysteriously disappeared during a voyage in the 1660s. Research at the University of Penzance established that the ship had been designed by a famous Portuguese craftsman, Mattias da Gama, and that many of its features were peculiar to Mediterranean trading vessels of the late seventeenth century. These preliminary investigations at the University were funded by the British Association for the Preservation of Maritime Monuments (BAPOMM). The discovery of the *Eldorado* generated a great deal of press attention and there was a considerable increase in the number of tourists visiting the area.

In April 1995 the *Penzance Express*, a local weekly newspaper, ran a story about a local businessman's proposals for the construction of a marina and the potentially detrimental effects on the remains of the *Eldorado* of the proposed development. The article came to the attention of Professor Lyons, who contacted the Society of Marine Archaeologists, Scientists and Historians (SMASH), an unincorporated association of distinguished academics in the field of marine archaeology and related disciplines. SMASH's members included the majority of the archaeologists from the University of Penzance who had investigated the discovery of the vessel and the Portuguese historian Leon da Braganza, who was the direct descendant of the *Eldorado*'s original owners. SMASH was gravely concerned that the construction of the marina would damage the remains of the vessel. Accordingly, SMASH wrote to the Secretary of State for the Environment requesting that he schedule the *Eldorado* under section 1(3) of the Ancient Monuments and Archaeological Areas Act 1979.

On 27th August 1995 the Secretary of State replied to SMASH's request as follows:

...the Secretary of State has considered your request that the remains of the Portuguese trading vessel *Eldorado* be included in the Schedule of monuments compiled by the Secretary of State under section 1 of the Ancient Monuments and Archaeological Areas Act 1979. The Secretary of State accepts that the vessel is a monument for the purposes of the Act. However, the Secretary of State considers that the vessel has no artistic, historical, archaeological or traditional connection with the United Kingdom and accordingly is not a monument of national importance within the meaning of section 1(3) of the 1979 Act. Therefore the Secretary of State has decided not to schedule the remains of the *Eldorado*. The Secretary of State has consulted the Historic Buildings and

Monuments Commission for England (English Heritage) in reaching this decision.

Upon receipt of this letter SMASH consulted English Heritage and BAPOMM with a view to instituting proceedings for judicial review. Neither was interested in making an application. Accordingly, on 1st October 1995 SMASH, through its president Dame Bonaventura Frampton, a historian specialising in seventeenth century mercantile history, applied for judicial review of the Secretary of State's decision. Leave to move for judicial review was granted at an oral hearing by Mr Justice Sullivan on 20th November 1995.

On 14th December 1995 the application was listed before Mr Justice Turtle. At the hearing Counsel for SMASH argued that the Secretary of State had misconstrued the phrase 'of national importance' in section 1(3) of the Ancient Monuments and Archaeological Areas Act 1979. Counsel for the Secretary of State argued that SMASH did not have *locus standi* to challenge his decision. Mr Justice Turtle delivered an *extempore* judgment, stating that:

I have been persuaded by the arguments of Counsel for the applicant that the Secretary of State's decision on the construction of section 1(3) of the Ancient Monuments and Archaeological Areas Act 1979 was wrong. I find, albeit with some hesitation, that the words 'of national importance' do not require that there be a connection, be it historical, artistic or traditional, with our great and noble country. Accordingly, I reluctantly conclude that the Secretary of State for the Environment's decision was unlawful. However, I have listened with great attention to the arguments on behalf of the Secretary of State with respect to the *locus standi* of the applicant. I have been referred to the decision of Mr Justice Schiemann in *R v Poole Borough Council ex parte Beebee et al* [1991] JPL 643 and I note that neither English Heritage nor BAPOMM was prepared to bring this application. I consider that neither SMASH nor its admirable president Dame Bonaventura Frampton has the standing to move for a judicial review of the Secretary of State's decision. I therefore dismiss this application.

SMASH now appeals to the Court of Appeal from the Decision of Mr Justice Turtle on the issue of *locus standi*. The Secretary of State cross-appeals with respect to Mr Justice Turtle's conclusion that his decision was unlawful.

Richard Wilmot-Smith QC, *39 Essex Street, Temple*
Middle Temple Annual Mooting Competition

Public law — judicial review — *locus standi* **— reasonableness**

IN THE COURT OF APPEAL (CIVIL DIVISION)

R v UK Rail ex parte Hand

UK Rail, a private company responsible for running most of the United Kingdom's passenger railway system, is in considerable financial difficulties. Rumours have been circulating for some weeks in the City of London that several other companies are considering making takeover bids for UK Rail. As a cost-cutting measure, the Board of UK Rail took the decision temporarily to suspend the implementation of a new code of practice on signalling practice which had been recommended by an official inquiry into the Clapham rail disaster, and which the Board had publicly agreed to implement.

The news of this suspension of the code of practice became public only as the result of a 'leak' to the trade journal, *Railway News*. Industry and financial commentators have speculated that the real motive for the decision was to make UK Rail a more attractive target for acquisition. UK Rail has denied this and says that the decision was taken in order to smooth over imminent cash flow problems, and will be reversed as soon as circumstances allow.

Henrietta Hand, the mother of train driver Reginald Hand, is concerned for her son's safety while the code of practice is not being implemented. She therefore sought, and was granted, judicial review of UK Rail's decision when Marsh J granted mandamus both to quash UK Rail's decision on the grounds that it was unreasonable and to order that the matter be considered afresh.

UK Rail now appeals to the Court of Appeal on the grounds that:

(1)   Mrs Hand has no *locus standi*; and
(2)   UK Rail's decision was not unreasonable.

Public law — judicial review — *locus standi* **— judicial discretion**

IN THE COURT OF APPEAL (CIVIL DIVISION)

R v *Slough Borough Council ex parte Association of Taxi Drivers*

The Association of Taxi Drivers is an unincorporated association. Members of the Association were present at a Slough Borough Council meeting held on 20th May 1993 in which changes to the council's concessionary travel scheme were discussed. The Council decided that it would limit its scheme to wheelchair accessible taxis.

The Association applied for and, on 16th July 1993, was granted leave to apply for judicial review of the decision. The Council, in August 1993, reversed its decision to limit its scheme to wheelchair accessible taxis.

The Council argued before Finn J that an unincorporated association had neither *locus standi* nor capacity to apply for judicial review and that in any event there could be no review of the decision to limit the scheme to wheelchair accessible taxis because the question was now academic, as the decision had been reversed.

Finn J held that an unincorporated association could seek and be susceptible to judicial review and quashed the decision to limit the scheme to wheelchair accessible taxis because such a decision was so unreasonable that no reasonable council could possibly come to that decision. He went on to hold that he had a discretion as to whether to decide academic points; it was a public law case and he could see that the Council might need guidance in its further deliberations on the topic under consideration.

The Council appeal to the Court of Appeal on the grounds that:

(1)   an unincorporated association has neither *locus standi* nor capacity to apply for judicial review; and

(2)   there can be no review of the decision to limit the scheme to wheelchair accessible taxis because the question is academic; and

(3)   in the alternative to (2) above, if the judge does have a general discretion to review academic decisions, this particular academic decision was one which no judge properly exercising his discretion would have reviewed.

Richard Wilmot-Smith QC, *39 Essex Street, Temple*
Middle Temple Annual Mooting Competition

Scots law — validity of wills

IN THE SHERIFF COURT

Tinker Bell v *Bella Bell*

George Bell made a will ('Will 1') in 1980 leaving all his property to his sister Tinker Bell. He made a second will ('Will 2') in 1984 which left his entire estate to his wife Bella. Will 2 contained a clause expressly revoking Will 1; but George Bell forgot to destroy Will 1. Both wills were valid holograph documents.

In 1991 George Bell made a third will ('Will 3'). He typed this and signed it; there were, through an oversight, no witnesses. (Both parties concede that Will 3 is formally invalid.) It contained no clause revoking previous wills, but Bell afterwards tore up Will 2 in several pieces. He sent Will 3 to his solicitor with a covering letter stating: 'This is my new will. The one I made in 1984 is out of date and I wanted to replace it. Consequently I have now destroyed it.' The next day Bell died suddenly.

Tinker Bell raised an action against Bella Bell to determine the division of George Bell's estate (the details of the division are immaterial). Both parties are agreed that this depends on whether Will 1 or Will 2 (or neither) is effective. Tinker Bell argues that:

(i)   Will 2 is not effective, having been revoked; and
(ii)   Will 1 is effective, having been revived by the revocation of Will 2.

Bella Bell disputes both arguments, on the grounds that:

(i)   Will 2 has not been revoked; and
(ii)   even if it has been revoked, Will 1 has not been revived (and therefore intestacy results).

The Sheriff found in favour of Bella Bell on both arguments. Tinker Bell appeals to the Sheriff Principal on both points.

D R MacDonald, *University of Dundee*

Scots law — contract — offer and acceptance

IN THE INNER HOUSE OF THE COURT OF SESSION

Albanian Exports Ltd v Bloggs (UK) Ltd

Albanian Exports Limited ('the appellant') is a company which was set up in Dundee in 1990 to take advantage of new opportunities for doing business with Eastern Europe. It specialises in buying Albanian fashionwear for resale in Scotland. The market is rapidly-growing but (as is well known to traders engaged in this line of business) the prices and availability of goods tend to fluctuate very rapidly.

Since commencing business, the appellant on a large number of occasions sold goods to Bloggs (UK) Ltd ('the respondent'), a small business in Perth. On Tuesday 2nd July 1991 Mr Smith, the appellant's sales manager, sent a Telemessage to Mr Jones, the respondent's director, as follows:

> Albanian business going well. Have acquired 10,000 'Mao suits' at bargain prices, no longer popular there. As our best customer I am offering them to you at £50,000 in all. You will appreciate that this is a unique opportunity, but other buyers are interested and you must reply by 10 a.m. this Friday 5th July at latest. Regards, J Smith.

The appellant's office despatched the Telemessage at 9 a.m. and it was delivered by British Telecom at 12 a.m. Jones posted his reply by first class mail at 5.30 p.m. on Tuesday evening:

> On behalf of Bloggs (UK) Ltd I accept your offer. Suits should sell well in Dundee area. A Jones.

Unfortunately, for some unknown reason, the letter did not arrive until 23rd July.

On Thursday Jones reconsidered his decision. At 8.30 p.m. he sent a fax to Smith stating that he was not interested in buying suits. He knew that the fax was received on the machine in the appellant's office, which (though the office was then closed) had been left on. The fax was not handed to Smith until 11 a.m. on Friday.

The appellant raised an action against the respondent in the Outer House of the Court of Session for damages for breach of contract. The Lord Ordinary, Lord Muirburn, dismissed the action, holding that:

(i)   no contract was ever concluded between the parties; and
(ii)   in any event the respondent's fax message was an effective retraction of their postal acceptance of the appellant's offer.

The appellant appeals to the Inner House of the Court of Session against both grounds of the Lord Ordinary's decision.

D R MacDonald, *University of Dundee*

Scots law — trusts

IN THE INNER HOUSE OF THE COURT OF SESSION

Kipper v Trustees of Arbroath Anti-Smoking Society

The Arbroath Anti-Smoking Society was established in 1910 with the sole purpose of campaigning for the abolition of smoking. Its assets are held by Trustees on behalf of its members. Every six months the Trustees receive a report from their stockbrokers reviewing their current investments and recommending changes.

In March 1995 the stockbrokers' report recommends that the Trustees purchase Ordinary Shares in Megafags plc, a multinational tobacco company, because of their high dividends. The Trustees at their next meeting consider the report but decide instead to invest in Loan Stock issued by Auchmithie Burgh Council. This is known to be an extremely safe investment, which will keep its capital value but gives very low income. They reach this decision because of the Society's aims, their own views, and the likely views of its members.

Kipper, a member of the Society, strongly objects to this decision. He raises an action for declarator that the Trustees acted in breach of trust. The Lord Ordinary, Lord Monboddo, held that no breach of trust had been committed. Kipper appeals to the Inner House of the Court of Session.

D R MacDonald, *University of Dundee*

Scots law — trusts

IN THE INNER HOUSE OF THE COURT OF SESSION

Cash v *MacSporran's Trustees*

Mark MacSporran died in March 1990 leaving his whole estate of £1 million in a discretionary trust in favour of 'poor people in Dundee, or such of them as my trustees in their sole discretion may select'. The trust funds were to be paid to beneficiaries in March 1995. The trustees named in MacSporran's will died before him. Two trustees were appointed by the Sheriff Court under section 22 of the Trusts (Scotland) Act 1921 to administer the trust.

In March 1995 the trustees met to consider the distribution of the trust funds. They paid the entire amount to Jane Moneypenny, a young woman whose income was just above the level at which she would have been able to claim Income Support. Penny Cash is another Dundonian with even less income; as MacSporran's cousin, she would also have inherited his estate if he had died intestate.

Cash raised an action in the Sheriff Court for declarator:

(i)   that the trustees, having been appointed by the court, have no power to select beneficiaries of the trust, so that the trust purposes fail and intestacy results; or

(ii)   that the trustees' selection is invalid as unreasonable and should be set aside.

The Sheriff refused decree and held that the trustees' selection was valid. Cash appeals to the Inner House of the Court of Session on both grounds.

D R MacDonald, *University of Dundee*

Scots law — contract — breach — frustration

IN THE INNER HOUSE OF THE COURT OF SESSION

Hieland Haggis Co. Ltd v *Persia Porridge Co. Inc*

Hieland Haggis Co. Ltd ('the appellant') is an old-established firm who make black puddings, haggis, bridies, and other traditional Scottish delicacies. They are famous all over the world. In December 1990 they entered into a contract (made under Scots law) to supply 1,000 haggises to the respondents, a firm in Abadan (in southern Iran). In terms of the contract the haggises were to be supplied 'with all due despatch', though no specific date was specified for delivery. The respondent intended to supply the food to the Abadan Caledonian Society for use in their Burns Supper on 25th January 1991.

On 10th January 1991 the appellant despatched the haggises by air. Unfortunately (for reasons which are unexplained) they were sent to Aberdeen (in Scotland), where they were impounded by the customs authorities in the (erroneous) belief that they were ammunition intended for the notorious Iraqi 'supergun'. By the time that the true position was made clear on 16th January, the Allied forces had attacked Iraq. As a result:

(a)   while it was legally and physically possible to supply the haggises to the respondents, this would have to be done by a much longer and slower route avoiding the Gulf war zone; and

(b)   the Burns Supper was postponed indefinitely until the cessation of hostilities.

The appellant, considering that the haggises would not reach the respondent in the pristine condition they were in when they left the factory, disposed of them to a buyer in Scotland.

The respondent raised an action against the appellant in the Court of Session for damages for breach of contract. In the Outer House the Lord Ordinary, Lord Auchinleck, found in favour of the respondent. The appellant appeals to the Inner House on the ground that the contract was frustrated and they were thereby released from further performance.

D R MacDonald, *University of Dundee*

Scots law — contract — exclusion clause — arbitration clause

IN THE INNER HOUSE OF THE COURT OF SESSION

Dundee Denims plc v Juggernaut Transport Ltd

Dundee Denims plc ('the pursuers') are a small firm of clothing manufacturers who operate a mail-order business. About once every three months for
the last three years they have contracted with Juggernaut Transport Ltd ('the
defenders') to carry a lorryload of clothes to London.

On each occasion the procedure was for the pursuers' managing director,
Mr Brown, to telephone the defenders' director to confirm whether they had
lorries available for carriage. When they did, they made an oral contract over
the telephone. When the goods were collected by the defenders for
transport, they would hand over a previously-completed 'Receipt Note'
(which would be subsequently transmitted to the pursuers' accounts
department for filing) acknowledging receipt of the goods. At the foot of the
receipt, beneath the description of goods, it was stated that 'All goods are
accepted and carried subject to the rules of the Angus Road Haulage
Association', of which the defenders were members. The Rules contain a
provision that:

> In any contract made by a Member under these Rules, (i) liability for any
> loss caused by the Member's negligence shall be limited to £10,000 in
> total; (ii) any dispute arising out of the contract shall be resolved by an
> arbiter appointed by the Federation, and the parties agree to exclude the
> jurisdiction of the Scottish courts.

On 3rd July 1991 the parties made a similar oral contract. Two days later
the pursuers handed over goods worth £50,000 to the defenders, and the
usual note was given in return. On the way to London the lorry was in an
accident due to the driver's carelessness, and all the goods were destroyed.

The pursuers brought an action for breach of contract against the
defenders. The defenders claimed that in terms of the contract:

(i)   their liability was limited to £10,000; and
(ii)   the court had no jurisdiction to hear the case.

The Sheriff upheld both aspects of their claim. The pursuers appeal to the
Inner House of the Court of Session on the grounds that the Rule did not
form part of the contract.

It is conceded that (if the Rule forms part of the parties' contract) its
provisions breach no rules of law and must be given full effect.

D R MacDonald, *University of Dundee*

Scots law — delict — psychiatric illness

IN THE INNER HOUSE OF THE COURT OF SESSION

Austin v *Ferguson*

Alison Austin (the 'appellant') was driving her Reliant Robin motor car along a country lane near Dundee on 15th March 1995. She was driving at about 15 mph with care and attention. John Ferguson (the 'respondent') drove a large tractor out of a field without looking, into her path. She could not avoid colliding with the tractor. The car suffered some damage to the driver's door. Alison received no physical injuries whatsoever. However, the incident reawakened memories of a severe car crash in which she had been a passenger 20 years earlier. As a result she developed an acute anxiety state which made her unable to go out in public; a month later she had to resign her post as managing director of a major Scottish company. It was conceded that no psychiatric problems would normally have been expected to ensue as a result of the collision with the tractor.

Austin brought an action for damages against Ferguson in the Sheriff Court. The Sheriff held that no damages were recoverable because Austin's psychiatric problems were not a reasonably foreseeable consequence of the accident. Austin appeals to the Inner House of the Court of Session.

D R MacDonald, *University of Dundee*

Scots law — contract — offer and acceptance

IN THE SHERIFF COURT

Hill v Mansell

Graham Mansell advertised his vintage 1950 Lada car for sale in the 'Dundee Courier' on 15th January 1995 at a price of £1,500. Mary Hill replied asking for further details, and came to inspect the car. She arranged with Mansell that she would let him know before 3rd February whether or not she wanted the car; in the meantime Mansell would not sell it to anyone else.

On 21st January Hill telephoned Mansell saying that she would not be prepared to pay more than £1,300. Mansell, commenting that 'it would be cheap at £3,000 — you won't find another one like it in the whole of Dundee', refused to lower his price. Hill said 'Fair enough, but I'll let you know if I change my mind', and the conversation ended somewhat curtly.

On 1st February Hill telephoned again, saying 'OK — I'll take the car'. Mansell, who had had second thoughts and was overcome at the prospect of selling his cherished Lada, refused to sell. However Hill telephoned again on 2nd February, saying that 'I really want that car — we can discuss the exact price later.' Mansell replied 'That's fine by me', and they arranged to meet on 5th February 'to finalise details'.

On 4th February Mansell decided once and for all that he could not bear to part with his Lada. He told Hill this when they met.

It is accepted by both parties that the normal market price for a second-hand Lada of this age would be £1,400.

Hill raised an action in the Sheriff Court for damages for breach of contract, pleading that a binding contract of sale had been concluded, either by:

(i)   the conversation of 1st February, to sell the Lada at a price of £1,500; or alternatively by

(ii)   the conversation of 2nd February, to sell at a price of £1,400.

The Sheriff dismissed the action and held that no contract had been concluded. Hill appeals to the Sheriff Principal on both points of law.

D R MacDonald, *University of Dundee*

Scots law — delict — malicious prosecution

IN THE INNER HOUSE OF THE COURT OF SESSION

Watt v *Hardman*

Wendy Watt made a complaint to the police alleging that she had been assaulted by Harry Hardman. The incident was alleged to have taken place in her flat at 10 p.m. on the evening of Friday 14th October 1994. The police interviewed Hardman who provided an alibi stating that he had been drinking in Frew's Bar, Dundee at the time that the assault was alleged to have taken place. Hardman gave the names of two parties with whom he said he had been drinking at the relevant time, Bill Bloke and Ned Norris.

The police interviewed Bloke and Norris who confirmed Hardman's alibi. No charge was brought against Hardman, but Wendy Watt was charged with wasting police time. She was found not guilty of the offence. In evidence it transpired that Frew's Bar closed down some years ago.

Wendy brought an action of damages in respect of malicious prosecution against Hardman, Bloke and Norris. She averred that the three defenders had given false information to the police, rendering her open to suspicion and arrest and which did result in prosecution.

Neither Bloke nor Norris defended the action. Hardman's defence was that absolute privilege attaches to the statements which he made to the police.

The judge at first instance repelled Wendy Watt's pleas on grounds of relevancy and assoilized the defender. Wendy reclaims.

Gordon Cameron, *University of Dundee*

Tort — misrepresentation — Misrepresentation Act 1967, s. 2(1) —
damages — *novus actus interveniens*

IN THE HOUSE OF LORDS

Airsales (Eastend) plc v Poynings Guaranty

The plaintiff, Poynings Guaranty, is a finance company of experience and
repute. The defendant, Airsales (Eastend) plc, sells executive aircraft.
Airsales (Eastend) plc induced Poynings Guaranty into entering a finance
agreement for the purchase of a second-hand Lear Jet with Maxpoor
Enterprises. Maxpoor Enterprises was an ostensibly substantial company
whose prime mover, Mr Maxpoor, was a man of strong personality well
known in the City as a doer of big deals in shares. The purchase
consideration was £100,000. It was Poynings Guaranty policy, of which
Airsales (Eastend) plc knew, only to enter into such a finance agreement if
the customer paid a deposit of 25 per cent of the purchase price. Maxpoor
Enterprises had only £22,000 in cash for a deposit. Airsales (Eastend) plc
presented false figures to Poynings Guaranty indicating that the precondi-
tion for the 25 per cent deposit had been met.

Mr Maxpoor on behalf of his company took possession of the Lear Jet and
flew it to Ruritania 48 hours later. Following this flight he and the aircraft
disappeared and his financial empire, including Maxpoor Enterprises,
collapsed. No payments beyond the original £22,000 were made. The Lear
Jet was never recovered.

Poynings Guaranty then sued Airsales (Eastend) plc for misrepresentation under section 2(1) of the Misrepresentation Act 1967. As against
Airsales (Eastend) plc the judge awarded the difference between the sum
advanced by Poynings Guaranty for the purchase of the Lear Jet, and the
sum they would have advanced if the deposit had in truth represented 25 per
cent of the purchase price of the Jet. Inclusive of interest, this was agreed by
the parties at about £16,000 (the lesser sum).

Poynings Guaranty appealed to the Court of Appeal, which allowed the
appeal and said that Poynings Guaranty were entitled to be put into the
position in which they would have been had they not entered into the finance
agreement at all. They were therefore entitled to recovery of all the sums
advanced to Maxpoor Enterprises: this sum was agreed by the parties at
about £98,000 inclusive of interest (the greater sum).

Airsales (Eastend) plc appeal to the House of Lords on the grounds that:

(1) the proper measure of damages for misrepresentation was such as to
put the representee in the position in which he would have been if the
representation had been true, so that the lesser sum as awarded by the trial
judge should have been awarded; and

(2) the greater part of the losses arose from the disappearance of Mr
Maxpoor and the aircraft, which was a *novus actus interveniens*.

Richard Wilmot-Smith QC, *39 Essex Street, Temple*
Middle Temple Annual Mooting Competition

Tort — negligence — nervous shock — damage to property

IN THE COURT OF APPEAL (CIVIL DIVISION)

Aldridge v Agmoco plc

The Great Yopshire Show is the largest agricultural show in the United Kingdom to be held on an annual basis. In 1989 Agmoco plc was allocated a stand near the central showring. The company placed a combine harvester on display on the stand. On the final day of the show, Nigel Pargetter, one of Agmoco's salesmen, started up the machine to demonstrate the level of engine noise for an interested farmer. Unfortunately he failed to check that the engine was not in gear and the harvester lurched forward, with its blades rotating, into a bull being led from the main showring by its owner, Brian Aldridge. Blood was spattered everywhere as the bull became entangled in the blades of the machine. The bull died in agony, making a great deal of noise. Blood was spattered liberally over Mr Aldridge and a group of schoolgirls who were passing at the time. Amidst the terrified bellowing of the bull and the screams of some of the bystanders, Mr Aldridge fainted. Mr Aldridge has since suffered severe bouts of depression, headaches, general irritability and a loss of interest in farming, all of which, according to medical evidence, have resulted from witnessing the death of the bull.

Five of the eight schoolgirls were treated afterwards for shock as a result of witnessing the death of the bull, but one of them, Lucy Perks, aged 13, has since suffered lack of sleep, inability to concentrate on her schoolwork and depression. Her psychiatric disorder led to an absence from school lasting seven months.

Brian Aldridge and Lucy Perks claimed damages in negligence for their psychiatric illnesses, and Mr Aldridge also claimed damages for the loss of his bull. At first instance Gabriel J found that the death of the bull was the direct result of the negligence of the defendant's employee, for which the defendant was vicariously liable. He awarded damages for the loss of the bull.

In respect of the psychiatric illness, Gabriel J found that, on the evidence, it had been caused by the fact that the plaintiffs had witnessed the death of the bull. However, he also found that at no time did it appear that the plaintiffs themselves were in any danger from the combine harvester. The only case in which any English court had admitted the possibility of a plaintiff recovering damages in negligence for nervous shock suffered as a result of witnessing the destruction of property was *Attia v British Gas plc* [1988] QB 304. In that case the property destroyed consisted of the plaintiff's home and personal possessions. The decision of the Court of Appeal in *Attia* could not be taken to extend the duty in respect of nervous shock beyond the destruction of such intimate and personal property. In the instant case, it was business property. He therefore found that the first plaintiff's illness was outside the scope of the duty of care owed by the defendant's employee. The second plaintiff, Miss Perks, was not even the owner of the property, and she was not, therefore, owed a duty of care in respect of damage to the bull.

Mr Aldridge now appeals to the Court of Appeal on the ground that the decision of the Court of Appeal in *Attia v British Gas plc* [1988] QB 304 allowed for the possibility of damages for psychiatric illness suffered as a result of destruction of property in appropriate circumstances and left it as an issue for trial whether, on the facts, the plaintiff's claim should be allowed. It is therefore open to a court to consider whether there are other appropriate circumstances, such as those obtaining in the instant case, in which damages should be awarded.

Miss Perks appeals to the Court of Appeal on the ground that the House of Lords in *Alcock and others* v *Chief Constable of South Yorkshire* [1992] 1 AC 310 expressly left open the question of liability for causing nervous shock to bystanders, and that, in appropriate cases such as the instant one, such claims should be allowed.

M B Murphy, *University of Huddersfield*

Tort — negligence — duty of care — misrepresentation — Misrepresentation Act 1967, s. 2(1)

IN THE COURT OF APPEAL (CIVIL DIVISION)

Babb v *Slobb*

David Dibb decided to put his house up for sale. Having heard about the current tendency of would-be buyers to put in a bid for a house only to reduce it after they receive a surveyor's report, Dibb decided to circumvent this problem by himself instructing a surveyor to survey his own house and report on its condition. He chose Sam Slobb and told Slobb that he would show Slobb's report to any prospective purchaser of his house. Slobb agreed and carried out the survey for a price of £500. He reported that there were no serious defects and that everything was much as one would expect in a house of this age and type.

Bobby Babb (a cash buyer) looked round Dibb's house and read Slobb's survey report. As a result he did not think it worthwhile to instruct a surveyor of his own. He made an offer for the house which Dibb accepted. The contract between them specified that £500 of the purchase price was by way of reimbursement to Dibb for the cost of Slobb's survey. Soon afterwards Babb moved in. Six months later the chimney collapsed because of a defect which Slobb's survey should have revealed.

Babb sued Slobb both for negligence and under section 2(1) of the Misrepresentation Act 1967. Hogg J held that Slobb owed Babb no common law duty of care, and that section 2(1) of the Misrepresentation Act was inapplicable because Slobb and Babb had not entered into a contract with each other. Babb now appeals to the Court of Appeal against both these findings.

Tort — negligence — vicarious liability — employer — course of employment

IN THE COURT OF APPEAL (CIVIL DIVISION)

Boulton v *Post Office*

John Boulton was a postman. His friend, Simon Crabtree, worked as a van driver for Deluxe Vans Ltd. In order to cope with the extra burden of parcel deliveries in the run-up to Christmas, the Greenside Main Post Office contracted with Deluxe to hire several of the latter's vans and drivers (including Crabtree) during December 1993.

The contract included the following terms:

(6) Any tortious liability arising during delivery of Post Office parcels is to remain the responsibility of Deluxe Vans Ltd.

(7) All working instructions to drivers are to be given by authorised officers of the Post Office.

(8) All drivers' pay is to be paid by the Post Office to the drivers at the conclusion of the contract.

One of the working instructions given to Deluxe's drivers was:

No unauthorised personnel are to be carried in any vehicle.

At the end of his shift on 18th December 1993, Boulton was given a lift home by Crabtree as the latter knew he would be passing Boulton's house on his way to the railway station to pick up more mail. On the way Boulton sustained severe injuries in an accident caused by Crabtree's negligent driving. Deluxe Vans Ltd has now gone out of business.

Boulton claims compensation from the Post Office on the grounds that it is vicariously liable for Crabtree's negligence. The Post Office contends, however, that it was not Crabtree's employer and therefore could not be vicariously liable. It further contends that Crabtree had not been acting within the course of his employment in giving a lift to Boulton since the latter was off duty and therefore not an authorised person.

Brightwell J found in favour of the Post Office on both counts. Boulton now appeals to the Court of Appeal.

Tort — public nuisance — special damage — private nuisance — nuisance and negligence

IN THE COURT OF APPEAL (CIVIL DIVISION)

East Bungleborough District Council v Sam's Bookshop

East Bungleborough District Council, having insufficient money to repair the large number of potholes in one of its town centre streets, decided to paint the potholes with a luminous green paint so that motorists could see them better and avoid them more easily. On 1st April, council workmen arrived in a van, blocked off both ends of the street and erected notices stating that all access was prohibited until the following day. As a result shopkeepers in the street suffered a loss of business. Sam's Bookshop was especially affected, since it had invited the famous pop star Jingo to the shop to autograph copies of his new book which was released on that day, and large numbers of people had been expected in consequence. Whilst the workmen were in the process of painting the potholes, a sign above Sam's Bookshop fell onto and damaged the Council's van which was parked outside the shop. The falling of the sign was not due to any negligence on the part of Sam's Bookshop but was due to a latent defect in the sign's construction.

In the High Court, Generous J held that:

(i)   the Council had no authority to close the road, the closure amounted to a public nuisance and the plaintiff's loss of business constituted special damage for which he was entitled to be compensated; and

(ii)   the plaintiff was also entitled to succeed against the Council in private nuisance, since the Council's activities constituted an unreasonable interference with the plaintiff's use and enjoyment of his land; but

(iii)   the defendant's counterclaim for damage to its van would succeed as constituting special damage resulting from a public nuisance, notwithstanding the absence of fault on the part of the plaintiff.

The Council concedes that it had no authority to close the road and that the closure amounted to a public nuisance but appeals to the Court of Appeal on the following grounds:

(1)   the learned judge was wrong in law in holding that the plaintiff's loss constituted special damage, since to constitute special damage a plaintiff had to suffer loss over and above that suffered by the rest of the public and the plaintiff's loss was no different from that suffered by other shopkeepers in the street; and

(2)   to amount to a private nuisance, the interference had to emanate from adjoining land in private ownership and could not emanate from land such as a highway that was open to the public at large, so that the learned judge was therefore wrong in law in holding that the plaintiff had a cause of action against the Council in private nuisance.

Sam's Bookshop cross-appeals on the ground that liability for public nuisance is not strict but can only be established if negligence can be proved and the learned judge was therefore wrong in law in allowing the Council's counterclaim for the damage to its van.

C D Manchester, *University of Birmingham*

Tort — misrepresentation — negligent misstatement — vicarious liability — damages
Contract — implied warranty — damages

IN THE COURT OF APPEAL (CIVIL DIVISION)

Carling Associates Ltd v *Hastings Bros Ltd*

Carling Associates Ltd is an advertising agency which counted among its clients a firm of undertakers known as Bradley, Murphy & Co. until the latter went out of business in October 1993.

In January 1993 Bradley, Murphy & Co. were concerned at their recent dramatic loss of business, which they believed was due to the success of a new firm of undertakers, Evans & Rayer, which had just set up in the same locality. In order to overcome this problem Bradley, Murphy & Co. instructed Dean Moore, a director of Carling Associates, to devise a television advertising campaign to be screened on the local commercial television channel. Mr Moore delegated this task to Jason Rodber, whom Mr Moore described to Bradley, Murphy & Co. as 'one of my ideas men'.

Mr Rodber held a series of long meetings with representatives of Bradley, Murphy & Co. at which he learnt that Bradley, Murphy & Co. were in a very serious financial position and were dependent on the success of the proposed campaign of advertising. By August 1993 Mr Rodber had devised a campaign with which Bradley, Murphy & Co. were happy and so he reported to Mr Moore that it would be necessary to contact a television production company in order that the proposed advertisements could be filmed for screening. It is accepted by all parties that Mr Rodber never thought to mention the financial position of Bradley, Murphy & Co. to Mr Moore.

Mr Moore chose to instruct Hastings Bros Ltd to make the necessary commercials. Hastings were at first rather taken aback at the thought of making television commercials for a firm of undertakers. They therefore questioned Mr Moore at length about Bradley, Murphy. In fact, it is accepted by all parties that Hastings Bros agreed to go ahead with producing the commercials only when Mr Moore faxed them a letter which included the following words:

> There is no need to worry about the campaign for Bradleys. This is a serious proposal drawn up by a reputable company in good financial health (unlike its clients!). This is a campaign which will really put you on the map by showing your ability to break new ground in the world of television advertising.

Hastings Bros therefore signed the contract with Bradley, Murphy & Co. at a price of £20,000 and went ahead with the booking of production facilities, studios, crew and actors at a cost of £10,000. However, Bradley, Murphy & Co. went out of business in October 1993 without the commercials being completed or any payment by Bradley, Murphy & Co. to Hastings Bros having been made.

In the High Court, despite accepting that on the basis of the information known to him at the time Mr Moore had not made an unreasonable statement, Hastings Bros sued Carling Associates both in the tort of negligent misstatement and for breach of warranty. Beaumont J found in favour of the plaintiffs on the first ground, following *Hedley Byrne & Co. Ltd v Heller & Partners Ltd* [1964] AC 465 and *WB Anderson & Sons Ltd v Rhodes (Liverpool) Ltd* [1967] 2 All ER 850. He also found that Carling Associates had given Hastings Bros an implied warranty that Mr Moore's representations had been made with reasonable care and skill, following *Esso Petroleum v Mardon* [1976] QB 801, and that this warranty had been breached by Carling. Beaumont J declared that as a matter of policy it should make no difference whether the plaintiffs were successful in tort or contract and awarded Hastings Bros damages of £20,000.

Carling Associates now appeal to the Court of Appeal on the following grounds:

(1)   *WB Anderson & Sons Ltd* v *Rhodes (Liverpool) Ltd* was wrongly decided, so that it is possible for an employer to be vicariously liable for negligent misstatement only if a specific employee could be identified as a primary tortfeasor. Since that was not the case here, it therefore followed that Carling Associates could not be vicariously liable for negligent misstatement. Moreover, even if Carling were so liable, the appropriate measure of damages under this head should be £10,000.

(2)   There was no implied warranty that Mr Moore's representations were given with reasonable care and skill. But even if such a warranty had been given it had been satisfied because Mr Moore had not been negligent. Moreover, even if Carling were so liable, the appropriate measure of damages under this head should be £10,000.

Tort — negligence — duty of care — standard of care — contributory negligence

IN THE COURT OF APPEAL (CIVIL DIVISION)

Chappell v *Boyce*

Christopher Chappell was an opening batsman for Northamptonshire County Cricket Club. During a match against Warwickshire County Cricket Club, which took place in the summer of 1993, he was hit in the face by a beamer bowled by fast bowler Darren Boyce. Boyce was playing in his first match for Warwickshire, having been called into the side at the last minute from his local club, Harborne. In a sworn affidavit unchallenged by Chappell, Boyce said that he had had no intention to injure Chappell but that he was so nervous about making his debut for Warwickshire that he had let go of the ball too early in his bowling action, causing the ball to fly out of his hand in a trajectory almost parallel to the ground until it smashed into Chappell's face.

Chappell sued Boyce in negligence for damages for personal injury and the consequential loss of income that had resulted from his career being terminated by the injury. Boyce resisted on the grounds that:

(i)   he owed Chappell no duty of care;
(ii)   he had bowled as any débutant might do, and had therefore complied with any tortious standard of care which might be imposed; and
(iii)   Chappell was contributorily negligent in not wearing a helmet while batting.

Dexter J held that Boyce did owe Chappell a duty of care and that, since Boyce's bowling was to be judged against the standard of a reasonably competent professional county bowler, Boyce had failed to meet that standard. He did, however, hold that Chappell was 50 per cent contributorily negligent in not wearing a helmet.

Boyce now appeals on the ground that the standard of care should be judged against what would reasonably expected of an amateur club bowler. Chappell cross-appeals on the grounds that his decision not to wear a helmet was reasonable in all the circumstances and therefore could not be contributorily negligent.

Tort — libel — fair comment — qualified privilege

IN THE COURT OF APPEAL (CIVIL DIVISION)

Daily Clarion v *Bea*

Bertha Bea is the mother of Brenda Bea. When Brenda became old enough to go to school, Bertha filled in the form sent to her by the local authority to indicate her preferred choice of primary school for Brenda. She chose Bluegates School, but the council replied that that school was full and allocated Brenda a place at Redstile School instead. Bertha appealed against that decision in accordance with the statutory procedure but it was confirmed by the appropriate appeal committee.

Bertha then made an application for leave to apply for judicial review. She said that since Brenda could already read fluently, Redstile School was unsuitable since none of the reception children could read and that the teacher would therefore be unable to pay Brenda sufficient attention; whilst most reception children could read at Bluegates School. The judge indicated that he was minded to grant leave, whereupon the local authority undertook to consider the matter again, and the application was withdrawn.

In its report of the court proceedings, the *Daily Clarion* stated:

> Bertha Bea succeeded in her claim against the local authority. She said that as 90 per cent of the children attending Redstile School were Asian and did not speak English as a first language, that school was unsuitable for her daughter who was already reading fluently.

It is now admitted both that Bertha has never made any comment about the racial composition of the pupils attending Redstile School, and that the comment attributed to Bertha had, in fact, been made in an affidavit sworn by the Headmaster at Redstile. It is accepted by everyone as factually accurate both that 90 per cent of the children attending Redstile School are of Asian extraction, and that most of them do not speak English at home.

Bertha sued the *Daily Clarion* for libel, claiming that the passage quoted above suggested either that she was generally racist, and/or that her preference for her daughter's school was based on racist views. Green J rejected the *Clarion's* submission that the passage was not capable of being defamatory. He also ruled that the *Clarion's* defences of fair comment and qualified privilege for the fair and accurate reporting of the judicial review proceedings in the High Court were inapplicable on the facts.

The jury found that the *Clarion* had libelled Bertha and awarded her £15,000 damages. The *Daily Clarion* appeals to the Court of Appeal on the following alternative grounds:

(1) the judge should not have allowed the case to go to the jury because the report was incapable of being defamatory; or, alternatively

(2) the judge should have allowed the jury to consider the *Daily Clarion's* pleas of fair comment and qualified privilege.

Tort — negligence — duty of care — omission — nervous shock

IN THE COURT OF APPEAL (CIVIL DIVISION)

Davies v *Simms*

Sid and Sadie Simms own a Victorian semi-detached house which shares a side wall with the house belonging to Donald and Doris Davies. As is typical in such houses, the loft space at the top is shared by both houses. Three years ago both couples' houses were very much in need of repair but since then Donald and Doris have spent a considerable amount of money renovating their house and making it more secure. The Davies' household is, consequently, protected by police-approved deadlocks and deadbolts on all appropriate doors and windows, and a new alarm system has also been fitted. Sid and Sadie Simms, on the other hand, have continued to neglect their own house, despite warnings from Donald and Doris (and from the local police station's Crime Prevention Officer) that their house would be easy for any would-be burglar to break into.

Last year, Donald and Doris decided to go away for a fortnight's holiday. They asked Sid and Sadie to 'keep an eye on the place while we're away' and the Simms agreed that they would. While the latter were out one night an unknown number of burglars broke into the Simms' house. However, they took nothing belonging to the Simms but instead made their way into the loft. They then crawled through the loft space until they were over the Davies' house. Finding the Davies' trap-door bolted from the other side, they simply cut their way through the ceiling and lowered themselves down. They then stole the Davies' television sets, their video recorder, their camcorder, a camera, some expensive chinaware and some jewellery.

When they returned from their holiday, Donald and Doris were so shocked by the burglary that Doris suffered severe clinical depression for which she has been receiving regular medication.

Donald and Doris sued Sid and Sadie for negligence in failing to take reasonable steps to protect their neighbours' property and personal well-being. Doughnut J found for the defendants on the following grounds:

(i)   their agreement to 'keep an eye' on the plaintiffs' house was incapable of amounting to the voluntary undertaking of any legal responsibility towards the plaintiffs and therefore the defendants could not be said to owe the plaintiffs a duty of care in respect of what was a mere omission; and

(ii)   Doris's suffering of a type of 'nervous shock' was unforeseeable in the circumstances and therefore too remote to be recoverable.

Donald and Doris now appeal to the Court of Appeal against both these findings.

Tort — negligence — duty of care — economic loss

IN THE COURT OF APPEAL (CIVIL DIVISION)

Goodness v *Gracious plc*

In 1976 Gracious plc built an estate of houses, including a four-bedroomed house purchased from them by one Cyril Offiah. In 1990 Mr Offiah sold the house to Graham Goodness for £80,000. One day in 1994 Mr Goodness came home from work to find that his house had suffered serious subsidence. Investigation by structural engineers revealed that the problem was caused by the laying of inadequate foundations by Gracious plc. This defect could not have been expected to be discovered by the surveyor whom Mr Goodness had instructed prior to his purchase of the house.

The work on the house deemed necessary to make it reasonably safe, stable and habitable included substantial underpinning and cost £45,000. In addition, the market value of the property has dropped by £20,000 as a result of its subsidence; and Mr Goodness has also found that his buildings insurance premiums have increased five-fold.

Mr Goodness sued Gracious plc in negligence, but at first instance Brickson-Mortar J found in favour of the defendants on the following grounds:

(i)   the loss caused to the plaintiffs by the defendants was purely economic and, since it was allegedly caused by a negligent act of the defendant Gracious, there could be no question of a duty of care being owed, following *Murphy* v *Brentwood District Council* [1990] 2 All ER 908; and

(ii)   even if he was wrong about (i) above and such a duty could arise in principle, it could not do so here because, again following *Murphy* v *Brentwood District Council*, there was insufficient proximity between Goodness and Gracious plc.

Goodness now appeals to the Court of Appeal on the following grounds:

(1)   the distinction between physical and economic losses in relation to the question of whether or not a duty of care exists is no longer good law, following *The Nicholas H* [1995] 3 All ER 307; and

(2)   the builder of a house and any successor in title to that house are in an analogous relationship to that between the manufacturer and consumer of ginger beer so that, following *Donoghue* v *Stevenson* [1932] AC 562, a duty of care was owed by Gracious plc to Mr Goodness.

Tort — negligence — duty of care — special relationship — 'just and reasonable' test — standard of care

IN THE COURT OF APPEAL (CIVIL DIVISION)

Gupta v *Windsor*

Ms Wilson has a small computer consulting company. She wanted to issue shares in the company to her ten employees in such a way that her employees would not have to pay any tax on the shares.

She asked her friend Mr Windsor, the son of affluent landowners and an articled clerk with a firm of solicitors, to structure the issue of shares so as to avoid tax. She did not want to pay the firm's regular rates, so she asked him to do the work over the weekend at home for free. He agreed to do so. Unfortunately, although it was possible to avoid tax altogether, he did not structure the issue of shares properly and Ms Wilson's employees had to pay a substantial amount of tax on the shares. Few fully-qualified tax solicitors would have made the error that he made but he was only in the first month of his tax rotation.

Ms Gupta, an employee of Ms Wilson's company, brought an action in negligence against Mr Windsor, seeking damages of £10,000 (the amount of tax she had to pay on her shares).

The trial judge, Connelly J, held that:

(1)   Mr Windsor did not owe Ms Gupta a duty of care because:

(a)   Ms Wilson only told Mr Windsor the number of employees to be issued shares and not their names;
(b)   Ms Gupta did not actually rely on any tax advice given by Mr Windsor; and
(c)   Mr Windsor's tax advice did not make Ms Gupta's position worse but only deprived her of an expectation of extra income.

(2)   Even if her decision on point 1 was wrong, Mr Windsor did not owe a duty of care to Ms Gupta because he did not owe a duty of care to Ms Wilson (whose reliance on his advice was unreasonable in the circumstances) and Ms Gupta cannot be in a better position than Ms Wilson.

(3)   Even if Mr Windsor owed a duty of care to Ms Gupta, he did not breach that duty because he took all the care in his research that a reasonably careful articled clerk would have taken in the circumstances.

Ms Gupta appeals to the Court to Appeal on each of these points.

Robert Wintemute, *King's College, London*

Tort — Occupiers' Liability Act 1984 — notice — exclusion — Unfair Contract Terms Act 1977

IN THE COURT OF APPEAL (CIVIL DIVISION)

Jones v Healthysport Ltd

Healthysport Ltd own a leisure centre in Birmingham. Just inside the entrance is a notice which reads:

> You use the facilities at this leisure centre entirely at your own risk and Healthysport Ltd can accept no liability or responsibility for loss, injury or damage to you or your property howsoever caused.

On 1st April 1990 Melanie Jones went to the leisure centre for a swim. She admits that she entered the centre by means of a fire exit which had accidentally been left open by one of Healthysport's employees, Mr Ron Marks. Mr Marks, a security guard, saw Ms Jones going in by the fire exit but apparently took no action to stop her. The fire exit is round the corner from the front entrance and it was therefore impossible for Ms Jones to see the notice quoted above.

While going down the stairs to the changing rooms, Ms Jones slipped in a pool of water which Healthysport, as they now accept, was negligent in failing to mop up. Ms Jones suffered several fractured ribs in the resulting fall and was consequently absent from work on sick leave for several months. This caused her financial loss since the sick pay to which she was entitled was considerably less than her normal salary for the same period would have been.

Ms Jones sued Healthysport in the High Court on the grounds of (i) negligence and (ii) a breach of section 1(4) of the Occupiers' Liability Act (OLA) 1984. Adamant J found for the defendant on the following grounds:

(1)   Healthysport Ltd owed Ms Jones no common law duty of care since she was a trespasser;

(2)   Healthysport Ltd owed no duty to Ms Jones under section 1(4) of the OLA 1984 because it had no reason to believe that Ms Jones was in the vicinity of the dangerous pool of water; and

(3)   even if Healthysport did owe a duty under section 1(4) of the OLA 1984, they had succeeded in excluding liability by posting the notice at the entrance to the leisure centre.

Ms Jones does not appeal against Adamant J's finding in respect of negligence. She does, however, appeal to the Court of Appeal on the following grounds:

(i)   since one of Healthysport's employees had seen Ms Jones entering the leisure centre, Healthysport themselves did have reason to believe that Ms Jones was in the vicinity of the dangerous pool of water, in accordance with section 1(3)(b) of the OLA 1984 and, accordingly, she was owed the duty under section 1(4); and

(ii)   the notice purporting to exclude liability was of no effect both because Ms Jones had not and could not have seen it, and because any attempt to exclude the liability imposed by section 1(4) of the OLA 1984 is ineffective.

Tort — negligence — duty of care — special relationship — public policy

IN THE HOUSE OF LORDS

Jones v *Chief Constable of Dangerville*

Ms Jones was assaulted in her first floor apartment by a serial rapist who had assaulted other women in apartments in the vicinity. The police had decided not to issue warnings to likely victims because they thought that warnings would cause hysteria and impede apprehension of the offender. Ms Jones brought an action against the Chief Constable of Dangerville in the High Court alleging negligence in failing to warn her and negligence in failing to apprehend the offender before the assault.

The trial judge found as matters of fact that:

(1)   it was the policy of the Chief Constable of Dangerville to use potential victims of rape as 'bait' for prospective rapists, and that this policy had had highly successful results in the past;

(2)   Ms Jones would have moved to stay with her parents had she been warned of the threat of the rapist; and

(3)   the police knew that the rapist only attacked women on the first floor of apartment buildings in the block where Ms Jones lived.

It was held (by the Court of Appeal, affirming the trial judge's decision) that Ms Jones' cause of action should be struck out for the following reasons:

(1)   there was no special relationship sufficient to impose a duty of care upon the Chief Constable; and

(2)   in any event, on the authority of *Hill* v *Chief Constable of West Yorkshire* [1989] AC 53 as a matter of public policy, no duty of care was owed to Caroline by the Chief Constable for activities in the course of investigating crime.

Ms Jones now appeals to the House of Lords on the question of whether a duty of care might be owed in the circumstances.

Kristina Stern, *King's College, London*

Tort—private nuisance—unreasonable user—abnormal sensitivity

IN THE COURT OF APPEAL (CIVIL DIVISION)

Christine v Julian

Julian has just moved into a new house, where the garden has been neglected for years. Julian, however, is a keen gardener who is especially fond of plants with a strong scent. Over the autumn months, therefore, Julian plants lots of sweet-smelling shrubs, perennials and annuals.

In the spring and summer, Julian's garden is a riot of colour and fragrance but Christine, Julian's next door neighbour who suffers from severe hay fever, finds that her life is now a misery because she cannot venture out into her own garden or open her windows in the fine weather without her eyes streaming, her face swelling and her breathing becoming so difficult that she has to resort to a special portable oxygen inhaler machine given to her by the local hospital.

Julian is sympathetic to Christine's plight to some degree and agrees not to plant any more plants known for their high release of pollen. He refuses, however, to pull up his fragrant shrubs and perennials on the grounds of both cost and aesthetics. Christine's allergy will therefore continue to make her life miserable for around six months of the year.

Christine went to the county court to seek damages in private nuisance for the injury and distress she has suffered; and also to seek a mandatory injunction ordering Julian to get rid of the offending plants. The learned judge found, however, that Julian's planting and enjoyment of shrubs and perennials was not an unreasonable user of his garden; and that Christine was abnormally sensitive. In the circumstances, therefore, he found for Julian and refused to order either the payment of damages or an injunction.

Christine now appeals to the Court of Appeal.

Tort — negligence — duty of care — meaning of 'proximity' — nervous shock

IN THE COURT OF APPEAL (CIVIL DIVISION)

Phillips and Another v Lifetime Magazines plc and Another

On 9th February 1991 Brian Phillips went to Aston Park to watch the association football match between Aston Town and Birmingham United, local rivals each with a large following of supporters. In normal circumstances the Aston Park ground could have accommodated 48,000 spectators but, due to building works necessitated by the Needleworker Report into public safety at sporting events, the capacity at Aston Park had been reduced to 32,000.

Mercian Constabulary, responsible for policing at Aston Park, had therefore drawn up a plan to escort supporters from Birmingham United into parts of the ground which they did not usually frequent at such matches. However, the size of the crowd — though no larger than could reasonably have been expected — proved too large to be easily managed by the police officers on duty at the match and, as a result, too many Birmingham supporters were ordered into the West Stand whilst much of the North Stand remained empty.

Brian Phillips was one of the Birmingham supporters ushered into the West Stand by police. As they struggled for room, hundreds were injured by being either crushed against barriers or trampled underfoot. Thirty died from their injuries including Mr Phillips.

Also in the crowd that day was Mr Phillips's estranged wife, Doris, who was standing in the North Stand with a clear view of the tragedy which befell her husband. As a direct consequence of seeing her husband being seriously injured, Mrs Phillips now suffers from the disorder known as post-traumatic stress.

During the tragedy the Phillips's daughter, Corinne, was away at university and could not be contacted by telephone. Indeed, she did not read or hear of the tragedy until the following Monday — two days later — when the weekly copy of *Lifetime Magazine*, to which she subscribed, was delivered. This carried on the front page a full colour photograph of the crowd in the West Stand at Aston Park, in which Mr Phillips's agonized face could clearly be seen. As a consequence of seeing this photograph, Corinne too now suffers from post-traumatic stress disorder.

Doris Phillips sued the Chief Constable of Mercian Police for negligence. In a separate action Corinne sued Lifetime Magazines plc for negligence.

At first instance Onion J found in favour of Doris Phillips on the grounds that the Chief Constable of Mercian Police owed her a duty of care since she was married to Brian Phillips and was herself in the ground at Aston Park when the tragedy occurred.

In a separate hearing Gherkin J found in favour of Lifetime Magazines on the grounds that they did not owe Corinne Phillips a duty of care because she was not sufficiently proximate and it would not be just and reasonable to reach a verdict which would, in effect, hold Lifetime Magazines potentially liable to all its readers.

In a consolidated action Corinne Phillips now appeals against the decision of Gherkin J on the grounds that she was owed a duty of care by Lifetime Magazines as a subscriber and was therefore sufficiently proximate. Since the number of subscribers must be inherently limited, she further claims it would not be unreasonable to hold Lifetime Magazines liable for negligence.

The Chief Constable of Mercian Police also appeals against the decision of Onion J on the grounds that since Doris and Brian Phillips were separated, there was no bond of 'natural love and affection' between them and accordingly Doris Phillips was owed no duty of care.

Tort — negligence — standard of care — causation

IN THE COURT OF APPEAL (CIVIL DIVISION)

MacDonald v *Acton School*

David MacDonald is a six-year-old boy who attends a local fee-paying school known as Acton School. In the summer term of 1994 he went on his class's annual school trip to Twycross Zoo, to which he and his classmates were transported on a coach hired by the school from Wellbeloved Travel, a local coach firm, which the school had used many times before.

Before the trip had been arranged, a number of parents had been to see Miss Haymaker, David's class teacher, to enquire whether the coach to be hired would have seat belts fitted for every child. They pointed out that Newcomer Travel, another local coach firm, could provide such a coach (though the hire charge would be £50 more than Wellbeloved's).

Miss Haymaker had replied that the coach would not have seat belts, and that most parents would not be prepared to pay their proportion of an extra £50 (approximately £4 each).

On the way back from the zoo, David's coach was in a collision with a car whose driver has never been traced. It is agreed that the accident was entirely the fault of the other driver. Most of the children were only slightly injured. David, however, suffered severe head injuries and will be handicapped for the rest of his life. It is agreed that he would never have suffered such injuries if he had been wearing a seat belt.

David's parents had not been among those who had approached Miss Haymaker about seat belts. In evidence which was accepted by the trial judge, Muller J, they said that the question of seat belts had never occurred to them until after the accident.

David's parents claimed on his behalf that Acton School were liable in negligence for those injuries which David suffered because he had not been wearing a seat belt. Acton School admit that they owed David a duty of care but deny liability on the grounds that it had not been breached.

Muller J held, first, that Acton had fallen below the standard of care required in failing to ensure that the coach hired had safety belts fitted, and so the duty of care owed to David had been breached. But he went on to hold that such a breach of duty had not caused David's injuries, which were caused solely by the negligence of the unknown driver.

David's parents now appeal against Muller J's second determination. Acton School cross-appeal against his first determination.

Tort — libel — justification — fair comment

IN THE COURT OF APPEAL (CIVIL DIVISION)

Daily Informer v *Minor*

Morris Minor is the current leader of the Christian Socialist Party (CSP), a political party with sufficient Members of Parliament to make Minor the Leader of Her Majesty's Opposition. In January 1994 a Royal Commission on Standards in Politics under the chairmanship of Grimm LJ reported that in its view Minor had been guilty of duplicity and of misleading the House of Commons when he had said in the House in November 1991 that: 'The CSP accepts no anonymous donations to party funds of more than £1,000.'

Minor refused to comment on the report and took no action in the courts. Since then Mr Minor's popularity rating in opinion polls has been at a record low, with the support of 10 per cent of respondents; whilst his party is consistently found to have the support of approximately 25 per cent of those respondents questioned.

In July 1994 the *Daily Informer* reported as the leading story on its front page that, contrary to Minor's recent statements that neither he nor the CSP could ever support the idea of proportional representation, he had actually advocated that very same idea in a by-election leaflet published in August 1989. The report went on to accuse Minor of being a hypocrite. A week later the *Informer* retracted this story on page three under the heading 'Apology' with the following words:

> On 6th July we reported that, contrary to Mr Morris Minor's recent statements that neither he nor the CSP could ever support the idea of proportional representation, he had actually advocated that very same idea in a by-election leaflet published in August 1989. We now realise that this was, and is, untrue. Mr Minor has never advocated proportional representation. The leaflet to which we erroneously referred was, in fact, issued on behalf of one of the candidates standing against Mr Minor at that election. We apologise unreservedly to Mr Minor, his family and the CSP for any offence and embarrassment which our report may have caused.

Minor nevertheless sued the *Daily Informer* for libel on the grounds that the *Informer's* report of 6th July expressly and by implication alleged that Minor was a hypocrite. The *Informer* defended the action on the grounds that:

(i)   Minor had no reputation to be lowered; and
(ii)   the report was incapable of being defamatory because there is nothing inherently wrong with being a supporter of proportional representation;

and, in the alternative to (i) and (ii) above, it alleged that:

(iii)   the story was substantially true since Minor is a hypocrite; and
(iv)   the newspaper had made a fair comment on a matter of public interest.

Short J ruled that the allegation that Minor was a hypocrite was a comment and that the defence of justification was therefore inappropriate. He further ruled that the defence of fair comment was inapplicable since the comment was clearly based on a report which was untrue. He allowed the case to go to the jury, which found that the *Informer* had libelled Minor and awarded him £1,000 damages.

The *Daily Informer* appeals to the Court of Appeal on the grounds that, for the reasons set out in paragraphs (i) and (ii) above, the case should not have been allowed to go to the jury; or, alternatively, that the judge was wrong in not allowing the *Informer* to put its defences, outlined in paragraphs (iii) and (iv) above, to the jury.

Tort — negligence — economic loss — causation — remoteness

IN THE COURT OF APPEAL (CIVIL DIVISION)

Napper v *Mitchell*

Neil Napper was a self-employed lorry driver, who contracted with George Gopher to deliver a cargo to Tilbury Docks by 31st January. Napper had never driven to Tilbury before, so he asked his close friend Miriam Mitchell, who is a cartographer by profession, to work out the best route for him. Mitchell did so by plotting the shortest possible route on Napper's road map.

Unfortunately, this route included some roads which are unsuitable for lorries, including the narrow and winding B13. As a result, Napper was involved in a collision with another motorist in which his lorry was so severely damaged that it cannot be economically repaired. Napper's business was already in difficulties and, since he no longer had a lorry, he was forced to declare himself bankrupt. The building society foreclosed on his mortgage (so that he lost his house) and he is unable to get credit anywhere. He is now living on social security in 'bed and breakfast' accommodation.

Napper sued Mitchell for negligence, alleging that her advice as to the route to be taken was careless. Harfeetch J held that Mitchell did owe Napper a duty of care in respect of the damage to the lorry, which was assessed at £3,000. He also held that Mitchell owed a duty to Napper in respect of the bankruptcy and the consequences of bankruptcy, but that nevertheless Mitchell could not be liable for these losses since:

(1)   her actions had not caused Napper's bankruptcy; and
(2)   even if Mitchell could be said to have caused Napper's bankruptcy and consequent losses, such losses were too remote to be recoverable.

There is no appeal in respect of the judge's finding concerning the damage to the lorry. However, Napper appeals against both adverse findings of Harfeetch J in respect of the bankruptcy and consequent losses.

Tort — libel — injurious falsehood — jurisdiction

IN THE HIGH COURT

Smith v Northern Chronicle

The *Northern Chronicle* is a newspaper published weekly in County Monaghan in the Republic of Ireland, with an audited circulation of 7,000 copies per week. Of these 7,000 copies, no more than 100 would normally be sold in Northern Ireland (such sales being approximately 70 in the Belfast area and the remaining 30 in South Armagh). The remaining 6,900 copies would be sold in the Republic of Ireland, principally in counties Monaghan and Louth. John Smith is a farmer in the townland of Rockfield in South Armagh, where he and his family farm 100 acres of good quality land, rearing beef cattle for slaughter; he is Northern Ireland resident and domiciled. John Smith is one of 10 farmers in the immediate vicinity of Rockfield in this line of farming, though there are very many more such beef farmers in South Armagh, probably numbering 200–300 holdings.

On 1st December 1994, after what is claimed by the newspapers to have been 'three months of exhaustive investigations', the *Northern Chronicle* published an 'exclusive' report entitled 'GREEDY ARMAGH FARMERS POISON US FOR PROFIT!'. The report, which occupies 75 per cent of the front page of the particular issue of the newspaper, claims to expose a 'secret ring of angel dust cowboys' who are feeding illegal growth hormones to their livestock 'and reaping huge profits in consequence'. The practice is alleged to be widespread and indiscriminate in South Armagh, where also 'informed sources say that there is a possible involvement by proscribed organisations'. The report states that the activity is centred on the townland of Rockfield, 'where, we can reveal, the most determined abusers operate with impunity'. It is clearly stated in the report that the alleged practices are endangering human lives, as the meat of these animals is claimed to be entering the human food chain. No person is identified by name as using any prohibited substance. However, the price paid for cattle from South Armagh drops sharply at markets in the following weeks.

John Smith categorically denies any involvement in such alleged activity and is incensed by the report. He instructs his solicitor in Armagh to issue proceedings for libel and injurious falsehood; a writ in these terms is duly issued by the High Court in Belfast on 15th December 1994. After unsatisfactory correspondence between the parties' solicitors (in the course of which the solicitors for the *Northern Chronicle* consistently deny any liability to John Smith, the plaintiff), the writ is served on the *Northern Chronicle*'s Belfast solicitors, who have been instructed to accept service.

The Board of the *Northern Chronicle* instructs its legal advisers to challenge the jurisdiction of the High Court in Northern Ireland to hear the action, and to argue particularly that:

(1) The appropriate and convenient forum for the litigation is the Republic of Ireland.

(2) (Without prejudice to the previous argument) John Smith, the plaintiff, is not sufficiently identified within the report to sustain the action.

(3) (Without prejudice to the previous arguments), such further points as occur to them.

John Smith has instructed his solicitors that he wishes the action to be determined by the courts of Northern Ireland, but that they (his lawyers) are also to plead publication both in Northern Ireland and in the Republic of Ireland and to seek damages accordingly. However, his further instructions are that this aspect of his claim should be dropped if thought necessary in order to sustain the action in Northern Ireland (i.e., to drop reference to publication in the Republic of Ireland if necessary).

Belfast solicitors for the *Northern Chronicle* have accordingly entered a conditional Appearance and have served it accompanied by an open letter which both contests jurisdiction and which argues the substantive merits of the action (as mentioned above) in the event of such argument on the jurisdictional question failing. Solicitors for the *Northern Chronicle* then bring a motion to contest jurisdiction, and it is agreed by the parties and by the Court that the Court will at that time hear argument from both parties on all issues relevant to the dispute and that the matter be determined by judges alone sitting without a jury.

Additional facts

(1)   Sales of the allegedly defamatory and injurious edition of the newspaper were as set out at the beginning of this recital of facts.

(2)   The *Northern Chronicle* is a limited liability company incorporated in the Republic of Ireland. It has one employee located in Northern Ireland; this individual is engaged on a market research project (see below). However, no editorial work or printing of the paper takes place in Northern Ireland. With a view to an expansion by the newspaper and a possible joint venture with a Northern Ireland based publication at a future date, the *Northern Chronicle* had taken a lease on a small office in Belfast for two years from July 1994. This is the office occupied by the sole employee of the paper in Northern Ireland. The *Northern Chronicle* otherwise has no assets in Northern Ireland.

(3)   Though only 100 copies of the relevant edition of the *Northern Chronicle* were sold in Northern Ireland, a large (though unascertainable) number of copies of the allegedly defamatory and injurious edition were purchased in the Republic of Ireland by Northern Ireland residents.

(4)   John Smith has had three convictions at Armagh Magistrates' Court within five years prior to the date of the publication of the offending article. Two of these convictions were for selling farm produce under weight (the penalty in each case being a fine of £50). The third conviction was for an assault contrary to section 47 of the Offences Against the Person Act 1861, the said assault having taken place during a fracas in a local public house (for which John Smith received a sentence of six weeks' imprisonment, though suspended).

Please note: While in a situation such as this it would be normal practice to sue the newspaper, the editor and the publisher, for the sake of clarity and in order to refine the issues, the company *Northern Chronicle* (the present defendant) may be taken as the representative of all such interested parties.

Anne Fenton, *Queen's University, Belfast*

Tort — negligence — duty of care — limitation period — Limitation
Act 1980

IN THE HOUSE OF LORDS

Thomas v Tramp Industries Limited and Pressgate Limited

Daniel Thomas is suing Pressgate Ltd and Tramp Industries Ltd for
damages for personal injuries. Mr Thomas was born in 1939. Throughout
the 1940s and 1950s his parents subscribed to a weekly newspaper called
The National Echo which was owned and published by Pressgate Ltd. Mr
Thomas regularly read his parents' copy of *The National Echo* throughout his
childhood. *The National Echo* regularly carried an advertisement for a
particular brand of high tar cigarettes called 'Wild West'. These cigarettes
were manufactured by Tramp Industries Ltd. The advertisement depicted a
cowboy on horseback galloping through the countryside, a 'Wild West'
cigarette dangling from his lips. The advertisement said 'Feel better and live
longer on the Wild West'. Neither the advertisement nor the cigarette
packaging carried a warning as to the dangers of smoking cigarettes.

In 1954, and at the age of 15, Mr Thomas started to smoke 'Wild West'
cigarettes. The advertisements carried by Pressgate gave him the assurance
and motivation to start. Since that time he has continued to smoke that
particular brand of cigarettes.

In 1983 Mr Thomas was diagnosed as suffering from lung cancer. His
doctor was confident that smoking was the cause of his cancer. In 1990 he
issued proceedings against Tramp Industries Ltd. Shortly after the issue of
proceedings his solicitors discovered that Tramp Industries Ltd were known
to be in severe financial difficulties and joined Pressgate Ltd to the action as
second defendants.

The case was tried by Gotham J in September 1991, by which time Tramp
had gone into liquidation and the action against them was stayed. Gotham J
made the following findings of fact:

(i)   the advertisements were at least partly responsible for Mr Thomas's
actions in starting to smoke 'Wild West' cigarettes;
(ii)   in the 1950s the tobacco industry was aware of the detrimental
effects of smoking cigarettes;
(iii)   it was not generally known by members of the public that smoking
cigarettes was dangerous; and
(iv)   in 1954, when he started smoking, Mr Thomas did not know that
cigarettes could damage his health.

However, Gotham J dismissed Mr Thomas's claim against Pressgate Ltd
on the grounds that:

(1)   Pressgate Ltd did not owe a duty of care to Mr Thomas; and
(2)   any claim by Mr Thomas against Pressgate Ltd was statute-barred.

Gotham J said:

Counsel for the plaintiff relies on sections 32(1)(b) and 33 of the
Limitation Act 1980. She accepts that the plaintiff knew that he had lung

cancer in 1983 and knew that it was likely that the cause of the cancer was smoking. However, she argues:

(a)   In 1982 an article was published in *The Sunday Chronicle* which revealed that Pressgate knew in the early 1950s of the risks of cigarette smoking. The article revealed correspondence between Pressgate and Tramp's advertising agency, Adline Ltd, in 1952 in which the possibility of including a health warning in the advertisement was discussed and rejected.

(b)   Pressgate had deliberately concealed their state of knowledge. In support of this proposition she relied on the fact that Pressgate had never disclosed their knowledge when questioned on this very issue on numerous occasions by journalists.

(c)   Pressgate's knowledge, in the early 1950s, of the risks of smoking was a fact relevant to the plaintiff's right of action within the meaning of section 32(1)(b) of the 1980 Act.

(d)   Prior to the publication of the article in 1989 the plaintiff did not know, and could not with reasonable diligence have discovered, that Pressgate knew in 1954 of the dangers of smoking.

(e)   Therefore, the period of limitation only began to run in 1989 when the article was published and the plaintiff discovered Pressgate's knowledge.

I find as a fact that Pressgate did know about the risks of smoking in the early 1950s. I also find that the plaintiff could not with reasonable diligence have discovered the fact or extent of Pressgate's knowledge until the publication of *The Sunday Chronicle*'s excellent article in 1989. However, in my view, the plaintiff cannot rely on section 32(1)(b) of the 1980 Act, since Pressgate's actions constituted only non-disclosure. In my view non-disclosure is not capable as a matter of law of amounting to deliberate concealment. Secondly, Pressgate's knowledge of the dangers of smoking was not a fact relevant to the right of action within the meaning of section 32 of the Act. In ascertaining the meaning of 'fact relevant to a right of action' I have had particular regard to section 14 of the 1980 Act. Pressgate's knowledge is not a relevant fact for the purpose of section 14 of the Act and is therefore not a relevant fact for the purposes of section 32.

Gotham J then considered whether to exercise his discretion under section 33 of the 1980 Act and decided not to do so.

Mr Thomas's appeal to the Court of Appeal was dismissed. He now appeals to the House of Lords on the following grounds:

(1)   Gotham J and the Court of Appeal erred in law in deciding that Pressgate Limited did not owe Mr Thomas a duty of care; and

(2)   Gotham J and the Court of Appeal erred in law in deciding that Mr Thomas was not entitled to rely on section 32 of the Limitation Act.

There is no appeal in respect of Gotham J's decision on section 33 of the Limitation Act 1980.

Richard Wilmot-Smith QC, *39 Essex Street, Temple*
Middle Temple Annual Mooting Competition

Tort — libel — negligence — quantum of damages — interest

IN THE HOUSE OF LORDS

Maria Taglioni v Henry Latrobe

Maria and Lisa Taglioni were twin sisters. In July 1993 both were beautiful and were 33 years old. Maria was a famous dancer with the Royal Ballet and Lisa was a schoolteacher in Balham. Henry Latrobe was and remains a critic with *The Sunny Newspaper*.

Lisa asked her sister to dance at her school in a solo performance before an audience of locals and parents to raise money for school books. The performance was at 7.30 p.m. on 22nd July 1993 and lasted one hour. Tickets were £30 each and 300 ticket holders crammed into the school hall to watch the famous romantic dancer perform. Latrobe, a parent, was in the audience. The next day's *Sunny* carried an article by Latrobe on page three under the headline, 'TAGLIONI RIPS OFF BALHAM PARENTS: £10,000 SMASH AND GRAB'. The story began 'Balham parents were conned by a gold-digging dancer who stole their money in exchange for a few lazy contortions. . .'.

Her sister Lisa was incensed at the slight to her sister and on the morning of the article drove to the offices of *The Sunny* in Shadwell in order to remonstrate with Latrobe. However, before she arrived, her Metro was hit by Latrobe's Bentley. Latrobe, drunk, was on his way into the office and his car collided with the Metro. Lisa lost an eye in the accident; Latrobe was unhurt. Maria, who had witnessed the accident from the bedroom window of the exclusive Shadwell penthouse to which she had moved anonymously the previous day, rushed to the scene whereupon she recognised the Metro as her sister's and suffered shock.

Maria sued *The Sunny* and Latrobe for libel. Lisa sued Latrobe for the personal injury suffered in the accident. Maria joined Lisa's action as co-plaintiff suing for the shock at the witnessing of her sister's injury. Latrobe retained the same Leading and Junior Counsel in both of the actions. Maria and Lisa also used the same Leading and Junior Counsel in both of the actions.

Latrobe defended the libel action pleading justification and fair comment at the trial before Jay J and a jury. The evidence was that Maria would lose no earnings as a result of the libel, since ballet audiences neither read nor believe. Indeed, the demand for her services increased after the article appeared. Maria's Counsel submitted to the jury that the article was 'an appalling calumny' and that 'nobody has suffered so grave a libel, albeit it is fortunate that her livelihood has not suffered'. The jury, in July 1994, awarded Maria damages of £125,000.

Lisa's action for personal injury was also contested. The trial was held one week after the libel action. The judge, Marshall J, found that Latrobe was negligent and that his negligence caused the loss of Lisa's left eye. Special damages were agreed in the sum of £10,000. Marshall J awarded Lisa £17,500. Latrobe did not appeal any aspect of this case.

However, Latrobe appealed the quantum of Maria's libel award. He accepted in the Court of Appeal that the libel was serious, but contended that the amount was grossly excessive having regard to the admitted fact that the dancer's career had not suffered. He asked that the Court of Appeal reconsider the amounts awarded by juries in libel cases when there was such a large figure awarded. He also asked the Court of Appeal for interest on any returned damages.

The Court of Appeal (Rutledge, Taney and Ellsworth LJJ) upheld the jury and Jay J. They did not therefore find it necessary to make a decision on the question of interest but said that they doubted that they had jurisdiction. They gave leave to appeal to the House of Lords. Taney LJ commented when giving leave that in his view the House of Lords was far freer to deal with the disparity between libel and personal injury awards than the Court of Appeal.

Their Lordships indicated that they wished to hear argument both on the disparity Taney LJ referred to and also on the power and discretion of both their Lordships and the Court of Appeal to award interest on returned damages following a successful appeal.

Richard Wilmot-Smith QC, *39 Essex Street, Temple*
Middle Temple Annual Mooting Competition

Tort — negligence — duty of care — economic loss

IN THE COURT OF APPEAL (CIVIL DIVISION)

Top Hat Hotels v Fat Quack Fitters plc

Lorryload Ltd took one of its tankers for a service by the local branch of Fat Quack Fitters plc. The fitter who serviced the lorry was called away to the telephone in the middle of changing the gearbox oil and forgot to check whether he had completely refilled the gearbox. In fact, he had not done so to the extent that the level of oil was left dangerously low when the Lorryload driver came to drive his tanker away.

The next day the tanker was filled with petroleum spirit and was being driven along the A1 when the gearbox seized, causing the tanker to jacknife and the petrol to catch fire. Because of the risk to public safety, the nearby five-star Top Hat Hotel had to be evacuated and, since it was felt that there was a risk that petrol vapour could still re-ignite for some time after the accident, the hotel was not permitted by the local authority to re-open for a further four days, which caused the hotel to suffer a considerable loss of profits.

The proprietors of the hotel sued Fat Quack in negligence. However, at first instance Turnover J found for the defendants on the following grounds:

(i)   they owed the plaintiff no duty of care since the case concerned an act causing pure economic loss, out of which no such duty could ever arise; and

(ii)   the plaintiff's loss was too remote.

Top Hat Hotels now appeal to the Court of Appeal against both these findings.

Tort — negligence — standard of care — causation

IN THE HOUSE OF LORDS

Whitten v *Brundle Air Ltd*

On 1st October James Whitten boarded Brundle Air Flight RU999 at West Midlands Airport. Five minutes later a bomb on board exploded, killing everyone on the 'plane. The bomb had been hidden in the suitcase of someone on the 'plane, who was later claimed to be a member of Terrorists Incorporated acting as a suicide bomber. He had checked the suitcase onto the 'plane in the normal manner, but Brundle Air's colour monitors had been out of action for three days, so that security staff had to rely on black and white monitors.

In evidence, experts agreed that someone watching the monochrome monitors stood only a 20 per cent chance of noticing the particular type of explosive used; whereas they agreed that the colour monitors would have increased the chances of discovery of the explosive to 60 per cent. It was also agreed that the only 100 per cent effective method of discovery was to unpack every item of luggage, as is the practice of the Israeli airline El Al.

Whitten's wife, Sarah, sued Brundle Air for negligence on the grounds that:

(1)   the colour monitors were not operative; and
(2)   Brundle Air should have searched every suitcase.

In the High Court Meek J held that it would be going beyond what was reasonable to expect every airline to search the luggage of every passenger. He also held that since use of the colour monitors would only have created a 60 per cent chance of discovering the explosive, this was not enough to establish that the failure to use such monitors had caused Whitten's death.

The Court of Appeal upheld Meek J's findings, and Sarah Whitten now appeals to the House of Lords.

Tort — private nuisance — unreasonable user — injunction

IN THE COURT OF APPEAL (CIVIL DIVISION)

Wilf v *Alf*

Wilf is a keen gardener who is particularly fond of conifers. Several years ago he planted several *Leylandii*, a variety known for its speed of growth, along the edge of his garden which adjoins Alf's garden. Whenever branches have protruded over Alf's garden he has pruned them off, and Wilf has never objected to this.

Now, however, the conifers have grown so tall that it is impossible for Alf to prune away any 'trespassing' branches. Alf is a pensioner and does not wish to pay a contractor to do this for him. Moreover, the height of the conifers means that Alf's garden no longer sees any sunlight, with the result that several of his own plants are now struggling where formerly they thrived; and some have even died.

Alf went to the county court to seek a mandatory injunction to order that Wilf cut his *Leylandii* down to a reasonable height on the grounds of private nuisance. The learned judge agreed that Wilf's user of his garden was unreasonable in the circumstances and thus a private nuisance but declined to grant the injunction sought, though he did award Alf damages of £3,000 for loss of plants and personal distress. Wilf now appeals to the Court of Appeal on the grounds that he is not committing a private nuisance. Alf cross-appeals, claiming that he should be granted the injunction sought.

BLACKSTONE HERBERT SMITH MOOTING COMPETITION RULES

1. The Competition shall be run under the auspices of an Advisory Board, which shall have the power to:
   (a) co-opt members;
   (b) appoint a National Secretary and Assistant Secretary to administer the competition; and
   (c) amend these rules as it thinks fit.

2. (a) The Competition shall be open to not more than one team from each participating institution.
   (b) Each team shall consist of two law students, who must be registered as such with the institution which they represent.
   (c) Undergraduates, postgraduates and those studying for CPE are all eligible to take part.
   (d) The members of each team may be changed from round to round.

3. (a) Each participating institution shall submit one original mooting problem dealing with a topic in an area of law specified by the National Secretary.
   (b) No entry will be accepted unless it is accompanied by the mooting problem specified in paragraph 3(a).

4. (a) The National Secretary shall have the sole power to determine the mooting problem to be used in each round of the Competition.
   (b) Any ambiguities or objections apparently arising out of a mooting problem shall be brought to the attention of the National Secretary within three days of receipt of the problem by the participating institution.
   (c) The National Secretary shall have the power to resolve the matter in his or her absolute discretion.

5. (a) The Competition shall be run on a knock-out basis.
   (b) Each team's opponents in the first round will be drawn by the National Secretary, who shall attempt to minimise the distance to be travelled by the away teams so far as is possible.
   (c) The first-round draw shall form the basis for each year's Competition (as in a tennis competition) and no new draw shall take place for every round.
   (d) Each participating institution shall receive a copy of the draw specified in paragraph 5(b) and the results of each round.
   (e) The first-named team in each round shall be the home team.

6.   (a)   The home team shall argue for the Appellant and the away team shall argue for the Respondent.
     (b)   The order in which speakers shall be heard shall be determined from round to round by the National Secretary.
     (c)   Leading counsel for each team will be permitted to speak for no longer than 20 minutes.
     (d)   Junior counsel for each team will be permitted to speak for no longer than 15 minutes.
     (e)   Time taken up by judicial interventions, and by counsel dealing with such interventions, shall not count towards the time limits specified in paragraphs 6(c) and (d).
     (f)   Time shall be kept on a stopwatch by a clerk, who shall warn counsel by some suitable means when they have:
           (i)   five minutes left;
           (ii)   one minute left;
           (iii) to conclude their speech forthwith.
     (g)   There will be no right of reply.
     (h)   There will be no speeches from the floor or by *amici curiae*.
7.   The home team in each round shall be responsible for:
     (a)   selecting the judge, who shall be a qualified barrister, solicitor or law lecturer who is not employed by or identified with the home team's institution;
     (b)   arranging a venue for the moot;
     (c)   faxing the details specified in paragraph 7(a) and (b) to both the away team and to the National Secretary at least seven days before the moot is to take place;
     (d)   faxing a copy of these rules to the judge at least seven days before the moot is to take place; and
     (e)   producing for the use of the judge a full copy of each law report and other literature cited by the participating teams.
8.   (a)   Both the home team and the away team shall fax to their opponents, the judge and the National Secretary not later than 3 pm on a day at least two working days before the moot is to take place:
           (i)   a list of authorities on which they wish to rely in the moot court; and
           (ii)   a summary (which must be typed or written in block capitals and no longer than one sheet of A4 paper) of the main points of their argument.
     (b)   No team may compile a list of more than SIX case citations.
     (c)   All other legal literature (including statutory materials, EC Directives, journals and textbooks) must also be cited on the list specified in paragraph 8(a)(i) and (ii).
     (d)   No team may compile a list of more than FOUR citations of the type specified in paragraph 8(c).
     (e)   Citations from law reports not included in Schedule 1, or from law journals not specified in Schedule 2, shall be admissible only if accompanied by a photocopy of the whole report or learned article to which reference is intended to be made.

(f) No mooter shall rely in his or her speech on any law report or other literature whose citation has not complied with the requirements of this paragraph.

(g) Each mooter shall, however, be free to rely on any case or other legal literature, whether it has been cited in accordance with this paragraph or not, when dealing with any judicial intervention.

9. (a) The judge shall not refuse to hear argument on any ground of appeal specified in the mooting problem, nor shall he or she allow either team to concede a point of law which is identified in the mooting problem as requiring legal argument unless the other team have already consented to such a course of action in writing.

(b) The judge should ask any questions of counsel that seem to him or her to be appropriate.

(c) At the end of the moot the judge shall adjudicate first on the points of law raised in the course of the moot.

(d) The judge shall then announce which team has won that round of the Competition.

(e) In reaching a decision under paragraph 9(d), the judge shall take into account in particular the following matters:

    (i) the quality of each team's summary argument specified in paragraph 8(a)(ii);

    (ii) the court room manner and etiquette of each mooter;

    (iii) the presentation and clarity of each mooter's speech, including whether each speech (or aspects of it) was too long or too short bearing in mind the confines of the Competition;

    (iv) the use made by each mooter of each authority or other literature cited; and

    (v) the ability of each mooter to deal with the judge's interventions.

(f) There shall be no appeal against the decision of the judge.

(g) Objections to the outcome of any round which are based on the allegation that the rules of this Competition have been infringed shall be faxed to the National Secretary no later than the working day immediately following the day on which the round took place.

(h) The National Secretary shall have absolute discretion to determine the result of any round of the Competition following any objection received within paragraph 9(g).

10. The National Secretary shall have absolute discretion to resolve any question concerning the interpretation of these rules.

Schedule 1: Law Reports not requiring to be photocopied

The Law Reports
All England Law Reports
Common Market Law Reports
Criminal Appeal Reports
European Court Reports
Industrial Cases Reports
Industrial Relations Law Reports
Weekly Law Reports

Schedule 2: Law Journals not requiring to be photocopied

Cambridge Law Journal
Common Market Law Review
Criminal Law Review
Current Legal Problems
European Law Review
Journal of Law and Society
Law Quarterly Review
Legal Studies
Modern Law Review
Oxford Journal of Legal Studies
Public Law